THE RIVALS

THE RIVALS

BY JERRY IZENBERG

A SIMON AND FLYNN BOOK

HOLT, RINEHART AND WINSTON, INC.

New York, Chicago, San Francisco

*Published simultaneously in Canada by
Holt, Rinehart and Winston of Canada, Limited.*

Current Printing (last digit)
10   9   8   7   6   5   4   3   2   1

LIBRARY OF CONGRESS CATALOG CARD NUMBER: 68-30512

Printed in the United States of America

For Stanley Woodward, who always had a viewpoint

The author wishes to respectfully acknowledge the valuable assistance tendered by Bill Brendle, Joe Cahill, John Farrell, Wellington Mara, Harry Markson, Barney Nagler, the National Football League office, Ken Smith, Frank Tripucka and Ed Weissman. Portions of the Barbra B. section originally appeared in an article by the author in Sports Illustrated. A deep bow of thanks also goes to Jim Hitchcock and George Bernet for their diligent research and to George Flynn for his tenacity in helping to ruin a freshly laundered tablecloth at Mike Manuche's where the idea for "The Rivals" was conceived. Finally, as always, there was the patience and understanding of the three Izenbergs, Victoria, Robert and Judith. When it comes to rivals, they have none.

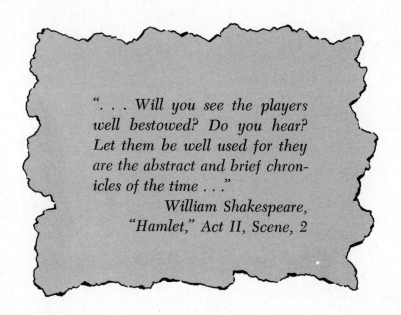

"... Will you see the players well bestowed? Do you hear? Let them be well used for they are the abstract and brief chronicles of the time ..."

William Shakespeare,
"Hamlet," Act II, Scene, 2

CONTENTS

"Oh, that my vexation were but weighed, and my calamity laid in the balances together! For now it would be heavier than the sand of the seas."

. . . Job, who may have been the first sports fan

ON VOLUNTARY SERVITUDE

When I was nine years old, my father, who was in other respects a sane, reasonably fair-minded man, nearly put his fist through the little Philco radio which traditionally stood on a plain wooden shelf he had built as a kind of perpetual shrine in the corner of our screened-in front porch. The radio always came out there in April no matter what the thermometer said because like the rest of the National League, the New York Giants always opened their baseball season during that month. It always began with dark, angry skies and high winds and occasional snow flurries. But the calendar says you are supposed to start in April and if the Giants were Pavlov's bell, then my father was his dog. If the Giants could play in it, he could drag out the screens, fit them into position around the front porch and sit in it.

He had painted the little Philco a kind of battleship gray, and, in truth, if a radio ever earned its Silver Star with Oak Leaf Clusters, it was that little Philco. The Monastary at Monte Casino took less pounding. The volume knob never seemed to do any good but you could get it to behave itself by whacking it on the side with the flat of your hand. Through an endless series of quick right-hand chops over the years before television, my father was able to breathe life into a strange mixture of voices which included people like Frankie Frisch, Jack Brickhouse, Mel Allen, Ernie Harwell, Russ Hodges and a cast of thousands. They were not, however, paint-chipping slashes. Those were done with the bottom of the right fist in an automatic punch-presser of a motion which he saved for moments when an umpire who was either blind or dishonest (George Magerkurth and Jocko Conlan were his favorite targets) had the gall to call a third strike against a Jewish catcher named Harry "The Horse" Danning. Things being what they were in his ethnic world, he took such decisions personally and invariably traced them back to the Czars, the Spanish Inquisition and Peter the Hermit.

At any rate, on the night in question, Leo Durocher, who managed the Brooklyn Dodgers, had succeeded in getting an umpire to reverse a decision which had previously been rendered in favor of the Giants. My old man dove off his old wicker chair and decked the Philco with one hell of a right cross. It shuddered and it wheezed and since in my nine-year-olds' wisdom I had viewed it as a living thing, I was absolutely certain that he had killed it.

"He was a lousy shortstop with the Cardinals," my father explained to the little Philco. "He was a cheap, banjo hitter and a big mouth and he is still a phoney." My old man rarely swore but he did manage to sneak in one very distinct "son of a bitch." Then he turned to me and he said:

"The Dodger announcers (they were on another station which he always tuned in with a burst of sadism on the rare occasions when the Giants were leading the Dodgers and immediately tuned out when Brooklyn invariably regained the lead) are lousy. Their players are lucky and Leo Durocher is a bum. Go to bed."

Later that evening (somewhere along the eighth inning which is how time was reckoned in my fathers' house) the doorbell rang and a policeman was standing there explaining that he hated to do this but a maiden lady (to use my mother's name for her) who lived across the street had called police headquarters to complain about the volume on the Philco. The reason I knew he was a cop was that this information occasioned my fathers' second "son of a bitch" of the evening and I had crept down to the second floor landing in my pajamas to see what it was all about.

I remember quite distinctly that my old man had said something about Leo Durocher and the cop had agreed and asked what the score was and then the two of them had gone over to the little Philco to suffer through yet another Giants' failure together. Giant fans were like that —particularly when the other team had "Dodgers" written across the front of its shirts.

This comes to mind here because nine years later when Leo Durocher crossed over the Brooklyn Bridge to assume command of the Giants in an incredible turnabout, my old man was particularly bitter since the late Mel Ott was fired to make room for him and my old man had helped Mr. Ott hit a great many balls into the right field seats at the old Polo Grounds when he was an active player with the Giants, although Mr. Ott had no way of knowing that.

My father's bitterness lasted a long time . . . I guess it was five or six hours but that night the Giants were playing the Dodgers and my old man was back at the Philco again. The Giants—miracle of miracles—won and when it was over my old man explained to me that baseball was like a war and the nice guys never won and since Mr. Durocher certainly was not a nice guy maybe we ought to give him a chance. Before the season ended, my old man was totally committed and when television finally came along, he even watched Laraine Day (the movie star who was then married to Leo) and her pre-game shows.

When you get down to the guts of what this country's great sports rivalries are or were all about, my old man's slice of personal history is about as relevant as you can get. Later when Horace Stoneham and Walter O'Malley tip-toed off into the purple sunset to sack California with their ball clubs, my old man gave up. The rivalry was dead for him. He just couldn't work up an affinity for San Francisco or, what is more important, a genuine hate for Los Angeles, a city he knew nothing about but which he could not realistically dislike on the theory that any place where Jack Benny spent a lot of time couldn't be all bad.

In a very real sense, this is what this book is all about. It is Max Schmeling coming over here to seek the world's heavyweight boxing championship while little Joseph Goebbels tried to scream himself up to six feet tall back home in Germany and made millions of Americans a very real part of the match with Joe Louis. It is the Giants and the Dodgers (when they lived back home where they were supposed to live) capturing a nation's imagination the way no two baseball teams did before or have done since.

It is that tiny corner of the refrigerator called Green Bay, Wisc., sending its football team off to the Goliath of Chicago to play George Halas' big, bad Bears on an equal footing. It is the glamour machine which is Arnold Palmer, the hero of those who cannot emotionally stand the strain of backing a loser, going head-to-head with Jack Nicklaus, who is physically everything that Palmer is not.

It is Sea Biscuit and War Admiral in the big showdown at Pimlico while the first real wave of post-depression money is returning to the race tracks.

It is all of these things and a lot more you will read about in the pages which follow . . . from an annual football game between two colleges (Notre Dame and Army) which became so emotional that one of the participants defied the Congress in order to break it off, right down to the supercalifragilistic pseudo Punic War which the combined noise of two major television networks thrust upon America's ear drums under the name "Super Bowl."

It is one part stubbornness and one part hysteria and no parts logic. It is the purest of pure emotions and you won't find it anywhere else in the world . . . not in England where the soccer fans brawl in railroad cars and not in Ireland where the counties of Kilkenny and Tipperary exchange bruises over a hurling match and not in Pamplona where they run the bulls. These are devotions to a single type of combat and the American dream of sports nonsense goes far beyond that.

Like my old man, there are millions of us who swing from one emotional sports rivalry to another and back again. The American spectrum is wider and higher in this aspect than anywhere else in the world. It has its roots in many things and not the least of them is geography. As a nation, we are the most hard-headed sports-minded people who ever existed. For the most part, we play our own games in our own way and the hell with the rest of the world. You can do that when you have the Atlantic Ocean on one side of you and the Pacific on the other.

We play football . . . they play soccer. We play baseball . . . they play cricket. We invented basketball. Our approach to boxing puts us in a vastly different world. Patty-

cake punchers can rule the British Empire with their foot-
work. The only thing a fighter who can't punch can rule
over here is the line in front of the unemployment office.

And on the occasions when we do play the rest of the
world's games, we play them and follow them with the
kind of violent passion of the newly-liberated colonials
which we are. Make no mistake about it. In 1952, an
American named Horace Ashenfelter won the 3,000-meter
steeplechase in the Olympics at Helsinki and the man he
beat was a Russian named Kazantsev. A steeplechase at-
tracts about as much attention in this country as a Sac
and Fox artifacts exhibit but even my old man took the
time to read about that one.

You could say that part of this hysteria stems from the
framework of what has come to be known as the American
Dream . . . a piece of fiction which insists that every boy
can become President of the United States or a captain
of industry or the quarterback for the Green Bay Packers.
The fact that he can't isn't really important here. The fact
that the myth puts such stress on competition, however, is.

Recently, I shared a ride out to the Oakland Coliseum
with a splendid actor named John Forsythe and the erudite
television commentator, Howard Cosell. We were on our
way to watch Jimmy Ellis and Jerry Quarry—a pair of
fighters whose rivalry was about as gripping as the Bryn
Mawr Inter-Sorority Field Hockey Playoffs—contest for a
tiny portion of what has now become the herniated heavyweight boxing title of the world.

"Nothing," Forsythe said, "seems to grip this country the
way sports does."

"And yet," Cosell interjected, "sports themes make lousy
movies. They simply do not make money and you would
think that something with that kind of grip on the public

would be sure box office." "Perhaps," he added, "it's because you simply can't tell the whole truth about the people involved."

That may be part of it. But the larger part . . . the thing which accounts for the kind of rivalries detailed in this book . . . is the fact that nobody wants to listen in the first place. Virtually every American male played baseball, football and basketball and had at least one fist fight as a kid. Ergo: every American male is an expert on the subject and every American male is going to see it exactly the way he wants to see it.

Some of them saw Gene Tunney down for eight seconds and some of them saw him down for 30 seconds during the famous "long count" fight with Dempsey. Some of them saw Sal Maglie deliberately throwing at the Dodgers' Carl Furillo and some of them saw Furillo freezing in the batters' box and failing to get out of the way. Some of them saw Army running up the score on gallant underdog Notre Dame during the war years and some of them saw Army settling an old score for the years when it could not cope with Notre Dame's massive recruiting program. Some of them saw Billy Conn making one fatal mistake in the 13th round and some of them saw Joe Louis setting Conn up for the inevitable.

And because they could see what they wanted to see, the hysteria took hold and grew into a voluntary servitude. When Harry Truman beat Tom Dewey, well, that was that. You couldn't say that Harry Truman was not the President of the United States. But when the Giants came from 13½ games back to beat the Dodgers out of the 1951 pennant you could, if you were so inclined, say that Charlie Dressen blew it and that next year would be different. A lot of people did.

My old man wasn't one of them. He had better vision. He saw it all and a lot more on his little Philco.

On soft, warm summer nights when a gentle breeze and the finicky volume control formed an uneasy alliance, the maiden lady across the street and the cop in the doorway saw it, too.

"Rocky didn't foul him. He didn't do nothin' wrong. What the hell they booin' him for?"

Puzzled ringsider after Marciano kayoed Louis, Oct. 26, 1951.

THE SECOND TIME AROUND

His name was Joe Louis Barrow and on the night of Oct. 26, 1951, he lay on his side, one leg twitching slightly within the tight geometrical confines of the Madison Square Garden ring while the rest of him sprawled despairingly across the ring apron. On the other side of the ring, Rocky Marciano, the man who had put him there, and Al Weill, Marciano's manager, danced in a grotesque embrace while visions of large, green bank notes tip-toed through Mr. Weill's brain. But even the ring announcer was having difficulty because the Niagara of noise which cascaded down from the balcony was a strange and over-powering mixture of joy and bitterness.

Joe Louis was 37 years old on that night and he really didn't belong there then. The calendar had made a liar of his body. He would never again climb through those same ropes as a professional fighter. He would never again shuffle across the ring on slow, flat-footed feet in that creeping-death style of his . . . never throw the left hook just below the heart, a punch so deadly yet so swift and direct that most people at ringside could only see the right which followed it.

Rocky Marciano had murdered innocence and identity and a great many people's youth. It would be several years before they would forgive him. There were deep and valid reasons.

If there is any validity to the cherished folk myth of Horatio Alger and the American Dream, the people of this country have always been able to nurture it at thousands of ringsides from the tiny Legion Hall smokers to the big ball parks and the large stone-cold arenas. Harvard fellows and stock brokers' sons do not become heavyweight champions . . . they don't even try, which is just as well for generations of alumni club treasurers yet unborn. Poverty is the boxers' common denominator in an inner world where all men are created equal but those with good left hooks are more equal than others.

It is not a complicated thing for the novice to comprehend. He doesn't have to learn a pseudo-language which deals in non-sequiturs like "red dog," "zig in" and "square out." He doesn't have to strain his neck out of joint to watch giants struggle for a basketball and wait for a little man with a whistle to tell him what *might* have happened. When a man gets belted in the chops by the only other athlete in the ring, you don't need a slide rule to realize that he is in serious trouble.

You hear cab drivers and bartenders and lawyers and accountants tell you that there are no real fighters any more but when the heavyweight title goes on the line, they all show up . . . more of them than ever before, in fact, because of the ubiquitous closed circuit TV screen. And for many who watched the end of Joe Louis as a fighter that night in 1951, the wake was very real and very emotional. It was a family affair.

Twice in his lifetime—and in most of theirs—Joe Louis

had been a part of a brutal rivalry which had gripped this country from one coast to the other. First there was Max Schmeling and then there was Billy Conn and each time the world—not just the world inside the arena but that great, larger one outside it—changed as it had never changed before.

And because of these changes—coincidences of history which were both political and social—nobody was ever going to be the same again. In both cases, Louis has stood for something which was warm and comfortable and which people could understand in a world where old values crumbled every day and a large, gray area of doubt was beginning to interpose itself on a national system of values which had previously only allowed for everything in life to be either right or wrong.

In June of 1938, the string was running out on normalcy. The new Plymouth was selling for $685 (including tax), Clark Gable was off on a vacation before returning to play Rhett Butler in "Gone with the Wind," Katherine Hepburn and Cary Grant were starring in "Holiday" at the Radio City Music Hall and 570 students sang their last "Whiffen-poof" and picked up their degrees at Yale.   •

But as Louis himself would say before the second Conn fight eight years later: "He can run but he can't hide." For the great mass of isolated, indolent America there was no hiding from what was just around the corner. This was the year of Neville Chamberlain and his last pitiful attempt to hypnotize himself into "peace in our time." Munich would settle the Sudetenland's fate and all of Czechoslovakia would soon follow it behind Hitler's twisted, degenerate curtain. Austria, the Ruhr, the Rhineland were already gone. In 14 months, Warsaw would be in flames. In two years, France would fall and in three, Pearl Harbor would go up in smoke and the United States would sweep aside the cotton-candy curtain of isolationism forever.

Hours before Joe Louis and Max Schmeling would climb through the ring ropes at Yankee Stadium, 18 American citizens would be indicted on charges of spying for Nazi Germany. A group called "American First" was about to appear in defense of what it called the good, old American principle of "minding your own business." And in Germany, a collection of mental cripples was already sitting down to discuss what it euphemistically called "the final solution to the Jewish question."

Against this backdrop, Max Schmeling set sail aboard a German liner for the United States and his return match with Louis. He had been there many times before. From 1928 through 1933 he had campaigned there almost exclusively with infinite boxing skill and a murderous right hand. He had both won and lost the world title and ultimately returned to fight there again in 1936. It was on that last trip that Max Schmeling had inadvertently become a focal point for millions of Americans in the madness which was beginning to sweep the world.

On June 19, 1936, Max Schmeling had knocked out Joe Louis in the 12th round at Yankee Stadium. Louis, who was previously unbeaten, had been an 8–1 favorite but he had victimized himself with a costly reflex action. Carefully studying films of other Louis fights, Schmeling had observed that Louis always feinted with his left before he threw the right. Schmeling would look for that on the night of June 19, 1936. He found it in the fourth round and dropped Louis with a straight right hand. He found it again in the 12th and finished him.

But a new element had crept into that fight. Only the day before it, Adolph Hitler had selected a man named

Heinrich Himmler to head something called the Gestapo. Gestapo . . . it sounded like an imported deodorant. But when Schmeling and Louis would meet again in 1938, Americans would know a lot more about what was happening in Berlin. They began to learn the morning after Schmeling's right hand had crumbled Louis. "I know," a telegram released by Max's handlers read, "that you fought for Germany. This is a German victory. Heil Hitler." Signed: Joseph Goebbels.

In the two years between the first and second Louis-Schmeling fights, America watched and waited for the rematch. Louis was now the world champion. But boxing had little to do with this thing. In parts of this country, grown men with deep psychological difficulties bought para-military uniforms, opened rifle ranges and called themselves the German-American Bund. They were Nazi, not German and they were surely not American in their intentions. They met openly with the Ku Klux Klan, a group which most Americans thought had been consigned to limbo by the invention of the rubber bedsheet. Meanwhile, the Communist Party began to make loud organizational noises through a great many organizations whose letterheads purported to be something else.

For the first time since the Depression years, America was torn by doubts and fears and violent emotions. The stakes in this fight transcended the heavyweight championship. For many, Schmeling became the symbol of all that confused and angered them.

There was a certain sadness to this. Max Schmeling was basically not a political animal. Later he would fight in the German army but as a soldier rather than as a Nazi. He was not a party member. Just before the first Louis fight back in 1936, Harry Markson, then a sports writer and now the managing director of Madison Square Garden's boxing division, engaged Max in polite conversation on the porch of the wooden bungalow which was his training base at Napanoch, N.Y. Max had noted in the newspaper that day that the American Socialist Party had again chosen Norman Thomas as its presidential candidate.

"This man, this Herr Thomas," Max asked, "he is important?" "Not really," Markson said. "He ran four years ago and he polled under a million votes."

"Under a million votes," Max said thoughtfully. "We had one like that," he added, his voice tinged with bitterness. "Under a million votes . . . and now he runs the country."

"I don't have the slightest doubt that he was speaking about Adolph Hitler and I don't have the slightest doubt that he was not being very complimentary. He was not a Nazi. Max was kind of in the middle of all this. He wasn't a man who seemed to hate anybody."

But whether Max Schmeling liked it or not he became a symbol and there was justification for it. Back in Germany, Joseph Goebbels, the propagandist who was so efficient that he could look in the mirror and convince himself that his twisted, puny body was really the personification of the six foot, blond Aryan he preached about, had mapped out the thing quite clearly. Max was married to a beautiful movie star named Anny Ondra, in whom it was said that Goebbels' interest was more than patriotic. He was the fighter who would win the world title and return home to his beautiful wife in triumph. Then he would be named head of the Hitler Youth Movement. In conquering Louis he would destroy both an American and a black man. Goebbels was a dwarfish, mental cripple, who used his black full dress uniform like a comfort blanket. It would all happen and it would happen for him. He would be seven feet tall. It would be his greatest triumph.

Never before had the American people felt so deeply involved in a boxing match, or, perhaps, any athletic contest. In New York, which housed the country's largest Jewish population, the garment center was off on an emotional binge. A group called the Anti-Nazi League to Champion Human Rights threatened to picket the fight. This was 1938 and nobody ever picketed anything except factories.

And then in a town named Speculator, N. Y., a man named Harry Sperber opened a closet door and made Pandora's box look like a 10-cent grab bag. Mr. Sperber was a reporter for the German-American newspaper Staats-Zeitung. On a hot June afternoon, he found himself alone in the Osborne Hotel in the room of a man named Max Machon.

Max Machon takes a little explaining. He was Schmeling's trainer and one his closest friends. He was a lean, sharp-spoken man and there was a tacit understanding between him and the American sports writers. They wouldn't like him if he promised not to like them. It was one of the few agreements ever to stand up in boxing. A month later, when the German party would sail for home, an American boxing writer named Murray Lewin would slip a mickey into Max Machon's coffee at a farewell press conference. The Americans would cheer as Max Machon stumbled from the room. It may be the last time more than two American boxing writers ever agreed about anything.

At any rate, Schmeling was established at the Osborne Hotel and on this particular afternoon Harry Sperber opened Max Machon's closet door. Nobody knows why he did it and in the tumult which followed, nobody cared to ask. There, hung neatly on a hanger, was Max Machon's party uniform and his swastika armband. Harry Sperber was a German-American Jew. He wrote the story. The prize fight was no longer a prize fight. The Germans, who were fearful and trying to remain as unobtrusive as possible before the fight, dropped the game. Everything was out in the open now.

The North German Lloyd Liner Europa came steaming into New York Harbor that week, carrying a load of dignitaries to the fight. Among them was a man named Arno Helmus, a blocky, powerfully built beefy-faced German, who would broadcast the fight back to the Third Reich in the mother tongue. Herr Helmus did not kid around. You didn't have to open his closet door to know where he stood. He, too, had a charming relationship with the American press.

Meanwhile, back in Pompton Lakes, N. J., Joe Louis trained for this fight as he had never trained before. He had always been a methodical workman in camp but this time he labored like a man obsessed. For one thing, people had questioned his courage after the first fight. For another, Jack Dempsey, who never missed a chance to take a shot at him, said after Schmeling's knockout victory two years earlier:

"Louis has a glass jaw and can't take a punch. All you have to do to beat him is to walk into him and bang him with a good, solid punch. I don't think he'll ever whip another good fighter."

And, finally, there was Schmeling himself. Louis did not like Schmeling. Max, who went through life with a perpetual scowl which was punctuated by his dark, bushy eyebrows, never said much to Joe. But through the good offices of Dr. Goebbels, the heroic pigmy who would take his punches from 3,000 miles away, Max was quoted as saying a great deal about him. The line which Goebbels fashioned and attributed to Schmeling which rankled the most said "The Negro will always be afraid of me."

Back in New York City, Arno Helmus kept the propaganda pot boiling. He filed a steady stream of invective back to Germany which he happily quoted for the benefit of anyone who would listen. His chief targets were American newspapers, which he said were trying to shake Schmeling's confidence by printing stories that he would be arrested back in Germany if he lost the fight and the "Jew governor (Herbert Lehman)" who had already insured Max's defeat.

"I don't think," Markson recalls, "that a prize fight had ever generated this type of emotion. People who knew nothing about boxing and cared even less were suddenly deeply involved."

The final spark for millions of Americans who were planning to hear the fight on radio was the indictment of the 18 American citizens as Nazi spies. On the night of June 22, 1938, extra police ringed Yankee Stadium in tight blue platoons as 70,043 people streamed through the gates and pumped $1,015,012 into promoter Mike Jacobs' cash register. It might have been a war of the worlds but for the man they called Uncle Mike it was a promoter's Nirvana.

At ringside technicians for the National Broadcasting Company ran their final tests and assured their own crews and Arno Helmus that all was in order. NBC would carry the broadcast coast-to-coast and its facilities would be used for Arno Helmus' German language report back to the Third Reich. Mrs. Schmeling (Anny Ondra, the movie star) would as usual, hear the fight alone with Goebbels in his apartment. Max was not reported to be happy about that. There is a limit to what a man should be expected to sacrifice for his country.

And then, quite abruptly, the way it always happens, there was Louis coming down one aisle and Schmeling down another. The noise spilled out in a rumbling crescendo. This is always the electric moment before a heavyweight title fight no matter how bad the actual fight figures to be. On this night of raw emotions, it was even more so. Louis came swiftly down the aisle followed by his trainer, Chappie Blackburn and a phalanx of policemen. Once he slipped off his robe, he confirmed what newspapermen had expected and what millions of emotionally-involved Americans had hoped. He was in magnificent physical condition. Across the ring, Schmeling waited with his beetle-browed scowl and the unbiquitous Max Machon, gently rubbing his back. Arthur Donovan, the referee, called them to mid-ring.

As things developed, that pre-fight conference was the longest look anyone had at Schmeling that night. The bell rang. Around the country, disorganized people slipped hurriedly off to the kitchen to get a can of beer. They didn't miss much . . . just the whole fight.

For several seconds Louis moved forward and Max retreated. Each pawed the air tentatively with his gloves. Then Louis landed two rapier jabs to Schmeling's head, hooked him to the body with a left and crossed with a right hand which landed high on the head and drove Schmeling to the ropes.

Schmeling was hurt. The Stadium was a wave of hysterical noise. Max grabbed for the top strand of the ring rope to steady himself and turned as Louis pumped to his body. Max turned in that daze and caught the blow in the kidney area. His third lumbar vertebra had been shattered by its force.

"I was there," Harry Markson says, "and I heard Schmeling scream. I was in the fourth row and I heard him. I have never seen anything like it. The crowd was positively devastated by the destruction which followed."

Schmeling went down three times in less time than it

takes to write about it. The third time, Max Machon looked at the crumpled heap which was one of his closest friends and heaved a towel into the ring, the traditional European request to the referee to stop the fight. But New York had no such rule. With his right hand, Arthur Donovan continued to toll the count. With his left he backhanded the towel out of the way. It caught on the ring ropes and hung there, flapping grotesquely; a kind of punctuation mark to Donovan's count. He could have counted to 500. The fight was over. The whole thing took just two minutes and four seconds.

Down below at ringside, Lovable Arno Helmus, his beefy red face even redder, a throbbing blue vein pulsing on his forehead, was shrieking wildly into a dead microphone. Back home in Germany, someone had pulled the plug. The German people were not going to find out what had happened to their man and to Joseph Goebbels' plans, at least not until Goebbels had time to frame his alibi. Even for Goebbels, it would not be easy.

But he tried. Schmeling was in the hospital. He was a mess. The pain from his shattered vertebra was excruciating but it could be repaired. Not so anyone can notice it, Goebbels ordered. He framed his stand quickly. Schmeling had been hit with an illegal punch. He might be crippled for life by it and the Jewish governor (Lehman) was a part of the scheme. Max was under orders not to walk again on American soil. Stick to it. Max did. After his stay in the hospital, Max Schmeling sailed for Germany aboard a Lloyd liner. He was carried up the gangplank on a stretcher. Doctors insisted he could have walked.

So Schmeling sailed away and no man had ever been beaten more decisively unless it was Max Machon that same day when they slipped him the mickey. The world would never be the same. The real war had begun to close in on America. Joe Louis and Max Schmeling had played out their tableau on a vanishing stage and thus had become an integral part of that era's history.

Few men ever get the chance to leave that kind of footprint. On the night that Joe Louis put it there, there was no way of knowing that in Pittsburgh, Pa., there was a 20-year old kid with a face like the map of Ireland who himself would be swept up in a similar emotional whirlpool and when the moment of truth would arrive seven years later, Joe Louis once again would be a part of it. His name was Billy Conn.

It was supposed to be just another fight. Billy Conn was a flashy light heavyweight with a dancer's feather-light feet and a boxer's stinging jab. In 1941, still five years removed from what would become the focal point of this hysteria, he found himself a heavyweight challenger by default.

Joe Louis never looked back after the second Schmeling fight. He fought often and he fought over-poweringly well. People ceased betting for or against him. The ultimate finishes were foregone conclusions. The only thing left to bet on was the round in which Louis would do it. A man named Johnny Paycheck had to be carried into the ring to face him. Two rounds later he was, for all practical purposes, carried back out. The field of potential opponents shrank faster than a pair of Brand X overalls. In Mike Jacobs' New York office, the names on it had dwindled down to just two.

Jacobs was the canny promoter who had found Louis and who had built an empire with him, dislodging Jimmy Johnson from his post as Madison Square Garden promoter by the simple but irrefutable maneuver of "owning" the heavyweight title through Joe. Now it was 1941 and Selective Service was a household word, Charley The Bug Workman drew a life sentence for the intra-tribal murder of Dutch Schultz, and Milton Berle and Vincent Lopez were packing them in at New York's Paramount Theater. Defense plants were booming. People were itching to spend money. And Mike Jacobs had a problem.

"Mike," a reporter said to him one day, "you only got two contenders left. I got a great idea. Let Lou Nova fight Billy Conn for the right to meet Louis."

"That's the lousiest idea I ever heard," Mike Jacobs replied exactly like a man who had been prodded into a decision. Mike Jacobs never went to college. Consequently, the justice of such a semi-final playoff never bothered him. With simple logic he thought to himself;

"Two fifty dollar tickets for two different fights are worth twice as much as one fifty dollar ticket for one fight. We will have two title fights."

First Conn and then Nova would get their chances. With any kind of luck one of them would not be a total disgrace and there might be a rematch, giving Mike a third fight. In any event, he would have 30 rounds of championship boxing before he had to plot a new course of action. So Billy Conn, a product of, by and for fight-minded Pittsburgh, Pa., would get his chance to fight Joe Louis.

The announcement thrilled nobody. Conn was a 4–1 underdog and he had to give away 25 pounds. Nevertheless, as Mike Jacobs shrewdly anticipated, the chance to see Louis and the lure of the heavyweight title combined to form a powerful magnet. On the night of June 18, 1941, more than 54,000 people packed the old Polo Grounds and what they saw left them pop-eyed. Billy Conn weaved and bobbed for 12 straight rounds, beating Louis to the punch often and then flitting away to live and fight some more. He may not have been winning the fight as later folk myths dictate, but it certainly looked that way to the large crowd which had come to the ball park expecting to see something quite different. They were, they firmly believed, about to see history made.

In the 13th round, Conn suddenly switched tactics and stood to slug with Louis in mid-ring, winning a brutal but brief exchange in which the champion backed off. But then, as the clock neared the end of its three-minute run, Joe Louis became his own referee with five straight right hands for which Billy Conn had no answer. The fourth one did it. It drove Conn backwards, his knees buckled and he was already out of it when the fifth blow landed. Only two seconds remained in 13 when Billy was counted out.

Those two seconds would become the backbone of a debate which would rage for five years. If Conn had managed to rise somehow, the bell could have saved him. Would he have won on points? Would Louis have swarmed all over him in the 14th and finished him even more decisively? Only one question could be answered about this strangest of boxing evenings. Would Mike Jacobs get them together again? Considering for a single second that he wouldn't was like asking the Mississippi not to roll.

Conn masked his disappointment in genuine logic. He had fought well. He had blundered by playing to Louis's strength in the 13th. Next time it would be different. Louis, obviously pleased with the outcome but with one eye toward a rematch, added that Conn might, indeed, have won it with more caution. And Mike Jacobs, well, Mike Jacobs was a positive one-man festival. He couldn't wait to set the date for the rematch.

But two days after the fight, Italy and Germany closed

the American Consulates in their countries and sent the employees packing. New York City began signing up and training air raid wardens. Louis fought Nova as scheduled and knocked him out in six rounds on Sept. 29. But time was running out. A little more than two months later, the Japanese bombed Pearl Harbor. Even Mike Jacobs couldn't straighten that one out.

And so this is how the thing took root. Louis and Conn both joined the Army. And the myth of what really happened or what nearly happened or what might have happened that night at the Polo Grounds took wings and soared. Mike Jacobs, his store-bought teeth chattering in pure trauma was a nervous wreck. What if one of them were shot . . . or decided never to fight again . . . or the war never ended . . . or . . . or . . . or . . . Sherman was right in Mike's view. War is hell.

But the public clamour was so great and the economy so flushed that Mike Jacobs never stopped trying. He enlisted the aid of sports writers John Kieran and Grantland Rice who proposed a bout in which both fighters would give all the money to charity. Well, at least that's what Jacobs told them. Upon closer scrutiny Robert Patterson, the Secretary of War, discovered that all the money couldn't possibly go to charity because $100,000 of it was scheduled to go to Mike Jacobs to pay off a debt which Louis owed him. Well, nobody is perfect. Mr. Patterson did not make allowances for human frailty. He threw everybody out.

Still, the public remembered. It remembered in a million bar rooms and at a thousand sports dinners and on a hundred radio shows. The war ended and Conn and Louis were discharged from the service. They did, indeed, plan to return to the ring. Mike Jacobs was back in the driver's seat. No other promoter in the history of war, love or boxing ever had

five years and the Star Spangled Banner to set up his act.
The only question to be resolved was when and for how
much.

In the spring of 1946, Mike Jacobs sat in his office at the
Brill Building, a spacious piece of luxury roughly the size
of one of the late Astor Hotel's pay toilets. It was a warm
day, the kind of day when nobody feels like working and
nobody felt less like it on this particular day than the now-
forgotten reporter who had dropped by Mike's office.

"Mike," he said, "I want to get home early. I need a story.
How much are you going to charge for the Louis-Conn fight
. . . I mean ringside . . . top ticket?"

"Who knows?" Mike said reflectively. "I have to see
what the traffic will bear. Could be 40 . . . 60 . . . 80 . . .
hell, maybe I'll charge 100 bucks. It's too soon to say."

The next morning, however, it had been said. Mike
Jacobs opened his paper and learned that Mike Jacobs was
planning to charge $100 for a ringside seat for the first time
in the history of boxing. "What the hell do I do now?" Mike
asked the ceiling. "Who the hell is gonna pay 100 bucks for a
fight?"

Then they brought in the mail and it was loaded with
$100 checks. It happened again the next day and the day
after that. "Well, look," Mike shrugged, "you got to bow to
the public in such matters. I mean, after all, the sport be-
longs to them." The tickets went on sale at $100 top. The
place would be Yankee Stadium. The date would be June
19. Louis would go back to Pompton Lakes to train and
Conn would be in Greenwood Lake, N. J. It was conceivable
that the gate could be close to $3 million.

It remained to be seen how many people would actually
pay to watch the thing but there was no doubt that it was
the dominant topic of conversation everywhere. It was a

happy time. People were convinced that the end of World War II had restored sanity to the order of things. Hell, hadn't General Motors announced it would start producing 2 million new cars . . . real cars . . . not those things that had to be held together with spit and twine and nerve during the war. In the spirit of the new international harmony, the United States announced that week that it would not try Emperor Hirohito as a war criminal. It was, for most Americans, a return to the way it was . . . a time of giddy relief. Joe Louis was back in the ring and all was once again right with the world.

Mike Jacobs, however, was not most Americans. Like all fight promoters, he realized that a situation like this was simply too easy and too good to be true. He kept waiting for somebody to drop the other shoe. The somebody who did was named Mike Jacobs and he stuck it in his own mouth.

As the fight neared, Barney Nagler, an incisive and extremely talented fight writer, had been assigned to do a piece about the making of a heavyweight title fight for Collier's Magazine. Mike Jacobs was expansive. "Take this fight," he said, "why in order to build a ringside setup appropriate for such an occasion, I am going to get the full production of two mills for two months. That's how much lumber I'll need."

Nagler wrote the story, an American Legion post commander in the Midwest read it. He called the FBI.

"Our boys fought and bled and some of them died for this country. Now they can't get lumber to build the homes they need. But Mike Jacobs gets it. What the hell is going on here? It's disgraceful."

Mike Jacobs blew his top. He had no quarrel with Nagler, who had accurately reported Mike's statements. He had no quarrel with the American Legion, whose absolute truth he was willing to recognize, particularly on occasions when they had sold—and hopefully would continue to sell tickets for him. And he sure as hell was not going to pick a fight with the FBI, which out-weighed him and thereby would have constituted very bad match-making. He took it out on the lumber.

As Nagler recalls, the wood was taken over to a warehouse in Glen Ridge, N. J., where it was soaked in water for 48 hours. Then they shoveled sand on it. Then they shoveled dirt on it. Then they called the inspectors.

"New lumber?" Mike Jacobs said, "gentlemen, you really hurt me."

The fight went on as scheduled.

It was staged, ironically, on the 10th anniversary of Joe Louis' knockout loss to Max Schmeling. The champion was a 12–5 favorite but sentiment around the country was sharply divided. This would be the first post-war sports spectacular, the end of a five-year wait. Radio would again carry it around the world but this time a new wrinkle had been added. In New York, New Jersey, Philadelphia and Washington, a limited number of hardy souls would get to see the thing on a brand new doomsday machine called television. NBC carried it, a man named Bob Stanton did the blow-by-blow and when it was over, viewers complained that long shots of the ring had reduced the fighters to dots. Less than two decades later this same medium in conjunction with hopelessly short-sighted promoters would combine through greed and mismanagement to reduce other fighters to absolutely nothing but that's another story.

So they came to fight on the night of June 19, 1946 . . . at least everyone assumed they did. Things do not always work out that way in the final act of a folk myth. Louis weighed 210 pounds and Conn weighed 182 pounds. Louis

was 32 years old and Conn, 27. Billy had problems with his
feet, not the least of them centered around a case of unfortunate blisters. Because of the high price scale only
45,266 paying customers were there . . . roughly 9,000
fewer than had seen the first fight. Still, because of the high
prices, Jacobs took in $1,925,564 that night.

From the moment the opening bell sounded, the tension
dissipated like the air shooting out of a ruptured balloon. In
a word, this flight of destiny, this two-man Armageddon
which had waited for a whole world to right itself before
it could resume, this five-year preamble to High Noon was
plain, old-fashioned lousy.

Louis was rusty. Conn had nothing left. For six rounds
they stared at each other, grunted and did very little fighting. John Lardner, the poet laureate of boxing, would say
the following morning: "It was the first live fight I ever saw
in slow motion."

If it had a saver, however, it was the ending, which was
accomplished with at least the residue of Louis' former
lightning. In the eighth round, he finally landed a right hand
and drew blood from just under Conn's left eye. He followed
with a right to the jaw and when Conn's knees buckled, Joe
Louis put together a left hook and yet one more right cross
to knock Billy stiff at 2:19 of the eighth round.

As heavyweight title fights go, this was a battle which
nobody would have remembered under normal circumstances. But normal circumstances were not what made it
the emotional thing it was. Nobody knew that better than
Mike Jacobs. Mindful of the horrendous artistic failure of
the thing, he rushed out and made another fight for Louis.
He wanted to get him into the ring so people would forget.
The man he chose was Tami Mauriello. Tami lasted one
round.

If a myth died that night in Yankee Stadium as Conn

lay spread out against the floor, so did an era. Louis was never the same. Except for one brief, burst of unbridled savagery two years later against Jersey Joe Walcott, his great moments were behind him. Conn fought only twice more. And roughly a decade later, boxing fell under the total domination of television. Then television pulled the plug. Places like Korea and Vietnam and names like Fidel Castro and Che Gueverra became household words. People began trying to fly to the moon.

The world which produced Louis-Schmeling and Louis-Conn was dead.

"There will come a time when nothing will be of more interest here in Brooklyn than authentic reminiscences of the past."

. . . Walt Whitman

"Baseball is trying to operate as it did in 1900. It can't be done. Population and business have moved West. Baseball must follow."

. . . Ford C. Frick, then Commissioner of Baseball, 1954.

A TALE OF TWO CITIES

In all of baseball, there was nothing like it. And since baseball is a uniquely American game, there was nothing like it in all of this country . . . not in the great focal point of the American heartland which is Chicago . . . not amid the smokestacks which form the guts of American industry in Pittsburgh and in Detroit and in Cleveland . . . not in the North, the South, the East or the West . . . not even in the marriage between San Francisco's dilettantes and Los Angeles' cerise stretch pants where it finally came to rest. The grip which the Brooklyn Dodgers and the New York Giants held on the hearts and—in one sad case—the trigger finger of the country can never be duplicated.

They have tried to regain it a full continent away in California but all they have fashioned is a pitiful carbon copy. The Lazarus which was this emotional catharsis each summer isn't going to take up its bed and walk. It died for all time on Oct. 8, 1956 when Walter O'Malley of the Dodgers and Horace Stoneham of the Giants announced they were moving their ball clubs off into the California sunset. The pieces they left behind can never be put together again.

Maybe it was the ball parks . . . the one a sprawling mis-shapen, misnamed architectural abomination called the Polo Grounds, hacked out of the side of Harlem with a set of dimensions that turned pop flies into home runs and home runs into outs . . . and the other, Ebbets Field where the Dodgers played, a positive caricature of a joint with a lobby like a circus tent, an elevator which counted each groaning trip from the ground floor to the press box as a slap at Sir Isaac Newton and a seating arrangement which gave both teams the impression they were trying to catch a ball with 32,000 people sitting on their shoulders.

Maybe it was the managers. There was John McGraw, the Irish-Prussian war lord and Mel Ott, the boy wonder grown suddenly old. There was Wilbert Robinson, who once was identified so closely with the Brooklyn team that it was called the Robins, and Casey Stengel, the linguist. There was Burt Shotton, who wouldn't put on a uniform, and Charley Dressen, who hated to take one off, and Leo Durocher, who blended day and night into one long siege.

Maybe it was the players . . . Van Lingle Mungo and Dazzy Vance, who threw pure smoke . . . Mel Ott with his impossible batting stance . . . Dolph Camilli and Dixie Walker, bouncing home runs out onto Bedford Avenue . . . Dick Bartell and Eddie Stanky, coming at the second baseman with spikes high . . . Jackie Robinson, all legs and muscles and pigeontoes, bouncing up and down off first base while the people yelled "go . . . go . . . go."

It was, of course, all of these things but most of all it was the customers and it was geography. There is only one Brooklyn and to a great extent even that one existed only in the minds of the people who lived there. Every Grade B war movie ever made had an infantryman named "Brooklyn" in it, who wrote letters to a girl named Mazie and, with appropriate musical background, asked the chaplain if he would beat the wound and get back home to boo the umpire again at Ebbets Field. It was pure, unadulturated corn but it was made for national consumption and the popcorn eaters in national audiences accepted it as what Brooklyn and no other place was all about.

It was a much maligned pseudo-city and if its Hessians were the Dodgers, Ebbets Field was its Maginot Line. No matter that the guns in the real Maginot Line and occasionally the guns in Ebbets Field were turned in the wrong direction. Nobody is perfect.

Even the idea of the stereotype Brooklyn resident drove them closer together. The stereotype was "dese" and "dems" and "doze." But in 1956 when the Dodger management abandoned Flatbush forever, the borough had eight colleges, 6,033 acres of parks, 700 churches, 500 synagogues and 7,500 factories. Still, through all of this, other New Yorkers, and consequently, the rest of America viewed it as a kind of comic strip no-man's land. Brooklyn, deprived of political autonomy usually associated with a population its size, rose to the challenge. It had a heart and a soul and it invested both in the Dodgers. Brooklyn fans were emotional, irrational, verbose, exhibitionist and unreasonable. The thing about which they were most irrational, verbose, exhibitionist and unreasonable was a New York Giants fan. It was a vendetta made in heaven.

Dodger fans were Dodger fans by geography. Giant fans were Giant fans by birthright. Long before the Yankees were born, the Giants owned the city. The glories witnessed by the father were passed down to the son. For a long, long stretch, beginning in the late 1930s and carrying over into 1951, Giant fans prided themselves on their dignity. Let the Brooklyns do the howling. The Giants could lose

with honor. Dodger fans contended that if the Giants were
to lose a little more over that period, dignity just might
not be their customers' strong suit.

Through all of this, New York was the only three-team
city in all of baseball. But the Yankees never figured in the
stress and strain of these moments. The only thing Dodger
and Giant fans ever agreed on was the fact that the Yankees
were off somewhere by themselves in that other league,
poised and professional and automatic. You could die rooting
for the Giants or the Dodgers . . . die of a broken heart.
You could also die rooting for the Yankees . . . out of sheer
boredom.

The Giants and the Dodgers lived in another world . . .
a world of fist fights and firecrackers, of bean balls and
amateur musicians. It covered the day Bobby Thomson hit
THE home run and the day the Dodgers flung Bill Terry's
knock on Brooklyn back in his teeth. The Yankees were
stockbrokers, making neat transactions on inside information. But the Giants and the Dodgers were sweat and
earthy smells and bottles thrown in a great many barrooms.
When they were good, they were thrilling. When they were
bad, they were magnificently lousy.

They were—the players, the customers, the managers
and, yes, even the umpires—part of a lusty, brawling fraternity and the truth was that their love and their hate
were interchangeable, which may be why adjustments were
so easily made whenever one of the troops crossed over
the bridge. Durocher managed both. Freddie Fitzsimmons
and Johnny Allen pitched for both. Casey Stengel played
for one and managed the other. Ducky Medwick batted for
both and when he was swinging successfully against the
Dodgers in a Sunday doubleheader at the Polo Grounds in
which the Giants had scored the amazing total of 23 runs

in the first game, a dejected Dodger fan perked himself up hurling an empty pop bottle at Ducky's groin as he climbed the centerfield heights during their intra-city squabbles. Bobby Rawn, a Giant infielder stooped under the weight of an .057 batting average, knocked a startling home run into the first row of the Polo Grounds' seats to lock up a doubleheader sweep. Packy Rogers, a transient third baseman whose major league career spanned all of 23 games, broke in against the Giants with two singles and a triple. Packy hit .667 against the Giants in a half dozen games and .097 against the rest of the universe.

It simply never mattered whether one team was leading the league and the other was seventh. Every game was played with a savage delight which rocked the ball park. There was Carl Hubbell at age 40 trying to throw the screwball past the Dodgers during a standing-room-only doubleheader at the Polo Grounds and getting away with it for seven innings. There was Tommy Brown, playing shortstop for the Dodgers during World War II when he should have been in his high school English class. There was Pete Reiser running into the wall in left center so often that they had to pad it with foam rubber.

The ball parks are gone now. After three false starts, the Polo Grounds finally came tumbling down and on the last day they sold the green chairs in the boxes, the lights and even the dirt. The joint was rotting away by that time (the Giants were already trying to function in a San Francisco wind-tunnel called Candlestick Park) and at night its remains belonged to the wild life of upper Manhattan—both two and four-legged—which prowled the debris.

Ebbets Field had gone to an earlier grave. Towering apartment houses now stand on both sites. For a brief period when the Mets first thrust their noses on the New York scene, the faithful (who had never switched their allegiance to the Yankees) came out to the park to see the return of Willie Mays and Don Drysdale. And then it was over. The teams belong to California now. Their series, which once moved a priest to pray on the steps of Borough Hall in Brooklyn, is nothing more than a provincial pillow fight. The things it used to be are gone forever.

But there is a legacy. You can find it in the photo morgue of any major newspaper . . . you can see three pictures taken on Oct. 3, 1951. There is Eddie Stanky, who once was a Dodger, wearing a Giants' uniform and leaping on the back of another ex-Dodger named Leo Durocher in the wildest of all victory hugs. There is Bobby Thomson, standing on the rickety wooden steps of the Polo Grounds' centerfield clubhouse and waving trance-like to the mass of humanity assembled down below. And there is Ralph Branca, sitting painfully before his locker, hands to his forehead in undisguised anguish.

Together they tell what this thing was all about. Together they tell the most emotional single story in the history of baseball and the mass hysteria it produced. It is the end product of an intense and complicated road which spanned decade after decade of a changing world and led to those three photographs.

The Giants and the Dodgers spawned their feud in bitterness. There were New York teams and Brooklyn teams before John McGraw came along. There were New York teams and Brooklyn teams during McGraw's early tenure as Giants' manager. But the well-spring from which this mass hysteria flowed really began to take shape when McGraw and his first base coach, Wilbert Robinson, had a violent argument in the spring of 1913. Robinson had been his friend. They had been teammates on the old Baltimore

Orioles, a brawling, lusty collection of early baseball heroes whose idea of medical attention for a split finger was to spit on it, rub it in the dirt and play the game.

Robinson drew McGraw's eternal wrath in a way which was common for people who worked for the Giants' manager. He insisted that the possibility existed that John J. McGraw might have made a mistake. The incident centered around Robinson's sending an injured player down to attempt a steal of second base which was aborted by some 10 ft. Robinson claimed that McGraw had flashed him the signal from the dugout. McGraw insisted this was impossible. Moreover, he added, it was also impossible for Wilbert Robinson to work for the Giants ever again. To prove his point, he fired Robinson at the end of the season.

Two years later, Charley Ebbets hired Wilbert Robinson to manage Brooklyn. In his honor the team became known as the Robins. Robinson immediately brought his club home ahead of the Giants in 1915 and 1916, the first time Brooklyn had finished ahead of New York since 1902, and won the pennant that second year. McGraw never forgave him.

Their battles were intense but toward the latter part of Robinson's career, the Dodgers began to acquire a different kind of reputation, one which would endear them as much to Brooklyn fans of that era as the proficiency of later years would attract another generation.

It began on April 15, 1926 in a totally inoffensive manner. The Giants beat the Dodgers, 9–5 and New York was buzzing because a man named Paul Emmanuel Hilton, 26, had been arrested in front of the park. Mr. Hilton had already killed one police officer and wounded three others during a spree of 29 robberies during which he had become known as "the radio burglar." He had stolen 14 sets because he said "I like music." History does not record whether he

was on his way inside the Polo Grounds to root for the
Giants or the Dodgers or to steal the scoreboard clock.

On that same day, the New York Times carried a story
which contended that in some strange way Prohibition was
actually causing drunkenness and immorality among youth
in Pennsylvania mining communities because "everyone has
a home-still and children have easy access to the drink."

What began on that day in 1926 would drive many a
Brooklyn Dodger baseball fan to drink—illegal or otherwise.
Virtually unnoticed, Babe Herman made his debut for the
Brooklyns and drew a walk.

In the years to follow, the Brooklyn baseball club would
bring a great many strange athletes into the Polo Grounds
on their regular invasions. The strangest of all would be
Babe Herman.

His square name was Floyd Caves Herman. Through
six seasons with Brooklyn as a once-in-a while first baseman
and a most unusual outfielder, Babe Herman would be all
major leaguer with a bat, his finest years producing batting
averages of .393 and .381. Unhappily, he is not remembered
for his hitting.

There are some who insist that he was the only major
league outfielder to alternate his defense between a fielder's
glove and a death wish. Tom Meany, a baseball writer with
the New York World Telegram wrote much of his attempts
to field fly balls with his head and one day Babe approached
him and said:

"I never get hit in the head. If I ever get hit in the
head with a fly ball you can be sure I will never show up
at Ebbets Field again."

"All right," Meany said, "what about the shoulder?"

"Shoulders," Babe replied, "don't count."

Brooklyn fans watched with horror on the day when

Babe Herman hit a line drive to the outfield with a runner on first, kept his head down, made a wide turn and charged for second base. For some strange reason the base runner decided the ball had been caught and retreated, head down, for first. And heads down they passed each other, moving in opposite directions.

Obviously, Babe Herman had a lot of help. He was surely on the right ball club. Nobody ever got the help Babe got one day from everybody in sight with a Dodger uniform. The opposition—more or less—was Boston. Some people say it was the rest of the Dodgers.

Brooklyn had the bases filled when Herman hit a tremendous fly ball to the outfield. It fell safely but nobody seemed to be sure.

One run scored and Dazzy Vance, who had been on second was now lumbering toward home, the man from first had reached third and here came Herman ploughing ahead toward third himself.

"Back, get back,' screamed the third base coach.

Unfortunately Vance and not Herman heard the order. He slid back into third base from the home plate side. Herman slid into third from the second base side and the third Dodger runner, standing on the bag, was nearly cut in half.

Yet, through it all, Brooklyn fans never wavered in their loyalty and the Brooklyn baseball writer of that era said, "overconfidence may cost this team seventh place."

But then it was 1934 and 1934 was a year that Dodger fans remembered for a long, long time. So, for that matter, did Giant fans. The Brooklyn rooters wouldn't let them forget.

Casey Stengel was about to be hired as Brooklyn manager and Bill Terry was manager of the world champion

Giants. In February, Terry stood in the lobby of the Hotel
Roosevelt and analyzed the forthcoming pennant race for
a group of baseball writers.

"What about Brooklyn?" asked Roscoe McGowen of the
Times.

"Is Brooklyn still in the league?" Terry replied.

That same week, Stengel, who had been a World Series
hero once for the Giants was installed as the new Brooklyn
manager and applied a very direct psychological needle.
"I am very happy to be back in town," Mr. Stengel said,
"and I can assure Mr. Terry that Brooklyn is still in the
league. He will be hearing from us shortly and he will also
be hearing from a pitcher I have, named Mr. Mungo."

The Dodgers were not expected to accomplish very
much in 1934 and they didn't let anybody down. They
finished sixth. Moreover, the Giants took their first six
meetings with them. But on Aug. 2, 1934 Bill Terry did,
indeed, begin to hear from both Brooklyn and Mr. Mungo.

Van Lingle Mungo was a pitcher of great speed and
even greater temper. He wasn't a bad hitter either. On
August 2, he singled home a run and shut out the Giants,
2–0, to cut their lead over first-place St. Louis to just 2½
games. It wasn't the last Mr. Terry would see of Mr. Mungo.

With two games remaining on the 1934 schedule, the
Giants and the Cardinals were in a dead tie for the league
lead. On a rainy afternoon at the Polo Grounds, Casey
Stengel sent out Van Lingle Mungo to warm up. He
would pitch this one for Brooklyn. The Giants would go
with their ace, Roy Parmalee. Because of the weather, the
crowd was held down to a mere 15,000 but almost half of
them had come up from Brooklyn carrying "Is Brooklyn
Still in the League" placards. They expected a very big
afternoon.

Mungo gave it to them. Just before he went out to pitch, Stengel read a telegram in the clubhouse which said: "You will earn the undying gratitude of Brooklyn fans if you knock Bill Terry and his Giants flat on their back." It was signed by 50 individual Brooklyn rooters. Mungo went out and pitched one of the finest games of his career. He drove in two runs and he set the Giants down, 5–1. The Giants fell out of first place for the first time since June 8. Every time Bill Terry stuck his nose out of the dugout he was hooted as only Brooklyn Dodger fans could hoot when the person they were hooting had "Giants" on the front of his uniform. They beat the Giants again on Sunday and when the game ended waves of Dodger rooters swept across the field chanting: "Is Brooklyn still in the league." It was almost enough to make Brooklyn forget that the ball club had finished sixth.

The vehemence of the feud never slackened after that. Rowdy Dick Bartell, an infielder whose temperament matched Mungo's joined the Giants. On one opening day he was hit in the face with a tomato. On another, Terry requested police protection for him. Twice he and Mungo punched hell out of each other. In 1948 an ex-Dodger named Goodie Rosen slid into Eddie Stanky at second with spikes high. Punches were thrown, the dugouts emptied and it took some time to restore order. Hardly a year went by without one such incident.

The emotions this series aroused were beyond any law of logic. The worst came off the field. It did not involve a single baseball player but it was the direct result of the hysteria which surrounded these teams and their rivalry. It happened in the wee hours on a blistering morning in Brooklyn.

Pat Diamond's Bar and Grill was a neighborhood Brook-

lyn bar where baseball was the main, and, often, the only
topic of conversation. Robert Joyce, a regular patron and
a violent Dodger fan, was almost always involved in it.
On the night of July 12, 1938 he sought solace from the
hot city streets in a glass or two of beer.

That afternoon, rookie Bill Posedel had beaten the
Giants and third baseman Packy Rogers had made his
auspicious if somewhat deceptive debut. It was Brooklyn's
first triumph over the Giants in 11 games that year. Frank
Krug, a Giants' fan at the bar, kept reminding Joyce of
that fact and just to keep the action moving, so did Bill
Diamond, the son of the owner. Joyce lapsed into a thought-
ful silence. He had another beer . . . and another . . . and
another. In all, he had 18 glasses of beer. Suddenly he
leaped to his feet and hurled an obscenity at Krug. Then
he left. Three minutes later he was back with a gun in his
hand. He fired twice.

Bill Diamond, 30, was wounded in the left side. Frank
Krug, 40, was shot through the heart and died instantly.
Joyce threw the gun at the bartender and dashed out of
the door. He was apprehended after a two-block chase.
Posedel, he told the police, was a very good pitcher.

Violence in a great many forms surrounded the Dodger-
Giant feud. But nothing—absolutely nothing—could have
shaken the faith of both sides as much as what happened
on July 12, 1948, exactly 10 years after Robert Joyce shot
and killed Frank Krug.

Leo Durocher was managing the Dodgers then, fresh
back from a year's suspension for what Commissioner
Happy Chandler had termed "conduct detrimental to baseball." He had brought Brooklyn its first pennant in 21 years
back in 1941. In so doing he had earned the undying hatred
of every Giant fan. After all, Leo was Leo . . . brash, out-
spoken, acid-tongued, a master bench jockey and umpire

baiter. Brooklyn loved him. Consequently, New York hated him. What happened that day was pure trauma.

Horace Stoneham, owner of the Giants, had grown impatient of his team's abject failure under Mel Ott. Stoneham decided that Ott would have to go. He held a secret conference with Branch Rickey, who was then running the Dodgers, and asked permission to talk to Burt Shotton, who had managed the Dodgers to the 1947 pennant during Leo's exile.

"No," Rickey told a startled Stoneham, "you cannot talk to Mr. Shotton. I have plans for him. If you want to talk to someone, talk to Leo Durocher. He is going to be available right now."

Stoneham did and when he had finished he set in motion one of the most incredible managerial exchanges in baseball history. Leo Durocher, that great hate-symbol of Coogan's Bluff, Leo Durocher, the man who had maligned their hero Mel Ott by pointing to him and saying "nice guys finish last," Leo Durocher was the new manager of the Giants.

Bill Corum broke the story in the late edition of the New York Journal-American. Players on both teams refused to believe it. But there it was. Burt Shotton had returned to the Ebbets Field dugout and Leo was the new man at the Polo Grounds.

Softly, like the bearded exiles at the Wailing Wall, long-suffering Giant fans gave vent to their emotions. So they hadn't won a pennant in 11 years. So they couldn't take a season series from the Dodgers. But Leo Durocher! It was too much even to consider.

In Peekskill, N. Y., a man named Leo Chefalo, who had rarely missed a Giant home game in 25 years and who claimed for himself the title of number one Giants' fan, told the Associated Press:

"That settles it, brother. I'm through. I'll never enter the Polo Grounds again."

Asked if he might reconsider if Leo Durocher should ultimately lead the Giants to a pennant, Mr. Chefalo replied: "That's impossible."

Giant fans, steeped in tradition, echoed his sentiments. They would take the players the Dodgers discarded. After all, that was baseball and it sometimes happened that the two clubs did make deals. Didn't they have Goodie Rosen now and hadn't Goodie put the spikes to Eddie Stanky? But to fire Mel Ott, who had been with the club since age 16 and who had set a National League home run record, well that was simply asking too much.

Over in Brooklyn, the reaction was less violent. There were those who remembered and admired Shotton for his handling of the 1947 team. They believed that his technique could deliver where Durocher's had failed. An incredible three and a half years was about to enfold. It would lead directly to Bobby Thomson and Ralph Branca. Durocher would become a Polo Grounds hero. As Hilda Chester, the number one Dodger fan often remarked: "Only in America."

For the rest of 1948 and through 1949 and 1950, Durocher would battle the Dodgers as individuals. He would bait Jackie Robinson. He would infuriate Carl Furillo and Brooklyn, well, Brooklyn would have no trouble at all learning to hate him. During the late stages of the 1950 season people would begin to notice an unlikely pitching hero named Sal Maglie. He had returned from hard times down in the Mexican League where he had played "outlaw" baseball. Because of the rarified air down there and with the assistance of a former Giants' pitching star named Adolph Luque, Maglie had actually developed an amazing variety of curveballs which he could make do different tricks.

Almost without warning, it became apparent that he could generally beat the Dodgers by simply throwing his glove on the mound.

1951 was going to be a dandy year.

It started as a near-disaster for the Giants, who lost 11 in a row very early. The Dodgers' batting order had been tailor-made for Ebbets Field's peculiar dimensions. It was so powerful that Furillo, who often batted eighth, actually hit .295 that year. It was packed with names like Peewee Reese, Billy Cox, Duke Snider, Gil Hodges, Jackie Robinson, Furillo, Roy Campanella and Andy Pafko, who was acquired as insurance from the Cubs in June. The pitching was thin in spots but Don Newcombe threw bullets, the bullpen was strong and with all those bats the Dodgers figured to be a mortal cinch.

The Giants fumbled and stumbled. Prophetically, they broke their 11-game spin against the Dodgers at Ebbets Field before a crowd of 33,962 when Maglie beat the Dodgers, 8–5. Each side accused the other of throwing bean balls. In the third inning, Jackie Robinson deliberately bunted toward first in an effort to draw Maglie over. The ball trickled foul but Jackie bumped Maglie anyway and the umpires had to step between them. After the game Durocher said "it was a bush stunt and Jackie Robinson is a bush player." "If it's bush," Robinson retorted, "he ought to know. He taught me."

The Giants were beginning to win games but the Dodgers continued to bomb their way through the National League. The Kefauver hearings were turning people like Frank Costello into television stars. Against that kind of show business nobody paid much attention to the Giants' hopeless efforts. On Aug. 11, they were 13½ games back of Brooklyn.

In less than a week they chopped it to 9½ after Maglie beat Newcombe, 2–1, for his 17th victory. Still, there was hardly cause for panic in Flatbush. The Dodgers were winning their share. The Giants would simply be too little and too late.

Durocher, however, had reason to hope. Stoneham had given him his head and it had taken him three years to do what he wanted with this team. The pitching, he knew, was excellent. Before the start of the 1950 season he had obtained an outstanding doubleplay combination from Boston in Stanky and Al Dark. Now he had taken a good hitter with a weak arm named Whitey Lockman and moved him in from the outfield to play first base. Monte Irvin had gone out to left field and Bobby Thomson had been shifted to third base. Finally, he brought up a whiz kid named Willie Mays from the Minneapolis farm club where he had been hitting over .400. Willie couldn't buy a hit his first 12 times at bat. Then he earned his varsity letter with a home run off Warren Spahn. Willie and the Giants never looked back again.

Willie Mays was more than help. He was the positive key. His hitting was vital but his fielding was unbelievable. In a late-season game with the Dodgers he made an incredible catch with his back to home plate, whirled and threw a perfect strike from the deep outfield to knock off the potential winning run at home. All season he gave them the big play. The Giants continued to roll. They won 16 in a row to neutralize the horror of that early losing streak. Down the stretch they won 37 of their last 44 games. The Dodgers lead grew thinner and thinner and thinner. By the final day of the season, it had disappeared completely.

On the morning of Sunday, Sept. 30, the Giants were tied with the Dodgers for first place. Larry Jansen beat the

Braves, 3–2, up in Boston. The Giants ran for the clubhouse and listened to the Dodger game with Philadelphia as they dressed. The Phils were leading, 8–6. Two cases of champagne were unopened in the corner of the room. "Take 'em along," Leo told the equipment man, "we'll drink 'em on the train."

They never did. The Dodgers tied the Phillies, 8–8, and went into extra innings. As the Giants' train rumbled down from New England the news came in sporadic bursts. The Phillies had loaded the bases. But the Phillies hadn't been able to score. Jackie Robinson had saved Brooklyn from total disaster with a diving catch of Eddie Waitkus' line drive. In the 14th, Jackie hit a home run off Robin Roberts. The Dodgers won, 9–8. The whole 1951 season would have to be played all over again.

This was not a New York street fight. It had become the most emotional baseball story the country had ever witnessed. And through the aegis of television it was being witnessed everywhere. The Giants, atrocious at the start, had captured the imagination of people everywhere who wouldn't know a baseball from an egg but who rooted with the passions Americans root with when they think an underdog can win. Both clubs were exhausted. Tempers were rubbed raw. Even mild-mannered Roy Campanella had tried to kick down the door to the umpire's dressing room in Boston after a close play had gone against the Dodgers. Suddenly it wasn't just baseball. Suddenly, the kind of thing these two clubs had been doing to each other for years had jumped off the sports pages and out to page one.

On Oct. 1, the Giants sent Jim Hearn out to face Ralph Branca before 30,707 Monday afternoon fans at Ebbets Field. Branca had the misfortune to make two bad pitches.

Bobby Thomson hit one into the seats with a man on and
Monte Irvin hit the other one there with the bases empty.
The Giants won it, 3–1. Nothing in the world could be
tougher for Branca. That was Monday. On Wednesday, he
would find out.

So they came back to the Polo Grounds the next day,
which was chill and overcast and Charley Dressen, who
simply could not afford to wait, decided on a daring gam-
ble. He would take Clem Labine, the bullpen ace who had
saved this club all year, and start him. If Labine could do
it, or at least keep the Giants at bay long enough to get
relief help, Don Newcombe would still be available to
pitch the deciding game. The Dodgers were now out of
first place for the first time since May 13. It would be up
to Labine to give them one more chance.

Early in that game, when the Giants were still alive,
Robert Brown Thomson struck out with the bases loaded.
Tuesday was no more important for Bobby Thomson than
it was for Ralph Branca. Labine was masterful. He beat
the Giants, 10–0, and the Dodgers who had been terrorizing
the National League with their bats all year looked just
like they were supposed to look. Gil Hodges and Andy
Pafko hit home runs and even Rube Walker, who was re-
placing the injured Roy Campanella hit one.

Now it was Oct. 3 and the Giants and the Dodgers
would have to play their season yet one more time. It was
a gloomy day and Dressen noted that with satisfaction. The
peculiar architecture of the Polo Grounds favored fastball
pitchers on days like this one. The shadow from the upper
deck of the grandstand lengthened quickly on such afternoons, making it increasingly difficult for the hitter to contend with a good fastball pitcher. Nobody in the league
threw as hard as Don Newcombe. The Giants, naturally,

would go with Maglie. Despite the mid-week date and oppressive cold and gloom, 34,320 people showed up at the Polo Grounds. Millions and millions watched in front of their television sets.

Branca and Thomson . . . on this day their names would be inextricably wed. You cannot think of one without the other ever again. They had each come a long way toward this moment although neither knew in the early moments of that chilly afternoon how far and for how long their names would be linked.

Ralph Branca was a big, strong righthanded pitcher. Later people would forget a lot of things he had done. As a college freshman at NYU, he was already pitching in the big leagues with Brooklyn. He had been with the club since 1944. He had won a lot of games. Even in the first playoff game he had pitched well. His teammates with their big bats had given him nothing to work on.

Bobby Thomson had been headed for this moment a long time although the Giants did not exactly turn cartwheels over his early minor league career. Incredibly, they even forgot they owned him and nearly signed him twice. The first time was in the heat of the mad scramble for warm bodies which began with the first wartime season. In 1942 they signed him out of St. Lawrence College. After 34 undistinguished games with their minor league affiliates at Bristol and Rocky Mount, Bobby Thomson marched off to join the other 19-year-olds at war. The Giants stuck him on their Bristol roster and promptly forgot where they had left him.

Toward the end of the war, reports on a big, power-hitting third baseman playing service ball drifted back to the Giants' office. One day an executive was on the telephone with a scout discussing the prospect whose name was Bobby Thomson. "Sign him," the man said, "even if you have to give him a bonus."

"Hey," an alert secretary interrupted, "you talking about Bobby Thomson?"

"Yeah, you know him?"

"No, but we own him. See his name is on the board under Bristol."

"Cancel that bonus," the man snapped into the phone, "and tell him to come home."

Bobby Thomson finally made it to the big club for a brief trial in 1946. He stayed on and his batting average fluctuated. He went through prolonged slumps. Nobody was sure how good he would be but in 1951 he hit .293 and on the morning he left his Staten Island home for what had to be the last game of this incredible season, he had already hit 31 home runs. Before this game would be three innings old, however, he would be the leading candidate for a set of unbreakable goat horns.

But now Branca was walking slowly out to the leftfield bullpen with Carl Erskine and Erv Palica and Clyde Sukeforth, the bullpen coach and Bobby Thomson had run out to third base as the Giants trotted onto the field and shivered in the chill breeze during the playing of the National Anthem.

And so it began.

In the first inning, Sal Maglie had trouble with his curve. He walked Reese and he walked Snider. Now it was Robinson, his arch adversary. Jackie lined the first pitch into left to score Reese. Sal Maglie had won 23 games for New York and he was down 1–0 in the one he needed the most.

In the second, the Giants got a single from Lockman and Thomson followed with a sharply hit ball down the line in left. Head down, he took a wide turn at first and dug for second. He looked up in time to see Lockman standing on the bag. They tagged him out in the rundown and the Dodger fans howled their approval. Babe Herman lives. He has only changed uniforms.

When the Giants came out for the third, they turned on the lights. The big shadow of the upper deck was already beginning to lengthen. Rube Walker, the Dodger catcher was satisfied. Newcombe was pumping in fastballs and they looked only slightly larger than an undernourished chick pea to the Giant hitters.

It was Maglie against Newcombe after that and they kept moving along. Newcombe, rocketing back from his huge stretch and darting strikes past the Giants . . . Maglie, unshaven, scowling as always, breaking his curveball off just enough to get by and doing it. Out in the bullpen, Branca and Erskine threw leisurely, more to keep warm than from any clear and present danger. They moved through the third, fourth, the fifth, the sixth and finally into the home half of the seventh.

Monte Irvin knocked one of Newk's fastballs into left-field for a double and when Rube Walker made a late throw to third on Lockman's bunt everybody was safe. Bobby Thomson flied deep to center and Irvin raced home with the tying run . . . 156 games and seven innings after it had begun, they still had to play the 1951 season all over again.

The next break was totally unexpected. Sal Maglie, king of the Dodger-killers, master of the curveball, simply could go no further. In the eighth inning he yielded a single to Reese and another to Snider, which sent Reese to third. Then he bounced a curveball into the dirt and away from Wes Westrum, his catcher. Reese scored and Snider raced all the way to third.

Jackie Robinson was next but Durocher ordered him

walked to fill the bases and to set up a force play at any base. He came reasonably close to getting it. Pafko rapped a hard ground ball toward third. Thomson lunged for it, for an instant seemed to have a chance and then it skipped over his shoulder into leftfield. The Dodgers led, 4–1, and nobody—but absolutely nobody—in that ball park thought that the 1951 season would have to be played any more. They were sure of it when Newcombe went out in the eighth and knocked the Giants off again.

The Giants came in with their number two pitcher, Larry Jansen, to work the ninth and he retired the side but they were down to just three outs now, they were three runs back and Don Newcombe was wheeling the ball low and outside through those shadows.

He did it twice to Alvin Dark and Dark was behind 0–2. Then he swung at the third pitch and got a piece of it. The ball bounced just to the right of first baseman Gil Hodges, it ticked his glove and slipped on past. The Giants had a base runner. Don Mueller followed with a similar hit sending Dark to third. Out in the bullpen, Branca and Erskine began to throw in earnest. 1951 wasn't over yet.

For an instant there was cause to think it might be. Newcombe got Monte Irvin to foul to Hodges and that brought up Lockman. He doubled to left, Dark scored and Mueller easily beat the throw to third. But he did it with a grotesque slide. His ankle twisted the wrong way. He lay on his back in obvious pain. Durocher ran towards him.

Now it was 4–2 and Hartung came on to run for Mueller, who was leaving the field on a stretcher, and out in the leftfield bullpen, Branca and Erskine ignored everything except the two catcher's mitts which were their targets. The bullpen telephone rang. There are several versions of what was said during that conversation. Nobody will ever know it all. But one thing was sure. Don Newcombe was finished and out from the shadows in deep leftcenter field, Ralph Branca was taking the long walk to the pitcher's mound with his royal blue Dodger windbreaker slung over one shoulder and his glove under his arm. The man in the batter's circle was Bobby Thomson.

So it all came down to this . . . 157 games . . . a month and a half to wipe out a staggering handicap . . . a ninth-inning rally to try to save it all. It all came down to Ralph Branca and Bobby Thomson.

As Branca warmed up, Charley Dressen stood behind him and said nothing. He had already made one major decision. Now he was faced with another. He could pitch to Thomson or he could walk him and try to set up a double-play which could begin at any base. The next hitter was Willie Mays. Dressen considered. Branca threw eight warm-up pitches to Walker. Then Dressen wheeled and said "pitch to him."

As Thomson started for the batter's box Leo Durocher whistled and hollered down at him "If you ever hit one, then hit it now." Thomson tugged at his cap and stepped in to hit. As was his habit, he danced slightly on the balls of his feet and then settled back to wait.

Rube Walker crouched behind him and gave the sign. On the mound, Branca nodded through the twilight. The pitch would be a fastball. Branca slipped it by Thomson hip high. Strike one.

Now Branca fidgeted on the mound. He took a deep breath and peered in again toward Walker. He had his first strike. The thing to do was to get Thomson to swing at a bad pitch. It was percentage baseball. Branca took his stretch and checked the runners. They weren't going anywhere. The whole game was right out there at home plate. He pitched Thomson high and tight.

Thomson went for it. His wrists whipped the bat around

and the ball shot off on an indefinite trajectory toward left field. Andy Pafko sprinted for the wall. "I thought I could get it," he would say afterwards. "I really thought there was a chance."

Reese, the shortstop, and Cox, the third baseman, turned sharply and mumbled "drop . . . drop . . . drop." Out on the pitcher's mound, Branca turned, too, and said one word over and over and over . . . "sink . . . sink . . . sink." Pafko, his shoulder-blades flush against the wall, kangarooed straight up. A fan, watching in either horror or prayerful admiration, leaned over the lower stand wall in fascination, unconsciously spilling the contents of a paper beer cup down toward Pafko. The ball carried the wall underneath the over hanging scoreboard. A woman who said her name was Helen Gawn, insisted that it landed in her lap.

Up in the radio-TV booth, Russ Hodges, the Giants' announcer who had broadcast every game of the amazing season, shrieked over and over into his microphone . . . "the Giants win the pennant . . . the Giants win the pennant . . . the Giants win the pennant."

Down below, out by the third base coaching box, Eddie Stanky leaped into Durocher's arms in a mad embrace, slipped and jumped on Leo's back. Giants were everywhere, tackling each other, dancing with each other and racing towards home plate to greet Thomson. Out in leftfield, Sukeforth and Palica and Erskine quietly gathered up their equipment and walked through the sea of humanity which spilled across the outfield grass, elbowing their way to the clubhouse. Of all the Dodgers, only Robinson remained. He stood there and made sure that Bobby Thomson touched every base. Then he turned and walked off in surrender.

The Giants' clubhouse was exactly what you would expect it to be. Players threw champagne at each other.

Bobby Thomson walked around saying "gee whiz . . . gee whiz . . . gee whiz." A brigade of newspapermen, who had been on the other side of the building in anticipation of the victorious Dodgers, thundered down one set of stairs and up another and engulfed Thomson. "I didn't touch the ground," he said. "I didn't touch it. I flew . . . I . . . I . . . I . . . Oh, gee whiz . . . good living . . . I don't know . . . It was a bad, inside high fastball . . ." He rambled on and an hour later he would be standing at the top of the steps in answer to the summons of the huge throng of spectators below who had chanted his name again and again.

Across the way in the Dodger clubhouse, Ralph Branca sat on a stool in front of his locker with his hands clutching his forehead. He spoke softly and his voice tore with the burden of it, a burden he would be a long time putting down. "Let me alone . . . let me alone . . . let me be, will you. You saw what happened. Things are tough enough . . . yeah, I knew it was gone all the way. All I kept saying was sink . . . sink . . . sink . . . it was like a curve ball and it was sinking down . . . he hit with overspin . . . All I remember was seeing Pafko up against the wall and then I was walking to the clubhouse and all I kept saying was why me . . . why me . . . why did it have to be me?"

A lot of people wondered the same thing. The battle raged all winter long. Why not Erskine? Branca had pitched the first playoff game only two days earlier. And why did they pitch to Thomson, who already had two hits in the game and who had homered off Branca in that first playoff meeting? and why . . . why . . . why.

Branca would never be the same. Thomson would never have another year like 1951. Sukeforth, the bullpen coach, would be fired that winter. Nobody would ever be the same.

The Giants and the Dodgers continued their war for five more seasons. The Dodgers beat them for the pennant in 1952 and the Giants returned the favor in 1954. Other heroes emerged among them. Durocher battled Furillo at the top of the dugout steps in a bean ball feud. Life was still violent and as always when these teams met, it was complicated.

And then in October of 1956, the Dodgers and the Giants announced that they were leaving for California. The Polo Grounds and Ebbets Field would disappear. The thing would be ended.

They would continue to play each other out in California. And in 1962 they would meet in another playoff series which would go the full three games. The Giants would win it. But who would remember how? Who would recall, even five years later, that a pitcher named Stan Williams had walked home the winning run?

Nobody except Stan Williams. And who would let Ralph Branca ever forget what happened when the real Giants played the real Dodgers in the real playoff? Nobody, not even Ralph Branca.

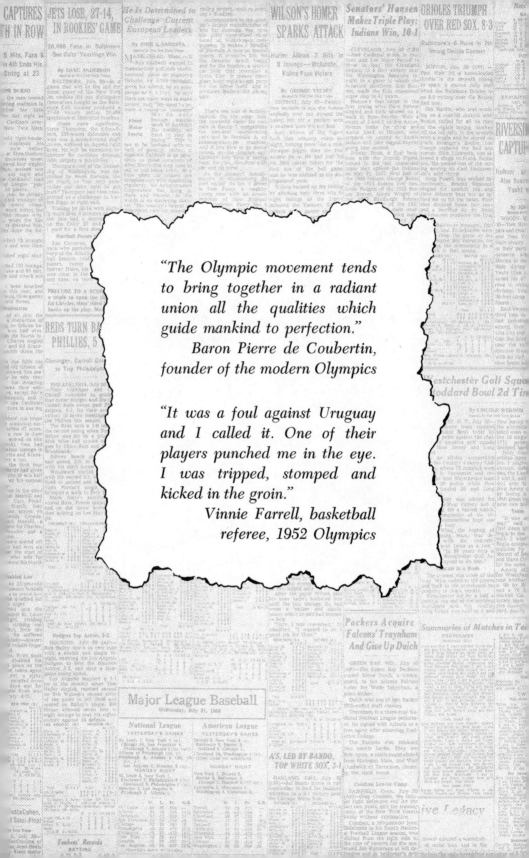

"The Olympic movement tends to bring together in a radiant union all the qualities which guide mankind to perfection."

Baron Pierre de Coubertin, founder of the modern Olympics

"It was a foul against Uruguay and I called it. One of their players punched me in the eye. I was tripped, stomped and kicked in the groin."

Vinnie Farrell, basketball referee, 1952 Olympics

THE STAR-SPANGLED SHAM

First there is the marching band. It can vary its stride, the color of its uniforms, even the number of oompahs and boompahs. It can even be invisible, spilling its counterpoint across the huge concrete stadium through a series of strategically placed amplifiers. But it must know the proper anthems. At an international soccer match between Ireland and Yugoslavia one muggy summer night in 1961 in Jersey City, N. J., the band played "God Save the Queen" in salute to the Irish team. As the IRA-oriented partisans began to advance on the bandstand, cooler heads suggested they change it to "God Save the Conductor."

Then there is the roar of the cannon. This is a must for any self-respecting international competition. Things being what they are when nations gather to compete on the fields of friendly strife, the day should soon be upon us when the opening salvo wipes out the Polish 400-meter relay team.

Finally, and most important, there are the pigeons; thousands and thousands of them, released simultaneously in one mighty whrrrr. The pigeons are vital. As they soar high above the stadium, bumping into each other in a maze of

concentric circles, they serve to put the whole spectrum of
international athletic competition into its proper perspective.
When pigeons soar above, somebody always gets rained
on down below.

You can be sure of this because whenever it comes to
making a choice between that Great Pyromaniac in the Sky
who keeps the Olympic Flame burning between semesters,
and pure, unadulturated chauvinism, you can safely bet
your money on national self-interests 11 times out of 10.
The athletes themselves—because they understand the genuine meaning of competition—might be able to beat the
rap if they didn't have to go home. Home may not necessarily be where the heart is but it is still the place you have
to go after the last race is run and the last point has been
scored. Home is not a very good place to go if you are a
loser.

The Greek poet Pindar (B.C. 522–448) hung it up on
the message board for generations of Olympic losers yet-
unborn when he wrote:

"By back ways they slink away, sore smitten by misfortune, nor does any sweet smile grace their return."

When it comes to long-distance perception, Mr. Pindar
holds the all-time Olympic record.

It is impossible to even attempt to catalogue the sham,
rule-bending and out-right cheating which has marked the
Olympic Games since Baron Pierre de Coubertin arranged
for their modern rebirth in Athens back in 1896. Dainty
creatures with all the feminine graces of unwashed lumber-
jacks win events consistently and then suddenly disappear
on the day the Olympic committee decrees that henceforth
women athletes will have to prove they are women . . . and
the test isn't all that hard. The amateur code becomes a
shame and a scandal for most of the countries through non-

enforcement and an even bigger one for the American entry, which by some nebulous divine right of kings is run by people who still think the Yale-Harvard crew race and Sunday Polo at the Meadowbrook Club is where it's happening.

How can you possibly give credence to poor, old de Coubertin? The old Blue Baron writes an Olympic oath in which he says: "The important thing in the Olympic Games is not winning but taking part. The essential thing in life is not conquering but fighting well."

Well, at least he's half right. You couldn't fight any better than the undetected competitor who sabotaged two American bobsleds in the middle of the night on the eve of the 1948 Winter Games . . . or the Brazilian water polo team, which was expelled in 1932 at Los Angeles after it attacked a water-logged Hungarian referee named Bela Komjadi and beat him damned near senseless to celebrate their defeat at the hands of Germany . . . or the Canadians and the Swedes who tried to score goals with each other's heads in the 1948 hockey competition . . . or . . . well, or Wilfredo Palaez.

Wilfredo Palaez was a Uruguayan basketball player . . . more or less. Most of the Uruguayan players that year were more less than more, which shows how lousy the French were when they only led, 68-66, in the closing seconds of the 1952 games. As basketball players, the Uruguayans were very good longshoremen. At this point, Vinnie Farrell, an American referee of excellent reputation and obvious guts, called a foul against Uruguay. If it reflected the character of most Uruguayan fouls that day, it was no more serious than attempting to maim and disfigure. The Uruguayans didn't need a referee. They needed the Sullivan Law.

At any rate, Mr. Palaez objected strenuously and the

thing he objected with was his fist, which he drove halfway
through Mr. Farrell's eye. The rest of the team objected,
too. They tripped him, they stomped him, and in the spirit
of international good will and fair play, they kicked him in
the groin. Having discharged their moral obligations, they
returned to Uruguay and, doubtless, an heroic welcome.

These things, of course, are not isolated incidents. They
are the real spirit of the Olympic Games no matter what
the American Olympic Committee tells you during its quad-
rennial hat-passing campaigns. The Americans ought to
know better because in 1908, the spirit of hands-across-the-
sea exhibited by the English was more like hands-across-
the-jugular vein.

On opening day, when brotherhood in this ace-bandage
charade is supposed to be at its highest level, the English
put the Colonists in their place by neglecting to exhibit an
American flag. Actually, the ring of flags around Shepherds
Bush Stadium included neither the American nor the
Swedish standards. The Swedes were disturbed. The Americans were livid. They bought their own flag and when the
American team passed by King Edward VII and his wife,
Queen Alexandria, Martin Sheridan, the color-bearer, did not
dip the flag in salute. "This flag," explained Mr. Sheridan,
a weight-thrower, who functioned as a kind of poet-laureate
in sweat socks, "dips to no earthly king." And *sic semper
tyrannus* . . . Dolly Madison is avenged.

It is worth studying the brotherhood and Olympic spirit
which dominated that particular year in England. Tom
Longboat, a professional marathon runner, was permitted
to run as an amateur by the British (in those days the host
nation ran the games, which was a dandy license to steal)
because he ran for Canada. The Americans had the 400-
meter race stolen away by dishonest judges, the Irish were

furious because the English wanted them to compete under the banner of Great Britain to swell that nation's point score when all the Irish wanted to do was go home and throw every Englishman into the Irish Sea. And the Finns, well, the Finns were sore at everybody because the Russian diplomats had made a deal with the British diplomats that the Finns would have to carry the Russian flag. They marched instead with no identification and were impossible to tell from the local sanitation department.

All right, that was 1908 . . . a long time ago . . . things are different now. Sure they are. They're different like this:

In 1960, during the zenith of the pitiless Roman summer, a Danish cyclist named Knud Enemark Jensen tumbles off his bicycle and pitches face down on the Olympic Velodrome track during the final stages of the 100 kilometer race. His pulse is faint. Sunstroke can do that to you. He was 22 years old and he was rushed to the hospital where he died. In extreme cases, sunstroke will do that to you, too.

But sunstroke did not kill Knud Enemark Jensen. National pride and stupidity did. It also sent two other Danish cyclists to the hospital but they recovered. The thing which put all three of them there was called Roniacol and it is used to stimulate blood circulation. The drug was administered by Oluf Jorgensen, the team trainer. Everybody was very sorry except for Knud Enemark Jensen who was very dead. Try working that one into your Olympic oath, Baron.

But the biggest single hypocrisy of this Star-Spangled sham is the very basis on which the teams compete. National Olympic committees need only certify that their teams have met the amateur standards of the individual nation. The most reliable way of putting it is that the standards in most cases are easily met because there aren't any. A Russian weightlifter who was listed as a military doctor comes to mind. After he finished describing his full-time, year-round training routine at a New York press conference, a bystander had to conclude that Russian medical health would stand at a make-or-break cross roads if he ever had to be pressed into service to treat a case of athlete's feet.

It is this way with all of the Iron Curtain countries which compete and with a great many of the so-called Free World countries. And then you have the United States.

Nobody seems to know how the people who agree upon the requirements to keep a man amateur in this country got there in the first place. Since they re-elect themselves it is not hard to figure how they stay there. As near as scholarly research of crude hand-lettered graffiti on the walls of several caves in Yellowstone National Park indicates, they have always been there. Moreover, they are still there and the way things are going they will remain there until that rapidly approaching day when the Nigerian water polo team drops the H Bomb on Uganda in a fit of rage over a bum call.

"Money," they tell us, "stinks." "However, if you are rich, you are welcome to compete and if you are not then go get yourself a college scholarship and let them keep you and we will borrow you every four years." It is a great system and it is so democratic that when the great debate over South Africa's apartheid policies split the International Olympic Committee, the U.S. representatives which none of us voted for, told the American public that it was none of its damned business which side it took in the balloting. Our business is to throw.in some money every time they pass the hat and sing: "Glory, Glory, Hallelujah."

It is only natural, therefore, that the American sports fan should not exactly go crackers over the Olympics unless some special situation exists. Despite the play the Games have received in American newspapers since their modern revival, it has always taken something extra for it to enable the American sports fan to respond with admirable insanity.

Avery Brundage's paeans to a world which went out of business when the last buggy-whip factory died will not suffice. Television, however, will. It was television which brought the dramatic and totally unexpected American ice hockey victory over the Soviet Union into millions of American living rooms in 1960. Since we won and the Russians lost, it didn't matter that the rules of the game were totally foreign to a great many of the viewers. Win, baby, win and give me that old-time Olympic spirit.

With the sale of the Games to the American Broadcasting Company, television asserted itself even more. This was accomplished by studiously inserting cameras and microphones into people's ear lobes and navels in order to get some thrilling picture coverage while totally ignoring the sham of the standards—or lack of standards—of many of the winners. There was a brief chance to expose these Games for what they are when Curt Gowdy, a fine announcer-commentator, casually explained how "amateur" Russia's "amateur" hockey players really were. At that point, or shortly thereafter, the cameras switched to something more esoteric even though the Russians were about to get beaten for the first time since only "Pravda" knows when.

America's adjustment to the level of international insanity which sports generates has been slow and sporadic. The reasons are fairly obvious. For one, there is a geography. It is almost impossible for a European athletic team to take a road trip without crossing a border somewhere. The United States, on the other hand, is sandwiched between two deep, wide oceans and it wasn't until World War II taught a lot of people how to cross them and the ensuing jet age burst upon us that we recognized the fact that other people existed and that they played games.

The games these people played were a second complication. With the exception of track and field, the vehicle which kept alive our flagging interest in the Olympics, we live in a totally in-bred sports society. We play football, baseball and basketball. The first is a hyphenated corruption of soccer and rugby, the second is a game so alien and so dull to everyone in Europe that it is almost impossible to explain, and the third we invented.

Consequently, it is difficult for Americans to work themselves into a positive frenzy over field hockey (which is swell at Skidmore but hardly has them lining up to get the bulldog edition of the Daily News) water polo (which used to belong to all the "correct" segregated clubs) and canoeing (which we try to ignore because we are afraid we may learn we have broken yet another treaty with the Indians).

But track and field, which was our first major interest in Olympic competition, has always had a stranglehold on a hard-core coterie of lunatics and a specialized interest on the right occasions for the large mass of emotional American sports fans. You do not have to be very bright to figure out the object of a foot race.

Which brings us to 1936 and the first harbinger of a changing world, a world in which nobody could go home again and because of that America's isolationist shell began to crumble in both politics and sports. The place was Berlin. The focal point was a marvelously talented track man named Jesse Owens. It was, in its way, the first total mass American venture into the spirit of the Olympics; ie: winning.

1936 was a very clear-cut kind of year. Nazi Germany was host to the Olympics and in this country there were people who said that maybe our athletes ought to skip the whole thing. The Nazis were not exactly the kind of people you could feel comfortable playing games with. There was talk of a boycott. Avery Brundage, who was then chairman of the United States Olympic Committee, was horrified. "When we let politics, racial questions, religious or social disputes creep into our actions, we're asking for trouble," Mr. Brundage said. He clearly and honestly believed these banalities and 32 years later when the same kind of debate would rage over the Union of South Africa's apartheid policy, Avery would gargle the same kind of drivel. In 1968, faced with the simple question of a unified national conspiracy against human dignity in that country, Mr. Brundage would be no closer emotionally to entering the 20th Century.

When Avery saw the great German facilities, the cleanliness of the cities and the Germans taking down their antisemitic signs, he was ecstatic. People can be that way when somebody gives them a chance to pretend something doesn't exist. He said "no nation since Greece has captured the true Olympic spirit as has Germany." The White Rabbit had presented the Croix de Guerre to the All-League Butcher.

The real world looked like this when the Games prepared to open. France was asking for a three-power conference on neutrality in Spain where Nazi pilots were hoping they could wipe out the last helpless civilians and get back to Berlin in time for the 100 meter dash. Rebel troops, supplied and at great length supported by both Nazi and Italian Fascist elements, were advancing on Madrid.

The Olympic torch was en route to Berlin through the efforts of 3,500 volunteer runners, whose route went from Athens to Salonika and then through Sofia, Belgrade, Budapest and Vienna, a route which the New York Times reminded its readers was the same line ". . . . which propelled

the Kaiser into the World War and in the past two years . . .
has been explored again as a path of expansion for the
Third Reich."

Back home, "Three Men on a Horse" and "Tobacco
Road" were packing them in on Broadway and a young man
named Ray Bolger was getting rave reviews in something
called "On Your Toes." It had been six long years since
anyone had seen Judge Crater, and Amelia Earhart, the girl
pilot, had just received a $70,000 Lockheed airplane, which
she planned to operate in conjunction with Purdue University. On the surface, the U.S. was still running away from
world involvement.

But 1936 caught America's imagination and the reason
centered around a young man who was born in Alabama,
raised in Cleveland, and had become a great track star at
Ohio State University. His role became clearly defined for
the large mass of emotional American sports fans when the
German propaganda machine began calling the 10 Negro
members of the United States' squad "the black auxiliaries."
It gathered momentum after a real or coincidental snub of
Owens by Hitler. Suddenly everyone in the United States
was angry. Nobody was going to push our athletes around.
What the Nazis did outside the stadium still had little inter-
est for most Americans.

The Games opened on August 2, 1936 in the 100,000
seat Olympic Stadium in the heart of the 325-acre *Reischs-
sportfeld* which Hitler had built specifically for them. Loud-
speakers boomed across the length and breadth of Germany
all day long:

"We await the Fuehrer at any moment. Never would
this field have been erected except for the Fuehrer. It was
created by his will. We can well understand the expec-
tations of the 100,000 awaiting the moment when the Fueh-

rer will enter the Stadium. ATTENTION . . . THE . . . FUEHRER . . . NOW . . . ENTERS . . . THE . . . STADIUM. . . ."

The rest is lost in an ocean of sound . . . a chorus of "Heil . . . Heil . . . Heil. . . ." In counterpoint to the massive full-throated roar, the strains of Wagner's "Hymn of Praise" fill the arena. Hitler is there . . . so is Hess . . . so is Goering. Germany is ecstatic. Like Avery said, who would dare inject politics into the Baron de Coubertin's ball game?

The massed teams marched by. Their approach ran a strange gamut. The Austrians gave the Nazi salute, the Bulgarians goose-stepped. The Americans did not even acknowledge Hitler. They did not dip their colors. Back home, the battle lines were joined. Even Mississippi rooted for Jesse Owens, provided he didn't plan to move on their block.

Owens, of course, dominated the Games. On August 3, he won his first gold medal by holding off a late bid by teammate Ralph Metcalfe, also a Negro, to win the 100 meter dash. He had set an Olympic mark in his heat, defeating a German rival and it was here that Hitler had allegedly snubbed him. In truth, the Olympic committee had warned Hitler against congratulating winners lest he discriminate against Negroes or Jews or anyone he might be inclined not to like. It wasn't that Hitler had snubbed Owens. It was that the Olympic powers had denied him the chance. But the news of the "snub" reached home and the grip Owens held on the American public only intensified.

The next day, he won the broad jump. On Wednesday, he captured the 200-meter title. Before the Games closed he also ran on the victorious U. S. 400-meter relay team. American athletes—black and white—had captured 12 of the 23 track events. And as usual, the Olympic spirit predominated.

The English immediately accused the Americans of under-
going secret surgery to make them run faster. The Germans
went them one better. With their paranoiac pre-occupation
with race, they claimed that American Negroes had won
their events because of "a certain peculiar conformation of
their bones."

America turned it on for Jesse Owens when he returned
with a massive welcome home parade. He was the vindication of the American dream and the American dreamers
expiated their consciences. Then Jesse, who had a degree
from Ohio State University, had his choice between a $2,700
a year teaching job at an all-Negro college or whatever the
traffic could bear in return for racing against horses and
whatever other sideshow attractions he could line up. He
never made a bitter statement in public over this. Obviously
whatever there was of Baron de Coubertin's spirit left, Jesse
had it all in this country.

No matter what else they did or did not do, the 1936
Olympics set a trend of American involvement. The frenetic
events leading to World War II wiped out the 1940 Games,
which had been scheduled for Tokyo. It wasn't until 1948
that everybody got together again and despite the fact that
the American bobsleds were sabotaged, there was no real
strong feeling about the Games in terms of the large mass
of American sports fans. That was going to change, however,
and in a way it began to change that very year. In the
grandstand at London there were Russian photographers,
Russian coaches, Russian athletes, Russian newspapermen.
The Soviet Union was getting ready to poke its nose through
its own Iron Curtain. When it did, it would drag the American sports fan along with it.

The Olympic Games by themselves were one thing. But
with the Russians, well, it didn't matter whether it was

chess, rocketry, or the 100-meter dash. Put a Russian in there and the American public began to root against him with all the timidity of a Holy War.

The 1952 Summer Games were held in Helsinki and for a long time there was doubt that the Russians would, indeed, compete. They spurned the Winter Games in Norway. They even refused to let the Olympic torch-bearers cross into Soviet territory at Talinn, thereby lengthening the journey from Athens to Helsinki by 2,000 miles. But in the end they came. If the American sports fan needed a rooting interest he now had one. The cold war was now the hot war in Korea, in Indo-China and in Malaya. The battle for nuclear domination raged unchecked. The Chinese had emerged as something else to worry about. Against this backdrop, the two great giants with their two diametrically opposite political viewpoints, took their battle to the playing fields of Finland. It was about as much a sports event as the St. Valentine's Day Massacre.

It began innocently enough. More than 70,000 packed themselves into Olympic Stadium and nearly drowned. It rained and it rained and it rained. But the enthusiasm was genuine when Paavo Nurmi, who had brought world honors home to Finland as a foot-racer of another era, trotted slowly down the track with the Olympic torch in his hand. The spectacle was breath-taking. There was fire below and there were thousands of soggy pigeons above. Suddenly, there was something else.

A well-upholstered blonde in flowing white robe vaulted the rail and started running down the track. She ran all the way to the box occupied by Joho K. Passkivi, President of Finland. Then she grabbed the microphone. At this point, Olympic officials who had stared at each other with an I-don't-know-I-thought-she-was-with-you expression on their faces made a grab for her. She got as far as "Ladies, Gentlemen, Friends" before they hauled her away.

Her name was Barbara Rotraut-Pleyer. She was 23 years old and insisted she was devoted to world peace. As motives go, this rates the all-time low on the Olympic Games Motivation Scale. Nowhere this side of Avery Brundage's raccoon coat are these countries in the stadium for any reason other than to beat hell out of each other.

The Russians proved this that very week. They set up their own private Olympic Village complete with fences and security guards. Subsequently, when it became apparent that they would win their share of medals, they permitted visitors to enter. Near the main gate they kept a huge scoreboard which gave their version of the team standings. No national point scores are kept at the Olympics but ever since the United States and the Soviet started going head-to-head, everybody keeps standings and the winner depends most of the time on which alphabet you are using. Ironically, on August 2 with the U. S. leading by both its own and the Russian scoring method, all figures disappeared from the huge board inside the Soviet compound. For the record, the U. S. won it by a very comfortable margin.

There was, however, genuine excitement to this first confrontation between the two political giants and the measure of it can best be gauged by what happened back in the United States after they ran the 3,000-meter steeplechase. The U. S. would win its big events and the stars who figured to be stars would be impressive. But the excitement generated in the United States by Horace Ashenfelter's steeplechase victory was typical of the emotional pitch to which the large American sports public can rise.

Consider the event. Back home the Bryn Mawr intersorority pillow fight gets more press coverage. Americans are creatures of violence and of comfort. The steeplechase provides neither except for the actual competitor. Running the steeplechase is like trying to spring through quicksand while somebody plays "The Stars and Stripes Forever" on your sternum with a sledgehammer. Enter, Horace the Magnificent.

Horace Ashenfelter was a 29-year old Penn State graduate who had gone to work for the FBI. It is not true, it should be said here, that he was more afraid of going back home and facing J. Edgar Hoover as a loser than he was of running against Vladimir Kazantsev. Vladimir was the one athlete the Russians felt absolutely sure would win a gold medal. He had already run the event in 8:48.6, a world record so startling that if he hadn't been a Russian the Russians would have thought the timekeeper was keeping score by trying to line up Mickey Mouse's big hand with his little hand.

Against this went Horace Ashenfelter, the pride of Glen Ridge, N. J., who by his own admission hadn't run the steeplechase more than eight times in his entire life. Moreover, he had never run it in less than nine minutes. What happened, therefore, was viewed by every American sports nut as a star-spangled, spiked-shoe kick at the Iron Curtain.

At the start, Horace Ashenfelter was dead last. He was seventh on the second lap and finally took the lead the next time around. Vladimir Kazantsev clung to his heels. When they finally wheeled off the back stretch, the Russian slipped by him. As they came to the final jump, the water hole, they were almost even again. The water jump is a bushcovered obstacle on the edge of a moat. The water is knee high on the inside of the pool and graded upwards for roughly 10 ft.

Horace Ashenfelter really didn't know a hell of a lot

about the steeplechase when he checked into Helsinki. Consequently, he set about doing his homework and the best teacher he ran into was a Finn named Olavi Rinteenpam. He told Ashenfelter that most Americans lost valuable time on the water jump by landing in the deep water. The way to do it, he explained, was to leap to the top of the barrier with one foot and push off into the shallowest part of the moat.

Ashenfelter remembered this as he gasped and hung on to Kazantsev's heels. He cleared the jump exactly as Olavi Rinteenpam had advised him to do. There was an audible gasp from the tens of thousands who found it hard to believe what happened next. Kazantsev had stumbled, lost his timing and his lead. The setter of records, the sure gold medal winner, the pride of the collectivist spiked-shoe set was in deep trouble—to say nothing of water. By the time he staggered out, Ashenfelter had opened five yards on him. Horace Ashenfelter had brought the United States a gold medal it neither expected nor understood. Back in the United States everyone with the price of a newspaper basked in his reflected glory.

It was the one event which insured a clean sweep. The Russian left for home without a single gold medal in the track and field competition. Back home the chauvinists hailed it as a victory for Free Enterprise. But the athletes weren't fooled. Those who planned to return in 1956 knew that the Russians had only begun their propaganda war. They were supposed to have been novices but they had been very, very tough.

In the four years which preceded Melbourne the United States continued to live well within its isolated sports cocoon, playing its own games, ignoring the rest of the world and waiting. But during that period something happened during a track meet at Oxford University in England, of all places. It changed the very face of foot-racing around the world and the United States was not immune to it. Its impact on the American sports fan was staggering.

Roger Gilbert Bannister, a 25-year old medical student, muscled his way onto the front page of every newspaper in the United States. It wasn't easy. Among the items he had to compete with on May 6, 1954 was a Western Big Three Conference about Indo-China and Sen. Joseph McCarthy, crusading against whatever it was Senator Joseph McCarthy happened to feel like crusading against on that particular day.

The Four Minute Mile was the kind of thing everybody talked about and nobody did anything about. Most track coaches conceded it could and would be run some day but it was like discussing the U.S. and Russian space programs. The time-table was very, very nebulous.

There were three outstanding milers in the world at the time. One was Wes Santee, an American of much talent who would later lose his amateur standing in an expenses clash with the AAU's you-can't-charge-to-run-but-it's-O.K.-if-daddy-pays-the-bills mentality. There was John Landy, an Australian college student who many said was the best. And then there was Bannister. In all of track, the mile run is for some unexplained reason, the premier event. The four-minute mile would be somebody's footprint on a very impressive landscape.

Roger Gilbert Bannister got there first. He did it under unfavorable wind conditions on the four-lap Iffley Road Track. "There comes a time," he said, "when you simply have to accept the weather as it is and have an all-out effort. I decided that today was that day."

The crosswind cut across the track at 15 miles per hour

with gusts up to 25. Nevertheless, running a planned race, he did it with quarters of 57.5, 60.7, 62.3 and 58.9. It added up to 3:59.4 and it fascinated the world's sports fans. Hell, he wasn't even a Russian. America had to wonder how long it would take one of its own to duplicate the feat,

It was still wondering a month later when word came out of Australia that John Landy had joined Roger Bannister. Joined him? Well, hardly. Landy had passed him, running it in 3:58. It was the two of them alone in the world now and the British Empire Games in Vancouver, B.C. that year brought them face to face.

The Empire Games are a great athletic event in the eyes and minds of the American sporting public and are followed by it with the intensity, say, of kayak racing. But this would be in Canada and it would feature Bannister against Landy. Moreover, it would be carried on American television. The barroom conversations and the money wagered in their support would have deeply pained the AAU.

The strategy was interesting and deceptive. Each ran just well enough in his qualifying heat to make the finals. The assumption most sports fans drew from that was that the emphasis would be on winning and the time would probably be slow. As is generally the case when sports fans make assumptions, the assumption was incorrect.

While 35,000 people watched inside the stadium and while millions and millions of others watched on American television, Bannister let Landy set the pace. With a lap to go, he shot by the Aussie, went into the lead and stayed there. He won it in 3:58.8. Landy finished in 3:59.6, the timers were so excited they nearly dropped their watches. The crowd was so excited it nearly dropped the security guards. It trampled its way onto the track and mobbed Bannister.

Then the television people switched back to their regular programming. It was a pity. They blew a dandy piece of nonsense which spotlights what international sports competitions are all about. In another race later in the day, a man named Stanley Cox, running in the marathon for England, had the misfortune to test a telephone pole. The pole won. He was knocked senseless in the collision at the 23-mile mark. As officials desperately sought to revive him, Mr. Cox showed signs of life, blinked his eyes and mumbled:

"Did Bannister make it?"

"Yes," said the guy with the smelling salts.

"God Bless him."

Then Cox tried to struggle to his feet, shouting: "I can't let England down. I've got to finish. Get these shoes off me. My feet are burning."

That's when they put him in the ambulance.

When 1956 rolled around, Roger Bannister had already retired and John Landy was going to get himself whipped in the metric mile by an Irishman named Ron Delaney. Horace Ashenfelter wasn't even going to qualify for the steeplechase. He would sigh and say: "I guess I'm just too old. That was as fast as I can run." The Americans again would have their share of heroes but this time the Russians would be ready for them. The Soviets would sweep off with 36 gold medals, 29 silvers and 33 bronzes. By any scoring total, the Russians would win the 1956 Olympics. Still, one event would grip the United States emotionally. Strangely, it would not involve a single American. It would be—of all things—a water polo match.

There was grimness to the 1956 gathering which even out-rivaled the Berlin Olympics two decades earlier. In the Mid-East, France, England and Israel were involved in semi-separate wars with Egypt. In Hungary, Russian

tanks rumbled through Budapest to crush a people's revo-
lution which had briefly over-thrown the Communist gov-
ernment. There was total sympathy for the Hungarians
throughout the United States. For the first time, Russian
aggression was being discussed at the U.N.

The 1956 Olympics, therefore, began with the usual note
of harmony and friendship which we have come to expect.
Egypt, Lebanon and Iraq walked out in protest against the
Suez War. Spain and the Netherlands quit over Russia's
treatment of Hungary. Red China quit when somebody
stuck a Nationalist Chinese flag on its pole in Olympic
Village. Holy William Tell, even the Swiss wanted to walk
out. Finally, it was learned that part of the Hungarian
Olympic team was traveling aboard a Russian ship with
the entire Russian squad. It was more fun than Chinese
checkers.

The name of the ship was the Gruzia and it was two
days overdue. When it finally docked it was met at the
pier by thousands of displaced Hungarians who had settled
in Australia. As the angry refugees closed ranks and sang
"God Bless Hungary" the betting was not on whether the
Russian team would win the Games but whether it would
survive the landing. The police finally hurried the crowd
and the Hungarian team off in the direction of the Olympic
Village.

Somehow, some way, all this emotion had to be turned
loose. To the discomfort of the Russia water polo team
and to the delight of millions of American newspaper
readers back home, it happened on the night of December
6 and it began as subtly as a left hook.

The Russian water polo team met the Hungarian water
polo team in the middle of the Olympic pool while a
pro-Hungarian crowd of 5,500 waited to pick up the pieces.

"How do you do," the Russians said. "Very well," the Hungarians said and then Peter Mchvenieradze of Russia threw a hammerlock around a Hungarian neck. He was caught and getting caught is considered very bad form. He went to the penalty box. Almost immediately, Dezso Gymati of Hungary popped a Russian on the chin and scored a goal all in the same motion. He was not caught. Hungary led 1–0.

The Hungarians scored four goals to none for Russia but such trivia is hardly worth mentioning. The real show had nothing to do with points. Left hooks and right crosses were barely noted because there were so many of them. Antol Bolvari of Hungary was noticed because he only had one serviceable eye after he was clipped and he humped along like a waterlogged Cyclops. Finally, in the late minutes of play, Valentine Popokov of the Soviet Union and Ervin Zador of Hungary got in a dandy scrap at the far end of the pool away from the semi-legal action. As they kicked hell out of each other, spectators rushed to the side of the pool cursing the Russian and the police had a nice little riot on their hands. Meanwhile, back at the other end people began belting each other above and below the water line.

In a moment of sudden silence Zador climbed out of the pool leaving a trail of blood in his wake. The Hungarian team followed him and caucused on the sidelines, debating who was going to even what for Zador. The Russians wisely stayed in the water as spectators leaned over—but not too far over—and cursed them. The joint was a mad house. With a great show of dignity and an even greater show of wisdom, the Russian team finally announced it had quit the match.

It had been a dandy Olympics. Iron Curtain judges had deliberately low-scored Gary Tobian, the American diving champ, and had cost him his title by 1/100 of a point. Clearly, attitudes never change in the Olympics. Only the names.

So the American public sat back to wait for 1960, stung by the worst defeat this country had ever suffered in an athletic competition it cared about. And 1960 would be a fascinating year of Olympic highs and lows for the United States. It would produce the biggest single disappointment in head-to-head rivalries this country had ever seen. That would come in Rome during the summer. But before that there would be an unexpected bonus.

Hockey is a game, as every American knows, played in large American cities for money by Canadians. It is basically alien to the large army of America's two-dollar bettors who also comprise the bulk of this country's sports-page reading public. It has absolutely nothing to do with what most Americans are all about . . . nothing that is, until the United States started winning.

The U. S. came in with a very fine "amateur" team. The rules of amateur hockey are somewhat more realistic than the rules of amateur track. There are ways you can get paid, and if you can get paid, you can afford to play. Consequently, the team which the United States put onto the ice at Squaw Valley, Calif., was not exactly helpless. It was, however, very lightly regarded.

There was no great excitement in this country when the team beat the Czechs or the Germans. But when goalie Jack McCarten made 39 saves to beat Canada, everybody within five steps of a television set suddenly became a hockey expert. Next on the schedule was Russia.

The Russian hockey team is a part of one of those dandy Iron Curtain arrangements which Mr. Brundage accepts as amateur whenever any country other than the United

States indulges in it. The players live together all year. They play together all year. They even vacation together at the Black Sea. A very nice co-incidental arrangement which is no better planned than the Japanese attack on Pearl Harbor. By the end of the first period, the Russians led, 2–1.

Midway through the second period, however, Bill Christian took a pass from his brother, Roger, and pulled the Americans even. Incredibly, he scored again in the third period, ramming the puck past Nikolai Puchkov, the Russian goalie, to win for the U. S., 3–2.

The American players threw their sticks in the air, total strangers hugged each other in the grandstand and some very dear friendships were immediately formed. The Russians stood silently by themselves at the far end of the ice in total disbelief and all around the country people who didn't know a puck from a taco were jumping up and down in front of their television sets. It was the first time since Horace Ashenfelter that the Americans had beaten the Russians at their own game. Strangely, the following day a Russian would try very hard to put the finishing touches to that triumph.

In order to clinch the gold medal, the Americans had to play the Czechs one more time. They had beaten them earlier but the enormous effort against first Canada and then Russia had taken its toll. After two periods the Czechs led, 4–3. And then along come Sologubuv.

It was one of those gestures of which there are many in the Games but which always seemed to be obscured by idiot team officials, judges and some coaches. Every time management gets its hands on the Olympic creed it manages to leave peanut butter stains all over Baron de Coubertin's parchment. The athletes, however, when left to

their own devices, sometimes generate genuine sparks of
what the old Blue Baron was dreaming about.

Nikolai Sologubuv was the captain of Russia's defeated
hockey team. In between the second and third periods he
visited the American dressing room. He spoke absolutely
no English but with sign language and some magnificent
method acting he finally told the Americans what he wanted
them to do. He wanted them to try oxygen. They did. There
is no evidence that it turned the tide although the Americans
did go out and score six goals to chase the Czechs off the
ice. But it was the gesture that counted and the Americans
never forgot it.

And back in the old living room, American sports fans
glanced at the story and said: "Nice guy that Russian. Now
let's get those Commies at Rome this Summer."

John Thomas was the man most generally accepted to
do the getting. He was, without doubt, the best high jumper
in the world on the day he left for Rome. As a student at
Boston University he had made a shambles of both the
indoor and outdoor track seasons.

What happened to John Thomas at Rome during the
1960 Games shattered the ego of American sports fans as
no individual defeat in the history of Olympic competition.
They expected the Russians to whip us in gymnastics and
canoeing and things like that. They even conceded that
the Russians might dominate the "unofficial" team scoring
although they never began to dream that the final count
against the United States would be a crushing 807½–564½.

But of two things they were chauvinistically confident.
The United States basketball team would easily win. It did.
John Thomas would probably leap over the top of the
stadium. He didn't even come close.

During a workout in Rome shortly before the official

opening of the Games, Thomas was preparing to test the high jump bar at 6–8 when he noticed a group of Russians approaching with cameras. With a stage whisper loud enough to shatter glass, he asked his trainer to raise the bar to seven feet. He cleared it twice with little effort and the Russians murmured: "zamechatelno" (wonderful). Valeri Brumel was one of those watching. He looked grim. "He is unbeatable," said Gabriel Korobkov, the Russian coach, about Thomas. "He just gave them a little handicap," said Bud Winter, Thomas' coach.

All America waited to read about it . . . and all America got sick.

The best Brumel had ever done before the Games began was 7–1½ to 7–3¾ for Thomas. But both Valeri Brumel and Robert Shavlakadze beat Thomas with jumps of 7–1. John went after that height three times and couldn't clear it. Shavalakadze was declared the winner by virtue of fewer misses. John Thomas barely salvaged third place.

It was shocking and it was compounded on the same day when the United States failed to qualify a single man for the 800-meter run, an event it had won every year since 1932, lost the 100-meter sprint final for the first time since 1928 and set the stage for other crushing U. S. defeats in events like the 200-meters and the hammer throw.

The United States team had collapsed and the biggest crash of all had been supplied by John Thomas. His decline had a peculiar postscript. In the winter of 1961, Valeri Brumel came to the United States for a series of three rematches. He won them all by large margins. When he and his Russian teammates left for home, Gabriel Korobkov, the Russian coach, delivered a quote which stung home at American sports page readers the next morning. "American athletes have a lot to learn. Many Americans could better their performances if they were trained with and by us."

Go argue with that one.

Ever since Baron de Coubertin got this thing going again there have been so many American athletes whose performances have excited the American sports fan . . . a list which they fully expected Thomas to join. The names before and after Thomas could and have filled books. Names like . . . Rafer Johnson . . . Bob Mathias . . . Jim Thorpe . . . Bob Hayes . . . Tom Courtney . . . Lee Calhoun . . . Bob Richards . . . Don Bragg . . . Al Oerter . . . Wilma Rudolph . . . Babe Didrikson . . . Mel Patton . . . and on . . . and . . . on . . . and on.

But the big ones, the ones who really counted in the eyes of the marginal Olympic fan who joined the hysteria only when the spirit moved him, were the ones involved head-to-head in vital competition with the Russians.

The nuances of the Olympic Games took on a new direction after the 1960 renewal. Man, the political animal, is father to man, the sports fan. Following 1960 there was a definite, if not conclusive, thaw in the cold war with Russia. Much of the sting left the rivalry at that point and perhaps most if it was transferred into the area of the space race, which—as the American press insists on handling it—is just a bigger ball game.

For that reason, the Olympic Games of 1952–56–60 stand as the high water mark in mass hysteria among the American sports fan. Now he has returned to his World Series and his Super Bowl and the Olympics will remain somewhere below that on the scale.

Of course, on the day when the Red Chinese come in. . . .

"There are other sports which could profit by the example of professional football and attract larger audiences and television revenues. But those responsible must first recognize the tremendous opportunities of, and the need to adapt, to television—adapt without effecting the integrity of their sports."

. . . Tom Moore, then president of ABC-TV, April 20, 1964

THE WAR OF THE WORLDS—I

In the beginning there was W2XBS. It no longer exists. If you shut your eyes and say the call letters fast enough, it comes on like Mickey Rooney operating a sub rosa ham radio station in the attic at Boystown or the last thing a champagne bottle sees before it splinters against the side of a brand new hull at the New London Sub Base.

W2XBS along with its equally anonymous competitors lies a'mouldering in a cathode-tube studded grave but its soul goes marching on. On a dramatic October evening in 1960, it frowns on Richard Nixon's make-up man, gently caresses a careless lock of hair high on the forehead of John F. Kennedy and a future president slips one foot inside the White House door. Three years later, it thrusts its big, red eye boldly into a stone cold corridor in Dallas, Texas, blinks once and who in this entire country could really serve on a jury to try a man named Jack Ruby and honestly say that he had not seen the very act of the specific murder committed?

Around the clock it pricks away at the American conscience, mores and pocketbook. . . . "Blondes have more

fun. . . . Why be old and gray when you can be a brunette?
. . . It's what's up front in a tobacco that counts. . . . Break
the cigarette habit painlessly. . . . Stretch your coffee break.
. . . Tea refreshes you best."

The Son of W2XBS is alive and doing well in everybody's living room.

This is the meaning of television in America today. If
it could elect a president, sell a breakfast food and enter-
tain both literati and cretin, it surely could create the one
synthetic sports rivalry capable of capturing the minds and
emotions of the American sports fans as nothing else before
had.

The date would be Jan. 15, 1967. The city, Los Angeles,
Calif. The decor, well, color it pickpocket-green and little-
white-lie white. And the name of the game. . . . call it return
of W2XBS or the Super Bowl.

It would match the Green Bay Packers, champions of
the league television helped to save, and the Kansas City
Chiefs, champions of the league television created. It would
also match the Columbia Broadcasting System and the
National Broadcasting Co. It would stumble off the drawing board after a peace conference which embodied all the
sanity of negotiations between Lilliput and Blefuscu. It
would slip quietly toward center stage with the subtlety of
Harpo Marx meets the Dance of the Sugar Plum Fairies.
It would be preceded by the combined hot air of two television networks, generating enough decibels to shatter
whiskey glasses in bar-rooms all over the country.

And it would end with all the drama of a tree forming
its annual ring.

The winding electronic trail which led from old W2XBS
to the first Super Bowl in Los Angeles had its genesis in
a chance conversation in the Spring of 1939 between a man

named William Burke Miller, a producer at NBC which
ran W2XBS as an experimental television station, and Bob
Harron, then director of public relations at Columbia University.

"Ever think of televising a sporting event?" Mr. Harron
asked.

"No," William Burke Miller replied, "why?"

"People might like it."

And so, on the afternoon of May 17, 1939, W2XBS took
its camera up to Baker Field on 212th Street in New York
to televise the second game of an Eastern Intercollegiate
Baseball League doubleheader between Columbia and
Princeton. There were just 5,000 television sets in the Metro-
politan New York area that day. Joe Louis was the heavyweight champion of the world. The Yankees were, well, the
Yankees. And television was absolutely nothing. If that
doesn't prove you can't go home again, somebody is telling
a very large lie.

A kid named Sid Luckman (later to become the premier
quarterback on professional football's premier team—the
Chicago Bears) played shortstop for Columbia and went
hitless. Bill Stern broadcast the game and a young man
named Don Carmichael gained a measure of fame by default, beating Columbia, 2–1, for Princeton and thereby be-
coming television's first winning pitcher. Nobody knows
where Mr. Carmichael is today but he really ought to go
out in the back yard and take another look at his fastball.
Things being what they are in sports' overexpanded and
under-staffed world today, he might be well-advised to
attempt a comeback.

Television had taken its first tentative step into a brave
new world. It never looked back. It fell in love with boxing
and killed it with over-exposure. It fell in love with wrestling

and that was a happier marriage because a script is a
script is a script. But most important, in terms of that great
Super Sunday in the distant future, it fell in love with a
man named Bert Bell, Sr., and the love affair was both
mutual and rewarding.

Ever since 1921 when a mixed bag of pioneers, vision-
aries, hustlers, and professional juveniles formed the National Football League, encompassing equally hyphenated
groups of cities which included Chicago and Detroit on the
one hand and Rock Island and Canton on the other, the
league's financial reports read like the hospital chart of
an acute chills and fever victim.

Stability was major league baseball's bag. Paying the
rent was the name of the game in the NFL. But with the
end of World War II and the emergence of Bert Bell as a
"strong commissioner," television leaned across the financial
Vesuvius which was burning on management's doorstep
and offered to beat it into cold, cold ashes with hot, hot
dollars. In 1949, just 10 years after W2XBS stuck its nose
into Baker Field, Bell sold the entire National Football
League schedule to the Dumont Television Network (flag-
ship station—WABD) for $75.000. He conceived a master-
ful plan which was to turn professional football into the
number one emotion-grabber in the country.

It was called the "limited blackout policy." Under this
strategy, Dumont would beam road games to the visiting
team's community, then reverse the procedure when the
teams met in the return game in the second city. The impact was two-fold. First, it reached the hard-core professional football fan and afforded him the chance to see a
game he could not otherwise attend. Second, it grabbed
large masses of dial-twisters who were willing prisoners of
this new television age and introduced them to a game

which combined the best sides of violence and excitement. Since home games were never carried, it brought a good many new fans to the ball park.

Unless you have been living in a cave somewhere, you undoubtedly know that it worked just the way Bell said it would. It set pro football off on a dizzy roller-coaster ride which has yet to take its first dip. The future of the National Football League—thanks to television's stranglehold on American recreation habits of the early 1950's was suddenly painted a splashy mint-green and edged in gold. The NFL had taken its first step along the road which would ultimately lead to Los Angeles and that great, synthetic moment of truth which the airwaves would immortalize as Super Sunday.

But television could never have produced its first monumental propaganda-spawned paper-tiger championship match without help. It got it from the very same place where every fast-buck operator who wants to crash the inner circle of sports' traditional establishments always seems to get it. It got it through the greed, arrogance and stupidity which marks sports' "haves" when they come face to face with the "have-nots."

Twice during the long, hard Grapes of Wrath-type years of the National Football League's fight for survival, the pioneers had beaten back rival challenges. In the late 1920's a man named C. C. Pyle (unkind people always insisted that the initials C. C. stood for Cash and Carry) had built a genuine challenger around the magic of Red Grange. Mr. Grange was the Golden Boy of the Golden Age, a magnificent football player out of the University of Illinois, who for a brief span pulled George Halas' Chicago Bears—and the teams fortunate enough to play them with Grange in the same ball park—out of a sea of red ink with his box office appeal. Mr. Grange could run like hell with a football. And Mr. Pyle, it was said with some validity, could run like hell with an ipso facto.

He had signed Grange to a personal services contract and peddled his talents to the Bears. When George Halas signed Red Grange he also got C. C. Pyle in the deal. And when C. C. Pyle, carefully noting the amount of money Mr. Grange had earned for Mr. Halas, asked for a piece of the action for his product, Mr. Halas told him to take a walk. The place C. C. Pyle walked was to a variety of empty stadiums in which he put hastily organized franchises, determined to challenge the NFL with a league built strictly around Grange.

They called themselves the American League and the touchstone of their movement was scheduled to play in Yankee Stadium just across the river from the entrenched New York Giants. Nobody succeeded. Everyone was hurt. But the Giants survived. Wellington Mara, president of the Giants today and the son of Old Tim Mara who founded the original team, used to sit on a desk in the Polo Grounds' office on game day and focus his binoculars out the window and across the river to where Pyle's team was playing. "It's O.K., pop," he would holler at Tim, "nobody's watching them either."

Within a year, C. C. Pyle was out of business and the National Football League remained the only wheel in the world until 1946 when a Buffalo trucker named Sam Cordovano, an actor named Don Ameche and a San Francisco businessman named Anthony Morabito were repeatedly rebuffed in their attempts to buy new franchises in the old league. "They could have accepted our bids for a later date . . . for a time when they would be ready to expand,"

Cordovano said one day in 1946. "But they just weren't interested. Now it's going to cost them."

The new league would be called the All-America Conference and among its stars would be an exciting quarterback named Otto Graham. Both leagues entered a bidding war for new college talent. The AAC fought the good fight and quite properly scared hell out of the old guard. It might even have succeeded if television had come along just a little earlier to help pay the bills.

But television wasn't ready for that. The first boom in home-set buying wouldn't come until 1948 and by that time the AAC was just a year away from its death rattle. They went down the drain but it proved an interesting point. It had fought so vehemently that three of its insurgent Montagues were grudgingly admitted into the Establishment by the National League Capulets.

Now it was 1960 and in a high-rent apartment with a Park Avenue address and a Lexington Avenue entrance, a man named Harry Wismer was saying some of the same things which Sam Cordovano had said about the NFL just 14 years earlier.

"They (the NFL) had Lamar Hunt in Dallas and Bud Adams in Houston and both of them wanted franchises. But they got horsed around. The NFL thought it didn't need them. Well, that's going to be a costly assumption."

For once in his life, Harry Wismer was right. Six years later, at a time when Harry Wismer was no longer a part of the AFL, one of the strangest peace treaties this side of Versailles would be consummated in a plush suite in New York's Warwick Hotel. It would come at a time when both leagues had come perilously close to stoning each other to death with their wallets and when the insurgents

were within an eyelash of launching a brand new weapon
which might have turned everything around only to suc-
cumb to the need to be loved and to give it all back at
the peace table.

But in 1960, the strength from which Wismer spoke
was a nebulous kind of thing, based on the over-powering
wave of pro football hysteria which was sweeping the country and the law of supply and demand (too many fans and
too few franchises). But there was one genuine and ultimately decisive hole card. Its name was television. In its
way, it was about to become an entrepreneur. The Son of
old W2XBS stood at major crossroads.

For years, Harry Wismer's voice had been a household
sound in living rooms across the country. As a sports
announcer, Harry brought a new dimension to radio—a
dimension of glamour and excitement (often self-manu-
factured) in which the facts rarely cluttered up the drama.
If Harry chose during some lull in the action to stage-
whisper a greeting to, say, Gen. Douglas Mac Arthur for
the benefit of his audience, well, that's what Harry did
and if Gen. Mac Arthur was off in Manila at the time, well,
that was the general's fault.

He was colorful, flamboyant, illogical and highly popular with his radio audience. Later, it would be said that
Harry Wismer was the only man in the world with nerve
enough to start a franchise to challenge the New York
Giants and the only one in the world capable of destroying
whatever chance it had once it was off the ground. But
there was a contribution that Wismer could and, indeed,
did make. As head of the league's television committee he
negotiated an inaugural contract with the American Broadcasting Company which he claimed would bring each AFL
club $200,000 that first year in television revenue.

In truth, a variety of escape clauses enabled ABC to hedge the bet in terms of numbers but the contract was an excellent one for a league which had yet to own its first football and without the long-range hope this television contact held out to the new lodge members, the league never would have emerged from Wismer's kitchen. There would be times after that first year, when people were not entirely sure it did.

The two disaffected NFL franchise-seekers of whom Wismer spoke were major factors in the league's puppy-hood. Lamar Hunt of the Dallas' Hunts and Bud Adams of the Houston Adamses had, indeed, attempted to buy their way into the NFL. Hunt had unsuccessfully attempted to purchase the Chicago Cardinals, a team which subsequently moved to St. Louis. After that abortive attempt, he and a former TCU All-American named Davey O'Brien met in secret with George Wolfner, the Card's owner, George Halas, head of the NFL expansion committee (which had no intention of expanding) and Bert Bell, Sr. the commissioner. The NFL, in all fairness, had experienced one hell of a trauma in 1952 when it had tried to resettle the defunct New York Yankee franchise in Dallas and threw up its hands after the club went broke in a single year.

"We met with Bell in January of 1959," Hunt once told a reporter. "When I asked about expansion, I was told that the league wasn't interested in us so we made no formal application."

Instead, Lamar Hunt of the Texas' Hunts went out to buy his own football. He lined up Adams and Wismer, a shrewd Detroit businessman named Ralph Wilson, hotel wheeler-dealer Barron Hilton and others. Among the others was a Minneapolis-St. Paul syndicate headed by L. P.

Skoagland and Max Winter. It was at this juncture that the National League took a giant step which would ultimately cost both sides millions of dollars. It didn't say "may I?" and if it had, the AFL most certainly would have said "hell, no." But on Nov. 23, 1959, while the AFL was holding its first major meeting in Minneapolis, the NFL seduced, abducted or extended the hand of friendship to the Skoagland-Winter group. Whatever language you choose to use, Minneapolis-St. Paul defected to the old guard. In desperation, the AFL which was having all kinds of organizational problems, accepted a ludicrous collection of owners who would call their team the Oakland Raiders. The second-string ownership of the Raiders distinguished itself by piling up points for enterprise. In their very first season, for example, they picked the one place in an otherwise empty ball park to air their intra-tribal vendettas—the press box. At that, it was more exciting than most of their ball games.

What followed the Minneapolis-St. Paul defection was a multimillion dollar lawsuit, a direct confrontation in San Francisco (where Oakland played its first season), New York and Los Angeles—all entrenched National League cities —and in Dallas, the city which the NFL had rejected and then fallen in love with when it (A) found its own Texas millionaire, Clint Murchison, to run the club and (B) claimed divine right of kinds when it learned that somebody else had the audacity to play there.

The battle lines were drawn and all hell broke loose when the rebels went out to sign their first players. The inaugural set of AFL owners was naive, in some cases stupid and in at least one case (Light Horse Harry Wismer) about as mature as a precocious 10-year old. The NFL owners were intransigent, greedy and short-sighted. But the college kids, well, the college kids were a joy to behold. The guards may not have known where Yalta was. The tackles may have thought Yeman was a name on the NFL expansion list. The halfbacks may have believed that William the Conqueror was a folk singer. But when it came to numbers, they played their own brand of new math.

They initiated six years of delightful holdups, playing one league off against the other and collecting staggering bonuses for talents which many of them simply did not have. The length of their contracts protected generations of their descendents as yet unborn. They accepted gifts from people they never planned to see again. The very first year, two of them—Billy Cannon of LSU and Charley Flowers of Mississippi—played it safe. They signed with both leagues. The height of the great captains of the professional football world's humiliation was clearly illustrated by an incident in a Mississippi courtroom. Flowers had signed with the NFL Giants and with the AFL Chargers (then based in Los Angeles). Jim Lee Howell, director of player personnel for New York, sat in court in a state which took its college football very seriously and where Flowers' exploits on local football fields had made him something of a folk hero. As Howell once recalled it:

"The Judge asked me if I was calling this fine young man a liar and then he said something like " 'Charley, where do you want to play?' "

The American Broadcasting Company (which had been shut off from the new pro football boom first by NBC and later by CBS' successful bidding) rubbed its hands, polished up its cameras and sat back and waited for people to come running over from Madison Avenue begging them to take their money. Nobody was killed in the rush.

The AFL opened its doors in 1960 and played game

after game after game before groups of people which one
writer reported "apparently came cleverly disguised as hundreds of thousands of empty seats." And in New York,
Harry Wismer cast himself in the role of Don Quixote and
played it with all the polish of Humpty Dumpty. This was
the one city where the league had to survive to stay in
business. Television was adamant about that but then it
was more than television. No major league had ever operated for any great length of time without a New York
franchise. The National Baseball League had tried it for
one and had returned.

Wismer called his team the New York Titans, confiding
to people who would listen: "What's bigger than a giant?
A titan, that's what." His playing field was the old Polo
Grounds, cited by public-spirited citizens as the Western
World's greatest challenge to Urban Renewal since the
Great London Fire. There, in total privacy, the sound of
toe against football blended with the drip . . . drip . . . drip
of the leaky comfort stations and echoed throughout the
empty park. Since home games were blacked out by ABC
and the league, New York's shrewder crop of philandering
husbands were said to have finally discovered America's
safest trysting place.

The Titans drew crowds of 3,000 and Wismer announced
them as anything from 12–18,000 depending on his mood.
He strode the side-lines, heaping abuse on the officials,
heckling rival players and occasionally moving his portable
chair onto the playing field. He fought with the other
owners. He fought with the press, which ironically had
welcomed the idea of a second wheel in town but which
after three weeks was willing to take up a collection to get
the Sherman Anti-Trust Act revoked in favor of the Giants.
Wismer had that effect on people.

"They used to introduce the players over the loud-speaker," Larry Grantham, a linebacker on the original Titans would later recall, "but you had the feeling that it was a waste of time and that you ought to run up into the stands and shake everyone's hand individually. The place was so empty that the players used to holler back and forth with their wives who were sitting in the upper stands."

Wismer ran his operation from his apartment. He even sold tickets from there—a master stroke when you consider that the address was listed as Park Avenue but the entrance was on Lexington Avenue. His living room was his business office. The coaches used the dining room and Ted Emory, the team's first publicist, used the butler's pantry. Unfortunately, his working area was so small that the mimeograph machine obstructed the bathroom door. Every time somebody needed a comfort break, Emory had to move everything. A single case of intestinal flu could have shut down the publicity department for a week.

This was hardly the kind of opposition designed to strike terror into the hearts of the affluent Giants or to be appreciated by ABC-TV which found itself "owning" the country's worst sports property in the country's largest city. Things weren't much better elsewhere.

Dallas—being Dallas—the population had split noisily over the warring factions, taken violent sides and proceeded to go to neither's football games. In Los Angeles, Hilton's Chargers won the league title, drew nobody to see them and fled in panic to San Diego. Boston's Patriots were lucky to have a place to play—although people who had the dubious distinction of watching them in the modern ruin called Braves Field might even argue that point. Houston survived in a high school stadium. The situations in Denver and Oakland were unspeakably confusing. The Denver people got off to a dandy start with their players by serving them hash for breakfast in pre-season camp. Only Buffalo, a football-wise Great Lakes town with a history of pro football left over from the defunct All-America Conference, showed any great promise.

But the league came back for more. It did have its television contract and it knew that if it ever came close to hitting, the big payoff would rest with that medium.

The battle could hardly be called Armageddon at that stage but like Topsy it just grew and grew and grew and the fact that people like Hunt and Adams and, for a time, Hilton were willing to spend big money to lure college All-Americans kept the rebels in the ball game. Through sheer attrition they began to test the National League where it was most sentimental—in its wallet.

It was costly. Nobody will ever know how many wretched football players—some of whom were never seen again—received bonuses completely out of line with their talents. Booze and broads, blackmail and kidnapping became standard operational procedures for scouts from both leagues. Everything short of barn-burning was tolerated by furious managements on both sides. Before it would end, lawyers (some sincere, some not) and fast buck agents would latch on to college prospects by the dozens and handle their negotiations. To spotlight the absurdity of it all, three University of Illinois football players would accept money for plane fare from the NFL, present themselves in New York where both leagues were drafting, point to their "advisor" and offer themselves to the highest bidder.

The National League firmly believed that it would drive the rebels out of existence. The AFL just as firmly believed that it could shoot its way into the Establishment and find love and happiness by forcing the other side to spend itself into exhaustion. Doves in each league talked peace. Hawks in each league continued to maneuver and cheat and fight. The legal battles mounted. A man on the sidelines watched mediocre football players become young millionaires and silently wondered if all the owners would be able to share the same case-worker when they were finally driven to the relief roles.

Then a series of fascinating things happened and not the least of them involved the Son of old W2XBS. Wismer, bankrupt, ridiculed but never silent, lost his ball club. He failed to meet payrolls. Towel companies and laundries demanded payment and it came to a head when the Titans faced the prospect of a Thanksgiving Day game in Denver without enough money to buy a single plane ticket.

The league stepped in. Ultimately, the club was sold to a syndicate headed by a man named Sonny Werblin, who had built a show business empire as the key figure for an outfit called the Music Corporation of America. He knew the value of publicity and he would later cash the biggest headline bonanza of all when he signed a kid quarterback out of the University of Alabama for what the papers accepted as a long-term $400,000 contract. He would mend his press relations, change the name of the team to the New York Jets and, best of all inherit the right to play his home games in brand new Shea Stadium.

At the same time, Wayne Valley, a tough, shrewd businessman, would assume control of the Oakland Raiders. He brought in a whiz of a coach named Al Davis, who made a specialty out of acquiring and rehabilitating some of the league's disaffected players. He was also a master recruiter and he had immediate success signing college prospects. He proceeded to build a fine young football team and as a plus the City of Oakland began work on a new home for the Raiders.

These things all contributed to staving off what surely would have been the end of the AFL. But television picked up the ball and ran with it. In January of 1964, Ralph Wilson, who owned the Buffalo Bills, was vacationing in Paris when he ran into an American sports writer he had known for some time. There, in a small restaurant just across from the Church of the Madeleine, he confided:

"I'm going to tell you something which is really going to knock your eyeballs out. The Columbia Broadcasting System just renewed its contract with the National Football League. What do you suppose they had to pay?"

"I have no idea."

"Come on, guess."

"All right, the Mona Lisa, the mineral rights to Chavez Ravine and Paul Hornung's Good Conduct Medal."

"You're not even close. . . . 28 million dollars that's what . . . 28 million and it doesn't even include the championship game. This is only the beginning. This is fantastic."

"That's very nice," the reporter said, "but unless there has been one hell of a revolt in the palace guard since we left home, I fail to see what this is going to do for you. The NFL isn't about to put you people on the dole."

"No," Buffalo Ralph admitted, "but just you wait and see what happens next."

A few weeks later, the National Broadcasting Company, the same business firm which had sponsored the original W2XBS, announced that it had taken the AFL away from ABC-TV. Taken is hardly the word. For the right to buy a league which was in desperate trouble, NBC would pay $34 million and change over a five-year span. The rebels had fresh money. The Super Bowl, that distant supercalifragilistic moment in the Los Angeles smog, began to take shape that very day.

The AFL fumbled in the television ratings but that was NBC's problem. It now went out to spend in earnest. It set the stage for the final showdown and while the American League was still not drawing people in fantastic numbers in most of its cities, its war with the NFL was dominating the sports pages. Of such things are emotional rivalries born in the minds of the American public.

The NFL was led by a man named Alvin Pete Rozelle. When somebody finally gets around to writing that master's thesis on the impact of professional sports in this country, he is going to flunk the course unless the name of Alvin Pete Rozelle leads all the rest. He is handsome. He is articulate. He is press conscious (he started in the business as a public relations man for the Los Angeles Rams). He is shrewd without offending and as tough as Attila. In short, if he ever decides to resign as commissioner, he can obtain gainful employment posing for the back of breakfast cereal boxes.

Rozelle has fought most of pro sports' battles in the Congress. He stole the Atlanta franchise from right under the American League's nose when it was supposed to have a lock on the town. He is a very good man to have on your side.

Against him, the American League had sent a man named Joe Foss, a former war hero and governor. In the league's early years, he did in many ways give it "image." He was courageous in war, scrupulously honest in business, successful in politics and dreadfully over-matched in professional football. NBC, the Big Daddy which was now paying a lot of AFL bills, found itself locked out of major markets in Los Angeles and Chicago. It wanted somebody to put American League franchises in those cities. It was getting very nervous.

The NBC ratings continued to hold at lousy despite the fact that it had television's best 1–2 announcing team in Curt Gowdy and Paul Christman. The National League's united resistance was in no way hindered in that same year when the AFL issued a challenge which said in essence: "We would like to play you in a championship game. By the way, we are appealing the verdict you won in our lawsuit."

It was clear that the biggest battle was yet to be fought and it was also clear, that the owners were not going to send Joe Foss against Pete Rozelle to fight it. They reached out for a new man. Brooklyn born Al Davis, the man who brought Oakland football its first genuine professionalism, was the surprise choice.

On Monday, April 25, 1966, the new man moved into his new office at 280 Park Avenue not too far from Rozelle's command post at 1 Rockefeller Plaza. It would be a matter of hours before both sides could begin monitoring each other eyeball to eyeball through high-powered binoculars. High noon at Rockefeller Center was just a matter of hours.

"I think you will find," Mr. Davis said in his first official statement, "that the commissioner's office will function a little differently than in the past. "You are going to see," he said as he double-parked his Sherman Tank on Park Avenue, "less and less rule by committee."

And there you have it. When the PTA debates the kindergarten zoo trip you need a committee. When the student council checks the pencils at the Happy Hour Nursery School you need a committee. But when CBS (through the NFL) and NBC (through the AFL) go to war, the only committee that pulls any weight is one which can operate an 81 mm mortar. Until this juncture, the AFL had dearly loved rule by committee. All it had to show for it was a set of tiger heads from one of Joe Foss' African safari and an empty julep glass from Atlanta.

While Mr. Davis was setting up his forward observers, a young man with a marvelously talented kicking foot was about to lay one right in the seat of Mr. Davis' pants. His name was Pete Gogolak. He was a Hungarian-born place-kicker who booted the ball soccer style, which is to say that he looked as though he were lining up facing the hot dog stand instead of the goal posts. But my, oh my, he got results. As a kicker for Ralph Wilson's Buffalo team, he was the best in the league—perhaps, for at least one season, the best in all of football.

Pro football takes a little explaining here. Like most American institutions, management and labor are created equal except that management is just a little more equal. Under a great piece of peonage which would make even the California fruit growers blush, pro football contracts are more than binding. If you sign one and choose not to sign another, you must sit at home for a year doing nothing and receiving no pay as a penalty or else play without a contract for a large cut in salary. At the end of a year of penance, the employee is free to make a deal if he can find someone to hire him. Pete Gogolak took that course. And where did he find the highest bidder? In the rival National League, naturally.

Even as Al Davis was unpacking, the Giants signed him and Pete Rozelle approved his new contract. Qualified football historians agree that there is one thing which Al Davis does better than anyone else in his particular business. He gets pro football players to sign contracts. The war had finally come to its moment of truth. Davis believed

that the ground rules had moved into his ball park. Later
Scotty Stirling, who replaced Davis as Oakland general
manager when Davis became commissioner, would say:

"There was nothing illegal about what the Giants did
but we felt it gave us the moral wedge to go out and
encourage a few people in their league to consider the same
course."

Since the National League had the better players and
the better box office attractions, it figured to risk more in
such a battle. Davis signed Roman Gabriel, the Rams'
quarterback, to an Oakland contract. So it shouldn't be a
total loss, Gabriel then turned around and signed a new
contract with the Rams. Pen in hand, Davis continued to
sweep through the NFL. Among the names which cropped
up most often as Davis signees who would play out their
options and subsequently jump to the AFL were Mike
Ditka and Rudy Bukich of the Bears, John Brodie of the
49'ers and a battery of lesser lights.

But suddenly, without warning and without Davis'
knowledge until the last possible moment, it was over. Rule
by committee was not dead. It was simply out for lunch.
Lamar Hunt was, again, the key figure. Lamar, soft-spoken,
dedicated to his football team, mindful of the price he
and other charter members had been forced to pay already, friendly, shy but in the ultimate oh so wanting to
be loved and to rub shoulders with the grownups in the
National Football League. Lamar Hunt carried the ball for
rule by committee. After it was over both Sonny Werblin
and Wayne Valley would charge that they had been spending the most money in the stretch run, they had the most
to lose because they were in head-to-head competition in
New York and the California Bay Area (Lamar had already
left Dallas for Kansas City while Hilton had shifted from

Los Angeles to San Diego), that they were unwilling to settle for anything less than total equality because they believed in Davis' technique and that they had been deliberately kept in the dark about peace negotiations until the wish had become a fact.

The talks had begun in secret in the parking lot at Dallas' Love Field, the municipal airport, in the spring of 1965. There, amid the faint aroma of carbon monoxide and Texas money, Lamar had represented certain American League owners while Tex Schramm, general manager of the NFL Dallas Cowboys—the team which chased Lamar out of town—spoke for the National League. They moved over the year to Washington and ultimately to New York. Because of them and some of the ridiculous peace terms to which the Americans agreed in their haste to be accepted by the Establishment, Lamar has since become known in certain quarters as the "Foundling Father of the AFL." Throughout the negotiations, Pete Rozelle knew everything that was happening. As they neared their conclusion, it is probable that CBS knew a great deal of it. As for NBC, well, it learned of matters near the finish, which was still considerably earlier than Davis was informed.

At 3 A.M., on the morning of June 7, 1966, Lamar Hunt was incognito in a New York Hotel, speaking to Tex Schramm in Dallas. Fifteen minutes later, Schramm telephoned Pete Rozelle back in New York to tell him the articles of confederation could be drawn at any time now. According to Lamar's poll of key league officials (less Valley and Werblin) peace was just around the corner.

Rozelle showered, shaved, checked the airline schedule and was back on the telephone to Dallas. He told Schramm that they could meet later in the day in Washington. Washington seemed like a nice city to meet in. It had the Lincoln

Memorial, the Smithsonian Institution and the Washington
Monument. It also had the Justice Department and the one
thing Rozelle most wanted to be certain about was that
he keep the Justice Department informed about what was
happening in a merger of this sort before somebody like
J. Edgar Hoover, Rep. Emanuel Celler (D-NY) or Bobby
Kennedy read about it in the morning papers. Rozelle told
Schramm that he would catch the noon shuttle from La-
Guardia. Schramm thanked him, then reminded him that
universal brotherhood has its limits. It might be 8 A.M. in
New York but "For Christ's Sake, Pete, it's only 6 A.M. in
Dallas. Good night."

That afternoon in Washington, Rozelle and Schramm
slipped off to the Sheraton-Carlton Hotel where another
highly secret meeting was scheduled with Hunt in a suite
which had been rented all year for business reasons by
Schramm's boss, Clint Murchison. After dodging, ducking,
weaving and sneaking along to the hotel they found Lamar
innocently waiting for them near the front entrance. It is
possible that Lamar's feet may have touched the ground
once before Rozelle and Schramm got him to the elevator.
It is possible but not likely.

The rest of the day was spent in secret communion.
Nobody will ever know what really happened that afternoon
and evening but the next morning all three went over to
the offices of Covington and Burling, attorneys for the
National Football League. Meanwhile, Jim Kensil, Rozelle's
astute director of public relations, had flown down from
New York with a list of questions which he as a former
newspaper reporter (and a good one) fully expected the
press to ask Lamar when the inevitable press conference
would be held later that evening in New York. The rehearsal
went well but the way things subsequently developed, the

show could have used a week's tryout in New Haven. Lamar then left for New York to meet with Billy Sullivan, president of the Boston Patriots, and Ralph Wilson.

And as this incredible six-year war raced towards its great and, as events proved, incredible moment of truth, things were absolutely crackers back in New York City. The news was out but the terms were not. Newspaper offices and their switchboards were about as calm as a television commercial. Everyone wanted the terms but nobody could find anybody. Meanwhile, reporters with friends in the American League office were having even more trouble with their telephone.

"What the hell is going on?" an AFL employee asked a close friend who writes a sports column.

"You tell me?"

"How the hell can I? Nobody here knows anything. Davis hasn't been in yet but . . . here he comes now."

"Sign this," Davis said to the underling. It was a formal contract. Several of the new employees—key men in Davis' plans for retaliation in the war of the signings—had been so busy signing players, they had not yet had time to sign their own contracts. To his credit it should be said here that Al Davis made sure they would not be left holding a large, empty and unemployed bag. Early that evening Santa Claus met the Wolf Man in the Essex Room suite of the Warwick Hotel.

Harry Wismer used to think of himself as Don Quixote and if manufacturing your own windmills is a qualification, then Harry deserved the part. Pete Rozelle never thought of himself as a cavalier but in truth he was the Three Musketeers all rolled into one. If he had really had the time to pick a joint for this first annual B'nai Hunt Brotherhood Award, he would have settled on the Essex Room

anyway. As it was, the site was dictated more by the logistics of assembling the key writers from all over New
York than it was by personal inclination. But if Pete Rozelle
in an alley fight is the Swedish Angel, Pete Rozelle before
the bar of history is one-part Beau Brummel, one-part
Clemenceau and two-parts Fred Allen. He has an amazing
sense of humor and timing.

Consequently, if you didn't know better, you would
have sworn that the wall-size mural behind Pete's shoulder
was of his own choosing. It was an old English garden, a
sprightly blending of hedgerows and lush green grass and
the ideal site for an Easter Egg roll. The American Football
League in its sudden rush for acceptance, was about to
get itself rolled. In the trade they call such sets type-casting.

The room was filled with press and National League
and American League employees. The last two groups
scattered to their respective side of the room separated by
a narrow aisle. You could almost hear the usher ask each
one at the door: "Friend of the bride? Friend of the groom?"

Up front, on a powder blue leather couch, Rozelle was
flanked by Schramm and Hunt. He held a portable hand
microphone. Occasionally he loaned it to Lamar Hunt to
answer a question. The terms of "peace in our times" or as
perceptive followers of American League history dubbed
the AFL's side of the document "The Commitment to be
Committed" were simple.

Pete Rozelle would emerge as commissioner of the world
and that's the way those things go, Al. All existing franchises would be retained. A common draft of all college
players into one dandy unified kettle of penal servitude
would begin next season. Assorted other goodies were inter-
league exhibitions and an inter-league playoff. game (ultimately named the Super Bowl), continued two-network
coverage (surprise) and finally all of this would cost the

American League the bargain price of roughly $25½ million in damages, initiation fees, marriage licenses, poll taxes, psychiatric care and comfort blankets. Rozelle agreed to let Lamar keep his mule for the spring plowing. There was no point in over-doing the thing.

In the long run, the peace would obviously benefit both sides. The Nationals had the most to lose at the finish when Davis began signing their players for the simple reason that they had the better players. The Americans were totally divided. Werblin and Valley wanted to fight on and so, for a time, did Houston's Bud Adams, who switched sides at the last moment. Ralph Wilson wanted to merge because he thought it was cheaper in the long run. The rest of the field never won any awards for anything in the matter of power politics.

As for the Nationals, well, the Giants and the 49'ers were reluctant signees. The Giants were particularly bitter because they believed they had suffered through the lean years and the Jets' organization would reap the benefits of their labors. This particular phase of the acrimony would be a long time dying in both New York front offices.

The meeting was of particular interest to the two television networks, which would both get to televise the Super Duper Super Bowl the first year and then alternate after that, and to devoted Biblical scholars who could now die happy in the knowledge that they had seen the lion lie down with the lamb. These were the Beatitudes as preached by Rozelle, ie: "it is more blessed to give than receive" and on this day the AFL was the most blessed group in the world. Hunt and Schramm did not hum a chorus of "Nearer My God To Thee," accompanied by Rozelle on the Hammond organ but then there was so little time to plan the press conference.

But for the Children of old W2XBS it was a glorious

occasion. CBS had been itching to prove that its league could lick NBC's league. It would have its chance the following January. NBC, on the other hand, was prepared to take that licking on the theory that once the American League was permitted to wipe its nose, get off the curb and play with the big boys, the American public and a great many potential television sponsors would take the league more seriously. NBC damned well had to take it seriously because its contract with the AFL was scheduled to run at least through 1969.

Throughout the country, sports writers debated the merits of who got what in this startling peace conference. Places like Denver and Boston breathed sighs of relief because dubious franchises were suddenly saved for them. The owners in both leagues were delighted at the prospect that the exhaustive spending battle for new talent was at last ended.

For the sports fan, the man whose emotions must be rubbed raw to create just the proper climate to manufacture the kind of enduring rivalry which can be translated into large sums of money for the rivals, the focal point was clear. Los Angeles would be the place and the Super Bowl . . . the very first war of the worlds . . . would be the game.

And along Madison Avenue, the people who know where it's really at, and just you ask them but ask quickly because if you don't they'll tell you anyway, debated the burning question:

"Can the National Broadcasting Company lick the Columbia Broadcasting System?" Around the water-cooler at B.B.D. & O. they were taking CBS and giving six points in the Nielsen ratings.

"Hate the other guy? Hell, I never even met him. How the hell are you going to hate somebody who is a complete stranger?"

Packer guard Fuzzy Thurston, three days before the game.

THE WAR OF THE WORLDS—II

On Thursday, June 9, 1966—less than 24 hours after pro football's shotgun marriage—the telephone rang at Judson 2–5265. This used to be the main telephone number at the National Football League but overnight, remodeled by the brave new era of football's universal brotherhood, it had become a kind of Mecca which former heretics in Kansas City, Boston and Buffalo were learning to face three times daily.

"I am calling from Denver, Colorado," the voice on the telephone said, "and I want to reserve 200 seats for the NFL–AFL championship game."

"We don't know when or where it will be played," the secretary explained for the 200th time that morning, "and we don't even know how much the tickets are going to cost."

"I don't care what they cost," the disembodied voice at the other end of the line passionately replied, "I just want to be sure that I'm not left out."

He wasn't the only one. The 1966 pre-season training camps wouldn't open for another month but the sound and the fury which six years of newspaper headlines and television commentary had generated immediately translated itself into the next phase of this furious debate. Professional football fans do not rate a high call on the scale of emotional stability even under the best of circumstances. Healthy grown men who won't even walk 10 steps to take out the garbage will dress up like something out of a fraternity initiation stunt, risk third-degree frost-bite and sit in a catatonic trance watching other grown men play a little boys' game for money. They will cheerfully allow themseves to be rained on, snowed on, hailed on and damned near blown out of their seats. They will sneeze, wheeze, cough and shiver for hours in physical circumstances normally prized by people who believe that a case of walking pneumonia is good for the soul. They will stagger off to their snow-covered automobiles, turn on their heaters, inch forward into a monumental traffic jam and then sneeze, wheeze, cough and shiver some more. They will enjoy every chill and fever that the subsequent week brings and seven days later they'll be back for more of the same.

So this super championship match would be for them. It would be called the Super Bowl and with a name like that a man couldn't be sure whether to bring along a hip flask or a shopping cart but what's in a name? Hell, this is history.

It would also be played for others who were not caught up in the fraudulent mystique of a brotherhood which speaks in the pseudo-language liberally sprinkled with "red dogs" and "zig-ins" and which operates on the theory that only a brain surgeon can understand the "real game" and what other event could attract 84,000 brain surgeons to Cleveland's Municipal Stadium on a snowy day? The Super Bowl would fascinate people who were simply interested in seeing the best a given sport had to offer. It would captivate others who would attach themselves emotionally to the rebel American Football League on the theory that all of America loves an underdog. For whatever reasons, it would grip the emotions of so many Americans—and television ratings would support this—that it would rank as the unquestioned sports event of the decade.

And there was yet another battle shaping up on a different telephone extension over at Pete Rozelle's office. The very morning after "peace in our time" was declared, two men, Bill McPhail and Carl Lindemann, would make enough telephone calls to Rozelle to pay all of Venezuela's phone bills for a year. Mr. McPhail was CBS sports and Mr. Lindemann was NBC sports. CBS carried the NFL schedule on its network. NBC had equal exclusivity to the AFL. Something would have to give on Super Bowl Sunday. Each wanted to televise the Super Bowl.

Rozelle handled them with the ease of a three-handed juggler. For three weeks neither side got the chance to sit down with him for face-to-face talks. Mr. Rozelle's concern —and properly so—was with his club owners and the ball game. If both networks were involved in one of the greatest gambles in the history of television, Mr. Rozelle wanted it clearly understood who the pit boss was before everyone stepped to the pass line.

CBS argued that it had spent millions of dollars to obtain the NFL schedule and its championship game—an event which suddenly had been reduced to the status of a semifinal match. NBC, on the other hand, was more flexible. Not from choice to be sure but from necessity. After all, CBS' Sunday telecasts had out-drawn it by roughly 2-1 for the simple reason that in June of 1966, the American Football League was still fielding a collection of Joe Nobodys in terms of national fan appeal. NBC would negotiate. The concessions it most felt it had a right to demand involved exhibition games between the two leagues and perhaps the NFL Pro Bowl (all-star) Game. But on the matter of the first Super Bowl both sides were determined to fight right down to their last Ivy League vest.

Rozelle finally brought them to the bargaining table in July.

The talks dragged on through the fall. Ultimately, he hammered out this formula. Both networks would carry the first Super Bowl at a cost of $1 million to each. Then CBS would have two exclusive Super Bowl telecasts sandwiched around one for NBC. Each would pay $2.5 million for each monopolistic telecast. Because CBS had the better property (NFL) and because it had paid more money for it, the four-year ratio of exclusivity, therefore, would be 2½–1½. For the first pickup, only CBS technicians would be used. Later, this last would become a major issue.

Privately, Rozelle would do something else to soothe the Columbia Broadcasting System. Over the next three years, NFL owners through a secret formula, would shovel back $2 million as balm to CBS. Nobody ever knew where the money came from. It is possible, however, that the NFL owners used some of the money which the AFL would pay it in damages under the peace treaty. That money had originally come from NBC, which had helped support the AFL. Now it was conceivable that NBC was in the position of subsidizing its most bitter enemy. Well, that's show biz.

The rival networks would take their war into the same ball park. So for that matter—among others—would Ford, which sponsored NFL games, and Chrysler, which sponsored AFL contests. This was going to be more fun than a good old-fashioned Biblical stoning. All they needed now were two ball clubs and a joint to play in.

The place they finally settled on was Los Angeles, Calif.

Well, that made sense. For one thing there was climate. For another, there was the Los Angeles Memorial Coliseum which could be altered to hold more than 90,000 people and which (much to Rozelle's subsequent regret) did not draw that many. Finally, there was geography. The proximity to Disneyland somehow seemed appropriate to whatever sane portion of the world still remained. Where else did a thing like this belong?

The teams would be the Green Bay Packers for the NFL and the Kansas City Chiefs for the AFL. There was poetic irony to Kansas City's role. This was the same team which Lamar Hunt had founded in Dallas and which had been chased out of town by the NFL Dallas Cowboys. Now Lamar was in his game of vindication. But for the length of three yards which the Cowboys had somehow managed to find a way not to negotiate against the Packers in the NFL final, it might have been Kansas City against Dallas. For dramatic impact, television would have liked that but even Peyton Place can't win all the time.

In a more rational time in space only a man determined to throw away his house, his car, his bank account and his sanity would have even considered betting as much as a quarter on Kansas City's chances. This was not, however, a rational time in space. This was Super Bowl time. This was the Son of the Punic Wars. . . . the Last Days of Pompeii. It had to be. Fifteen thousand television commercials said so.

In Las Vegas, where the home team is always rational, this flood of emotion was causing more than moderate concern. A Vegas actuary named Bobby, who stays in business by not making rash statements to people who want to challenge his opinions with money, was frankly troubled.

"You have to have the biggest betting event in history,"

a reporter said to Bobby over the telephone as Green Bay
and Kansas City were preparing to travel west to their pre-
game camps.

"Forget it," Bobby replied. "This one is for the amateur
betters. My people are concerned because they just don't
know enough about the young team to make a valid point
spread. Still, you got to please the public to keep the franchise. We make the Green Bays a 13-point favorite. We do
not do this from deep conviction. In fact, the less action
we get on this game, the better."

The Kansas City Chiefs, indeed, were an unknown
quantity as far as most of the country was concerned. It was
known that their quarterback, Len Dawson, had been something of a failure years before in the National League but
apparently had improved since joining Football Players
Anonymous. It was also known that their coach, Hank
Stramm, was an imaginative man who stressed offense and
who had had a playbook roughly the size of the complete
and unabridged Warren Report. Among the more familiar
faces on the KC roster were Mike Garrett, an All-America
running back from USC, linebackers E. J. "The Beast" Holub
and Bobby Bell and a huge defensive tackle named Junius
Buchanan.

This was not very much to go on for the astute gambler
but the astute gambler had long since decided to put his
money on Coach Vincent Lombardi and the Green Bay
Packers. As for the emotional man . . . the one who formed
the very core of the frenzied hysteria which now gripped
the country . . . well, if he hadn't been emotional, he
wouldn't have taken Kansas City seriously in the first place.

Green Bay was different. Green Bay was an automatic
punchpress of a football team . . . rich in talent, strong in
reserves, quarterbacked by a brilliant athlete named Bart

Starr and, most of all, coached by a man who had been able to convince the men who played for him that he had more answers than the Rosetta Stone. Men who remained unconvinced were buried at sea before the club left pre-season camp each summer.

In the two weeks which had elapsed since the respective league title games, America moved through life with its eardrums at halfmast. The teams were only moderately involved in this. After all, the winning players would only be competing for $15,000 a man and that just happened to be a world record for this kind of violence. The television networks, now that's where it was really happening.

All the losing team had to do was to go home and explain to everyone it met on the street what happened. But the losing network in the Neilsen Rating war, well, the losing network had to explain to Madison Avenue. "So, let's win, baby, or else we are going to have to put our explanation on the track and see if they kick it off at Scarsdale."

Each network massed its forces for the shoot-out. CBS would charge its sponsors $85,000 for each one-minute commercial. NBC, the underdog, would exact between $65–75,000 for the same service. No sooner had the prices been established when Variety, the Delphic Oracle of show business, announced that for CBS to win it would have to roll up at least a five-point advantage in the Neilsens. Both networks went to work promoting "Super Week." By game time, America was bleeding from its inner ear.

For a two-week span (the real promotional stretch run) CBS devoted 75% of its night-time promos and 50% of its daytime spots to Super Week. It ran living color promotions in various lengths from 16–60 seconds. It also fed special closed circuit TV color tapes to its affiliates, provided them with four different color films, slides, mats, glossy photos and everything this side of Vincent Lombardi's finger-nail parings. It pushed the fact that only its cameras would be permitted inside the ball park and it was going to have 11—count 'em—11 Norelco Plumbicon color cameras (what the hell is a Plumbicon?) to cover Super Sunday. The cost of all this hot air, including television time, newspaper ads and radio spots would run well over a million bucks.

NBC chose a different—but equally noisy—means of assault. Its champions—the Kansas City Chiefs—were hardly household names. It blew a reasonably intelligent excuse for all the noise when it chose not to let people in on the secret that Kansas City, did, indeed, have enough bodies to fill the bench. It could not fight the fact that CBS was franchised to transmit the pictures. It chose instead to strive for the dignity of image, which is a very popular word in that social set. In short, it would peddle its announcers.

In Curt Gowdy and Paul Christman it had an excellent combination. Since CBS used regional announcers around the country for its normal Sunday football telecasts and NBC used Gowdy and Christman nationally each week, its announcing team was better known. It would sell Gowdy and Christman as a kind of Huntley-Brinkley in cleats and "good night to you, Curt." This is not a bad approach for the Geneva Disarmament Talks but why be picky? By this time the name of the promotional game for both sides was sheer, unadulterated noise.

On Christmas Eve, in deference to the Ghost of a Belated Christmas Yet to Come, NBC introduced on-the-air crawls at the end of most of its night-time programs devoted to just that theme. By New Year's Eve it was devoting 50% of its evening spots to pushing the Gowdy-Christman team. It also utilized 1,400 direct mailers to TV newspaper editors around the country as well as a barrage of radio and newspaper advertisements. A week before game-time, most of America had bells ringing inside its head. More extreme segments of the population were considering a fund-raising drive to buy Super Sunday and lift it off the calendar before everyone went stone deaf.

Meanwhile, out in California, the Packers had settled down in Santa Barbara and the Chiefs in Long Beach and downtown in smog-covered Los Angeles, all hell was breaking loose. Mr. Alan Minter, a stock broker who listed his address as 5363 West Slauson Avenue, had challenged Pete Rozelle's one-world-indivisible-with-liberty-and-television-for-almost-all policy. Mr. Minter went to court.

The issue was the 75-mile area blackout which the commissioner had slapped on the televising of the Super Bowl. Professional smog-watchers when first informed that Los Angeles was going to be blacked out, asked "How can you tell?"

But Mr. Minter was serious and he had support from a great many people. Among them were newspaper columnists; radio and television commentators; City Councilman John Ferraro, a former USC football player; Frank G. Bonelli, chairman of the board of supervisors of the Los Angeles Memorial Coliseum; and the committee which had succeeded in bringing Super Sunday to Los Angeles in the first place.

Rozelle was not alone. Also brought into the suit were CBS, NBC, the National League and the American League. A show-cause was issued and somebody had to figure out the answer before Jan. 6—just nine days before the game.

Rozelle was adamant. The cause he would show was a simple one. It was called 60,000 empty seats. Harking back to Bert Bell's original TV blackout policy, the commissioner explained that it would be unfair to give the game away

to people at home and charge people who came to the park.
Moreover, there was a suspicion that nobody might come
to the ball game under a system where they could get it at
home for nothing. Cause? Rozelle had plenty of cause. Later
it would develop that the ball park had been set up for
a crowd of 90,000-plus and fewer than 65,000 would show
up. Had Rozelle lifted the blackout it would have been far
worse. U. S. District Judge William Gray ruled in favor of
the blackout. One television problem had been solved. A
new one began the same day.

This one had its genesis in the agreement which had
made CBS technicians the only team in the electronic side
of the ball game. NBC technicians belonged to a union
called The National Association of Broadcast Employees and
Technicians. CBS people belonged to a rival group called
the International Brotherhood of Electrical Workers.
NABET was positively furious. The Super Game was back
in Super Trouble.

NABET's track record in such cases was impressive. In
its last battle it had complained because Lyndon B. Johnson,
who only happened to be the President of the United States,
was using Signal Corps technicians on his White House telecasts. NABET threatened to institute its own blackout on
Mr. Johnson. Faced with the choice any politician would
have done the same thing. Mr. Johnson was going to find
a way to appease NABET even if he had to put it under the
Anti-Poverty Program.

But this wasn't that simple. In the first place, with ac-
credited press and other authorized personnel totaling 800
there simply wasn't enough room for two networks worth of
cameras. In the second, CBS was not about to throw away
a nonsense point in its advertising. Secretly, the pro football
people brought in Theodore Keehl, the Super Solomon of

Labor disputes, as their mediator. It was subsequently rumored that football made a donation to NABET's favorite charity and the crisis was solved.

Meanwhile, as the noise continued unabated on television each evening, the Green Bay Packers and the Kansas City Chiefs struggled manfully to prepare for a football game against a bunch of total strangers. It wasn't easy.

In the first place, the Packers didn't really want to be in Santa Barbara, California. To be precise, Vincent Lombardi didn't want to be there and since Vincent held all the voting stock in this family, that tells it all. Vincent had picked out a nice little monastery-type place out near Palo Alto where his troops could spend much time in silent communion and get to hate life sufficiently so that they could make the proper impression on the Chiefs—more precisely on their sternums, skulls and forearms. But when you are in Los Angeles, Palo Alto becomes one of those places where "you can't get there from here." Rozelle wanted as much press coverage for this thing as possible. He gave Vincent his choice: Santa Barbara or Santa Barbara. After much thought, Vincent chose Santa Barbara.

It had much to recommend it. For one thing, there was the University of California at Santa Barbara which had excellent stadium facilities. For another, there was climate. For the third—and in Lombardi's view most important—it was still a two-hour drive from Los Angeles, it was a small town and the joint did not figure to be overrun with spectators.

So on Sunday, Jan. 8, the Green Bay Packers flew out of the tundra which is Green Bay, Wisconsin, and set down softly in Lotus Land. It is a damned good thing that they did set down softly because when Vincent looked out the window there were 1,000 people running down the runway to meet the ball club. With great trauma, a police escort moved the Packers directly from the plane to waiting buses and ultimately to the Santa Barbara Inn where everyone settled down in his room, flipped on the television set and was instantly reminded in ear-shattering tones that Super Sunday was just around the corner. Well, if you want to live in the stereophonic, cathode-fed jet age, you have to learn to pay the price.

Still, this was a relaxed team. Their big quarrel had been with Baltimore and with Dallas in their own social set. They could not get worked up over people they did not know. Just two weeks before in their victorious locker room at Dallas, Henry Jordan, a veteran tackle of 10 years professional experience, put it into genuine perspective.

"Pressure?" Henry said, tapping his forehead which seemed to grow a little taller each week. "You think the pressure was on us today? You think it will be on us in the Super Bowl? Take a look at all the bald heads in this locker room. Each of them has been there before. Now you tell me who the pressure was on today and who it will be on in the Super Bowl."

If the Packers had any problem at all, they believed it was simply a matter of identity. They didn't know the Chiefs and they had to find a way to learn more about them.

To do it they went through the KC game films and then matched them against their own game-film file. They transferred personalities. Chris Burford, the KC split end, became Baltimore's Raymond Berry. Otis Taylor was Dave Parks of San Francisco. Fred Arbanas became Chicago's Mike Ditka. Mike Garrett was Gale Sayers of the Bears. Pick a man whose moves resembled the KC player's. It was more fun than pin the tail on the donkey.

Meanwhile, Lombardi began to conduct secret practice

sessions. There was no reason for this but old habits die slowly. It did create, however, the most activity the camp had because everyone had to go out and look for a canvas with which to cover the open storm fence at the end of the field.

The drive to Santa Barbara from Los Angeles for newspapermen covering the Super Bowl camps was a pleasant one. A half hour before the Santa Barbara city limits came into view they could see the first surfers outlined against a blend of brilliant sunlight and rich blue ocean, looking for all the world like separate but equal picture post cards. The Packers were quartered directly across from the beach. Given his choice, Lombardi, who built his Packers on discipline and precision, would have preferred to train them in either the Matte Grosso or the Arctic Circle. Since he was not given his choice he told a reporter "Yeah, it's beautiful all right. Too damned beautiful to train a ball club."

This was Lombardi's way and it had been a successful one. The team he would bring to Smog City on Super Sunday was a violent joy to behold, a polished jewel of a machine. The players knew it and Vincent knew it. He tried hard to give the press what it wanted to hear but the strain of repetition was not an easy thing to handle. Five hundred times that week he would be asked if this was the biggest game of his life . . . if Paul Hornung, the injured Golden Boy, would play . . . once he was even asked if he personally planned the menu for each press lunch. He did not. It was obvious that if he had, the questioner would have been on it, medium rare.

On a dazzling sun-lit afternoon three days before the game, Fuzzy Thurston, the veteran guard who was an integral part of the Green Bay Sweep, the power play in the Packers' arsenal, sat on the balcony overlooking the motel swimming pool (it had been placed off limits for swimming by Lombardi) and reflected on what all of this super-duper nonsense really meant.

He sat in a blue morris chair with the deceptive kind of stumpiness which belied the artistry of the man when he was at work on the football field. His receding hairline was flecked with gray and a faint reddish tinge showed just above the eyebrows, a kind of reminder of the hundreds of times he had forced his head into the tight cage which is a football helmet.

"You could let it get to you," he said. "I guess some people do. But the thing you have to realize is that it's still a game . . . a game of, say, 70 plays and you have to get the job done in that time or not at all. You can't hit your fist against the wall or stare into the mirror or lay around in bed and not talk to anybody.

"You can't even think about the other guy—the guy you have to go out and do it against—and hate him because it isn't true. Hate the other guy? Hell, I never even met him. How the hell are you going to hate somebody who is a complete stranger?"

The "other guy" was Junius Buchanan, the huge Kansas City defensive tackle who weighed 285 pounds and who was 6–7. He had seven inches and 40 pounds on Thurston. "He wishes I was five inches taller and I wish he was four inches shorter and between us we are going to have to decide what to do about it on Sunday. That's what I think about all week and I know damned well he's thinking about it too. That's our private little Super Bowl."

He was right, of course. Just a day earlier, Buchanan had sat in the coffee shop of a Long Beach motel where the Chiefs were quartered and he had said pretty much the same thing. Before the team had left for the coast he had

walked into a Kansas City bookstore and laid up $5.95 for
a marvelous book called "Run To Daylight", a kind of
biography of Lombardi and the Packers and what they are
all about, which is known in some circles as the Gospel according to Vincent. All week long Fuzzy Thurston and
Junius Buchanan would be shadow boxers looking for an
intangible edge.

But the best insight into what the Packers personally
felt about the impending showdown . . . an emotion totally
divorced from the emotions of America's sports fans, the
squawks of America's television sets and the purple-tinted
drool of some of America's typewriters . . . was explained
meticulously on that same day by Fuzzy Thurston.

"If we lose this game, our league gains nothing. If they
lose, their league gains nothing."

"It's not a game for losers," a reporter said.

"There *never* has been a game for losers," Thurston replied. "And I'll tell you something else. I don't know their
coach but I know that we have something they cannot
possibly have. We have the greatest football mind in the
world on our side. I don't know Hank Stramm but he's not
as smart as Vincent . . . if he were, he'd be God."

It was a feeling which was expressed freely and often
during the Packers' brief stay in Santa Barbara. The pressure
was indeed on that "other football team." A man named
Fred Williamson had finally given the Packers something to
pass the time of day.

Fred Williamson was a Kansas City defensive back out
of Northwestern. A flamboyant dresser both off and on the
field (turtle necks before they were "in" and white football
shoes), Williamson was never reticent to talk. The thing he
spoke about the most was something which he called The
Hammer, which, in fact, became his own nickname.

The Hammer, Williamson claimed, would make Thor blanch. It was an arm chop, delivered with great power at a receiver who was otherwise occupied with trying to catch a football. It was legal and in Williamson's view it was devastating. It had already shattered one enemy cheekbone and forced a key fumble in the recent AFL title game with Buffalo. Moreover, Williamson claimed it had broken 30 helmets.

The Chiefs were not enamoured of their teammate's talk. For one thing they secretly knew that their own major weakness rested with their cornerbacks, Williams and a man named Willie Mitchell. For another, they had no intention of drawing the Packers' attention to this. One of Williamson's teammates said to several reporters that week "If Freddie broke 30 helmets he must have taken them outside in an alley and stomped on them."

The Packers were positively delighted with Williamson's talk. All week long as Starr arched forward passes against the Packer defense during practice, Herb Adderly and Willie Wood flitted about the field tapping people on top of the helmet in a parody of Fred Williamson's 30 broken war bonnets. "31" Adderly would yell. "32" Wood would holler back across the field. "My God," Jim Taylor, the fullback would deadpan, "run". "It's the Hammer." Predictably, when Super Sunday would arrive, a Packer rookie named Gale Gillingham would run full tilt into the Hammer and leave him twisted at right angles. And with equal predictability, when someone would ask Lombardi after the game what took so long (Williamson was injured in the fourth quarter) Lombardi would reply: "Well, he never got close enough to anyone before that."

Meanwhile back at the rebel camp in Long Beach, the Chiefs were subdued. "My hands," E. J. Holub, the talented linebacker would say to a visitor in the coffee shop, "look at the palms. They sweat every time I think about this game." "It's a lot of money," Junius Buchanan would say. And every night when they turned on their television sets to relax they were hit in the ear with "Only X more days until Super Sunday."

Back in the rest of the world, Super Week rocked along at a furious pace. Out in Milwaukee, the Catholic Herald Citizen, the official weekly of the Milwaukee Roman Catholic Archdiocese would write "what a world it would be if all of us loved one another with the same ferocious loyalty displayed by the Packers . . . what better practical theology could there be." It went on to call Vince Lombardi a theologian. Well, that completed the cycle. Other people had called him just about everything else.

A Los Angeles radio station went to war with Pete Rozelle and filled 15,000 requests for its set of instructions on how to build a super aerial to beat the super blackout. Its key ingredients consisted of a broomstick and five wire coat hangers. Tickets (top price: $12) continued to move slowly and the State of California announced that each non-resident, non-married member of the winning team would leave the field owing the state $435 in income tax. Even on Super Week some things remain constant.

Down in Santa Barbara, Lombardi was telling the truth and the truth was not very good for television's purposes. "One football game proves absolutely nothing," the coach said. "I wouldn't say that this was the supreme test. I guess the thing it most lacks is tradition."

But back in Los Angeles that same afternoon Lamar Hunt disagreed. Swept away by the romance of the moment, Lamar, owner of the rebel team, had said: "This is the only fair test. The rest are all going to be hybrids. By the time the

two leagues play exhibition games they will have participated in a common draft, made player trades and exchanged
movies. This is the purest of the pure . . . the most important
professional football game ever played."

Holy Cataclysm! The Barbarians are hammering on the
gates of Rome. Ghengis Khan (or is it Sammy?) is charging
out of the East and move that Greek Fire a little closer!
You're on Candid Camera.

Earlier in the week both camps had been swarming with
television types, itching to bring America deep inside the
core of this contest which Lamar called the "purest of the
pure." In speaking about the war between CBS and his own
network, an NBC spear carrier remarked: "ABC? Who the
hell knows what they are going to run on Super Sunday? I
hear they are going to play old Ronald Reagan movies and
give away Green Stamps."

Even Lombardi graciously consented to be photographed
with Miss-Something-Or-Other of Some-Year-Or-Other holding a football for the benefit of CBS. This was a great coup
—as Madison Avenue counts its coups—but NBC got what it
deserved. It was out taping football players at the time.
Still, NBC got off cheaply. The real master stroke hadn't
come off. "Would you mind," a CBS supernumerary had
asked Chuck Lane, the Packer publicity man, "asking
Coach Lombardi if he would pose for us with his team on
top of a trampoline?"

"Yes," said Chuck Lane without a moment's hesitation,
"I would mind asking Coach Lombardi if he would pose
for you with the team on top of a trampoline."

And back in Kansas City, burglars provided the one
note of sanity which the week had to offer. They cleaned
out all the cash in the office safe of the Chiefs and left 2,000
Super Bowl tickets untouched.

The night before Armageddon, both leagues joined in a hypocritical staring match called a pre-game party in the Statler-Hilton. Love was supposed to be the theme. Sonny Werblin, the owner of the Jets who had opposed the merger, did not even bother to attend.

At that same moment over at Los Angeles' Sheraton-West Hotel, Paul Hornung and Max McGee were getting ready to go to bed. The Packers had already motored down from Santa Barbara. Under normal conditions it was a little early for the McGee-Hornung Axis to retire. There had been nights when this ceremonial act had finished in a dead heat with the sunrise.

But things were different for both of them that week in 1966. Hornung had a bad nerve in his neck and would never play another football game. McGee, at 34, was, with substitute quarterback Zeke Bratkowski, the oldest man on the team. He had been a pro for 13 years. The calendar was starting to catch him and he had played very little all season. Barring an unforeseen injury to someone like, say, Boyd Dowler, he did not figure to play at all in the Super Bowl. They tuned in the television set, caught another 10 commercials for Super Sunday and watched the Late Late Show, which was about as good as the Kansas City bench. By midnight, they were asleep.

On Super Morning both television networks held separate but equal staff meetings. NBC was unhappy with the picture control it had been forced to yield to CBS. Just as an insurance policy it determined that producer Lou Kusserow, a former Columbia football player, was the man physically best qualified to sit in and monitor the CBS remote truck. The Packers and Chiefs had already determined that they would go with the starting lineups which had brought them this far. Now a breathless world finally received the starting television lineups. Nobody was killed in the rush for carbon copies:

CBS

Position	Player	Ht.	Wt.,	School
Play-by-Play	Ray Scott	5-11	195	Connelsville (PA) H.S.
Play-by-Play	Jack Whitaker	5-11	180	St. Joseph's (Phila).
Pre-Game	Frank Gifford	6-1	192	USC
Post-Game	Pat Summerall	6-4	220	Arkansas
Producer	Jack Creasy	6-1	175	St. Lawrence
Director	Tony Verna	5-11	180	West Point
Publicity	Bill Brendle	6-0	170	Fordham
Head Coach	Bill McPhail	6-2	195	Swarthmore
Cheerleader	J. Walter Thompson Co.	$557,000,000		Lexington Ave.

NBC

Position	Player	Ht.	Wt.,	School
Play-by-Play	Curt Gowdy	5-10	180	Wyoming
Analysis	Paul Christman	6-0	190	Missouri
Post-Game	Charley Jones	6-0	190	Arkansas
Producer	Lou Kusserow	5-11	210	Columbia
Director	Harry Coyle	5-10	210	Paterson State
Publicity	Ed Weissman	5-10	165	Temple
Head Coach	Carl Lindemann	5-10	175	MIT
Cheerleader	Young & Rubicam, Inc.	$400,000,000		Madison Ave.

Morning betting line: Packers by 13; CBS by 5 Neilsen Points.

The battle lines were joined. There was no turning back. Out at the Los Angeles Coliseum, 10,000 balloons, 313 musicians, 80 girl baton-slingers, enough rockets and cherry bombs to wipe out Singapore, glee clubs, drill teams and 300 neatly crated pigeons were already inside the ball park. The Packers climbed into their chartered bus in front of the Sheraton-West at 11 a.m. As the players and several writers traveling with the team scrambled for seats, Max McGee stood in the doorway, raised his arms heavenward like Moses about to deliver the tablets and proclaimed: "This is Super Morning of Super Sunday. We are all going out to the Super Bowl and I am a Super End."

"You," an anonymous voice from the rear of the bus shouted, "are a Super bench-sitter."

"Quiet," Max replied, gesturing behind him where Lombardi stood. "The Super Coach is coming and I don't want to give any of the Super Writers on this bus the wrong kind of Super Idea."

As Henry Jordan had wisely pointed out two weeks earlier, pressure was a problem for "the other guys."

Meanwhile, the Chiefs were on their way in from Long Beach. Only Mike Garrett, who had starred in the Coliseum for USC and five veteran teammates who remembered it from the days when the Chargers used to play there before they moved to San Diego, had ever seen the ball park. Stramm wanted it that way and had, in fact, turned down the use of the field for a loosening up drill the day before. He believed that nothing could be gained but something could, indeed, be lost emotionally. Their bus ride was quiet and subdued. The Packers might indeed be strangers to them but just because a man has never seen a typhoon it does not mean that he is unaware it can blow him over the top of a sky-scraper.

As the Packers and the Chiefs were filing into their dressing rooms, the tempo of activity was increasing elsewhere both in and out of the building. Mark Duncan, the NFL's supervisor of officials, stopped by the room under the stands where his charges were changing and delivered last-minute instructions. Because the American League football's laces were $4\frac{1}{2}$ inches long as opposed to $4\frac{1}{4}$ for the Nationals, it was agreed that each team would use its own ball on offense. The feeling was that it would be unfair to ask a player to try to catch the other league's ball. Within two hours a man named Willie Wood would prove that he was a very rapid learner in such situations.

Down in the Packer dressing room, Max McGee had

hung his shirt neatly in his locker and was saying to Hornung: "I wonder if I'm going to get to play in this thing. If Boyd gets hurt again, I don't know how far I can go. When you start missing Sundays it's tough to keep in shape. I know I can beat their corner backs," Max said, "but I don't know how long I can go."

Across the country, the long countdown toward the kickoff had begun in earnest for what was later estimated as 62 million television viewers. The Grambling College marching band was quick-stepping across the field with its pre-game show and back in New York CBS was beaming out the Harlem Globetrotters as their Super Bowl lead-in while NBC was showing a taped review of the season with a round table discussion. The discussion NBC's viewers were hearing was nothing alongside of the impromptu and unwanted round table the NBC staff was holding back at the Coliseum.

For some fantastic reason the National Broadcasting Co., L.A. Coliseum Division was without electrical power. It could have been the costliest failure in the history of television. If the game had started at that precise moment, executives back at Rockefeller Center would have been taking flying leaps at the artificial ice skating rink across the street from 20 floors up. Less than a minute before actual air-time the power came back on. And even while they were waiting for it, the National Broadcasting Co., experienced yet another trauma. Somebody had set up a huge "Go Mustang" sign. Since Ford was one of the CBS sponsors and Ford makes Mustangs and all the cameramen were paid by CBS, NBC rushed at Jim Kensil, public relations director of the National League and charge d'affaires of press relations, hollering "foul." The sign came down. Innocent bystanders had to wonder amid all the sound, fury, electronic dike-plugging above and the horn tooting below if somehow, some way, someone was going to be able to sneak in a football game.

Back down on the Coliseum floor, Paul Christman of NBC and Frank Gifford of CBS came together, shook hands, snuggled their lavaliere mikes to their rapidly-beating bosoms and prepared to open a joint pre-game show. "Hey," Christman kidded, "I'm the senior man here. You ought to be on my left." Gifford moved over. Both of them laughed. The show began and from the NBC truck, a wounded forward observer screamed at Christman over his intercom:

"Get him the hell out of there. You got him blocking the NBC shield on your sports jacket."

And then as the Packers, resplendent in green jerseys with white numerals, gold pants and gold helmets with green and white trim, massed in front of their bench and the Chiefs, in white with red trim and red helmets, huddled before theirs, 63,036 super ticket holders stood and sang the National Anthem, and for a brief instant afterwards nothing happened.

"The pigeons," an harassed theatrical-type on the sidelines hollered, "where the hell are the damned pigeons?"

Dr. Ralph Waldo Emerson Jones, president of Grambling College, had proudly walked the sidelines while his school's band had staged its impressive pre-game show. Now he wanted to sit down and he chose a large unoccupied crate near the band.

"Hey, you have to get up," a Coliseum spear-carrier panted, "you're sitting on our pigeons."

With a whrrr and a flap, 300 pigeons soared toward outer space, a gesture allegedly symbolic of the super peace which prevailed on Super Sunday. Fortunately, they circled

once and headed off toward the sun before they had time
for anything else more accurately associated with pigeons.

Finally, the nonsense was over. A man named Fletcher
Smith moved forward and kicked the football down to the
Green Bay five yard line where Herb Adderley caught it
and returned it 20 yards before a covey of white jerseys
wrestled him to the ground. They had apparently decided
to play this game after all.

Cautiously, like a set of heavyweight boxers probing for
information, the two ball clubs went to work. The football
changed hands twice before Green Bay put it in perspective.

But before that something happened which was to shape
the very pattern of this football game. On the second play
from scrimmage, Elijah Pitts, Green Bay's dandy little runner, swept around left end for five yards. As Boyd Dowler
attempted to close down on linebacker E. J. Holub, he left
his shoulder back at the line of scrimmage somewhere. The
game was barely one minute old and here was Max McGee
picking up his helmet and trotting on to replace Dowler.
Max McGee, who was a pro when many of the Kansas City
players were still in high school and who had expected
to spend a quiet afternoon on the end of the bench, was
going to find out just exactly how far he really could go.

All week long, Max had slouched in his chair at the film
sessions and studied Willie Mitchell and Fred Williamson.
He firmly believed he could beat them. He wished he had
as much faith in his legs as he had in his diagnosis.

Midway through the first period Starr began to move
the Packers. In five plays, three of them successful forward
passes, he had taken them 43 yards to the Kansas City 37.
After the last play in that sequence, a successful pitch to
Carroll Dale, Max came puffing back to the huddle and
reported: "If they blitz, I'm going to be open in the middle.
You might want to keep me in mind."

As the Packers lined up for the play, Starr looked over the Kansas City defense and decided that they were, indeed, about to blitz him. This is a defensive maneuver in which a person or persons with violent intent comes rushing out of the linebacker position or the deeper secondary in an effort to split the quarterback into many pieces. Neatness does not count. Starr called what football players refer to as "an automatic." This is a pre-arranged auto call which indicates that the play selected in the huddle is off and a pre-arranged alternate is on.

Max McGee's defender in this instance was Willie Mitchell, who was no more over-matched on this afternoon than, say, Harold at the Battle of Hastings. He tried to play the ball instead of Max. Willie went up and Willie came down. Then Max went up about five yards and straight ahead 37 and the Packers had seven points on the board.

The Chiefs, however, fought the good fight as young Turks should. They got those seven back in the second quarter when Dawson, throwing out of a shifting pocket of body guards, hit Curt McClinton in the endzone. The rest of the first half was uninspired. Green Bay took a brief 14–7 lead when fullback Jim Taylor bounced into the endzone with the subtlety of a left hook. The run covered 14 yards. Kansas City cut the gap to 14–10 on a 41 yard field goal by Mike Mercer. As the teams left the field for intermission and half the Free World's entertainers jockeyed for position for the super halftime show, people in the Coliseum and around the country sat back and wondered just what the hell it all meant.

Well, for one thing they had seen a relatively close football game and for another they had seen the Packers experience some difficulty with Dawson's roll-out passing style and with KC's vigorous front-four linemen.

On the other hand, the Packers had played like the Packers generally play. They had probed to get the answers to questions they did not want to have to ask again in the second half. They had determined that they could do a little blitzing of their own with Dawson, confirmed the fact that they could shell the Chiefs at their cornerbacks and decided that Dawson had committed his team to a passing game.

Nobody is really sure what Lombardi told them at halftime and contrary to common belief the lecture was not delivered with a mace and chain. But it was preached, nevertheless, with great vigor. Meanwhile, up in the stands the AFL owners were delightfully surprised, the NBC announcing force was ecstatic and CBS was worried. Super Sunday was off to a dandy start.

The American League had sought merger in its intertribal warfare and had sent Kansas City out as its champion. Less than three minutes after intermission, the Chiefs would be merged all right—right into the Coliseum turf. Four plays into the third quarter, Lenny Dawson tried to throw the ball to Fred Arbanas, his tight end. For all intents and purposes, Super Sunday ended then and there.

"I can't give you the full name of the play," Arbanas would say afterwards, "but it's set up to get medium yardage against a man-to-man defense. We fake a run up the middle and I run what we call an 83 pattern, which is a short, outside move. I go down about five or six yards and cut to the outside and Len throws when I cut.

"I was man-to-man with Wood. I gave him a head fake inside, cut to the outside but the ball wasn't there."

Dawson couldn't have gotten the ball there with an 81 mm mortar. The Packers had put on a blitz of their own. Henry Jordan, the big Packer tackle and what looked like half the Chinese Eighth Route Army were chasing Dawson and gaining with every step. The pass was thrown behind Arbanas, Wood came up fast, swiped it at the Packer 45 and returned it all the way to the Kansas City five before Garrett caught him from behind. On the next play, Pitts cracked over left tackle for the score. The second half was just two minutes and 27 seconds old and the score now read: Old Guard, 21, Freshman Class, 10. It would get a lot worse.

Later in the period, waves of green jerseys pushed Dawson 24 yards in the wrong direction on two plays and set the stage for the next chapter in the Perils of Max McGee. This time he ran straight through the goal posts and right past Willie Mitchell. He stuck up his hands, juggled the ball once, then nestled it to his hairy chest five yards inside the end zone. As the period ended, Green Bay led, 28–10. Things became rather subdued in the NBC booth.

The final score would be 35–10. Old Max McGee, who had caught just four passes during the entire 1966 season, would catch seven on this day for 138 yards and two touchdowns. Bart Starr would be magnificent. And if, as Lamar Hunt had so sentimentally insisted, this game was the purest of the pure, then nobody challenged the fact that Mr. Clean would continue to get his mail in Green Bay, Wis., for a while.

Lombardi, asked over and over again to appraise Kansas City, finally said what everyone in the ball park knew to be true: "I do not think they are as good as the top teams in the NFL. A good team but still not that good."

As for the Kansas Citys themselves, they were whipped pretty good. Jon Gilliam, who had been with the club since its inception but who did not play because of an injury, said it best. "I'll tell you, mister, watching it happen, well, I feel like I got out in the back alley in a pretty good fist fight. I fought the good fight but I got my tail whipped."

It was over for Green Bay and for Kansas City . . . for the owners, who tried to keep their feelings to themselves . . . and for the people all across the country who had been emotionally involved in this strange many-faceted rivalry as perhaps no other sports rivalry of the past 50 years.

But for the Columbia Broadcasting System and for the National Broadcasting Co., it was just beginning. Early returns gave CBS the smashing five-point triumph in the Nielsen Ratings which Variety had decreed was the measuring stick. But a week later, Nielsen—good old infallible guide to Madison Avenue's jelly-fish division, reversed itself and holy market-media, the flap on Madison Avenue was enough to make a fella forget his vest. The great winking eye which is never wrong damned near had itself a super nervous breakdown.

On February 8, roughly three weeks after the crime, the Nielsen people officially announced that the Columbia Broadcasting System had wound up with a 5.2 advantage. A week later it corrected itself. The cities of Birmingham, Lexington, Durham and Dayton had been incorrectly tabulated. Birmingham, in point of fact, didn't even belong in the CBS column at all. Sorry about that coach but we'll make it up to you with the Beverly Hillbillies.

And when the last great gas attack finally wafted over Madison Avenue, out past the water coolers and over to the networks on February 27, the final Nielsen tabulation stood at 22.6 for CBS and 18.5 for NBC and make them mean whatever you want them to mean. The margin was 4.6. Each network immediately claimed victory.

In point of fact, there were only two clear-cut victories

to emerge from this electronic moment of truth which could only have been produced in the last half of the 20th Century. The Green Bay Packers, who knew exactly what they were doing out in Los Angeles, scored the first one and they scored it big.

The second triumph belonged to the American sports fan. If you doubt this, then consider that on the night of January 15, 1967 after the last great scorer had come to mark against the television screen, they could turn on their sets at night, serene in the knowledge that they would not have to hear the word "super" for another year.

"Ahnie just buhdied thuh'teen.
How d'ya lak that, Fat Guts?"
. . . Southern corporal in Arnie's
Army at the Masters

"I just guess, the sun don't shine
on the same dawg's tail every
day."
. . . Samuel Jackson Snead after
playoff victory over Ben Hogan

A GENTLEMEN'S GAME

It is the last thing any sane person could look to as a trigger for violent human emotion. It is played out on a lush, green stage, gently sprinkled with cool, clear water holes and smooth, yellow patches of sand. It is performed against a musical backdrop of bird calls, cricket chirps and the sound of growing grass. It is fresh, clean air and brilliant sunlight and the dewy-eyed duffer's prayer:

"Oh, Lord, if you have to push me into this world again, make me a Spaulding golf ball and lose me amid the yellow jasmine at the Augusta National Golf Club."

An Irish bar-tender, much addicted to the teeth-rattling lure of Gaelic football, put it another way for a reporter one night. "Golf," he said, "is a gentleman's game. Let them have it. Now here comes Arnold Palmer and he takes this great big club and he hits this tiny, tiny excuse for a ball and away it sails and everyone says 'oh, how lovey, oh, how thrillin'. And all the while he's doin' it, nobody, but nobody, is permitted to lay a finger on him. Now what the hell kind of game is that?"

It is this kind of game. It is a game where a man, given

enough time to frustrate himself will wind up trying to re-design the head of his driver with the help of the nearest oak tree. It is the kind of a game where a man will sweat and curse his way through 18 holes, blame himself, his caddie, his playing partners and the greenskeeper for his misfortunes, work himself into a case of galloping tremors and return home to his wife and snarl: "I had fun, dammit, fun."

And because there are so many public courses in this country today and because people play golf for fun, for exercise, for self-flagellation and sometimes in order to make a business deal, everyone is an expert and everyone who buys his way into a professional tournament will mug his way around the course just for the chance to get enough daylight between the two red necks in front of him to catch a fleeting glimpse of Arnold Palmer's backswing.

Golf is not simply an emotional game. It is a positive trauma. Because American sports fans measure performance by the amount of money at stake, once let loose at a golf tournament, they are not a gallery. They are a bermuda-shorts army of avenging angels. Its heroes are beyond reproach. Its villains, beyond salvation.

It wouldn't have reached this level of emotional intensity as a spectator sport without the runaway development of the golf professionals into a band of sun-tanned migrants, playing for stakes large enough to match Venezuela's annual budget. The boom in public courses and the advent of touring pros put everyone into the game. Before that it belonged strictly to the country club set, where 80 per cent of America was unable to play under the mores which then existed in this country.

For that reason it is vital to go back to a man named Walter Hagen. No matter what sentimental golf historians

tell you, it begins there because Walter Hagen is the man
who made it possible for the golf pro to come off the 18th
green and walk straight through the front door of the clubhouse and into the grill room. It may be only 100 yards but
it took more than three decades for the pros to take those
first tentative steps toward an ice cold beer with their
employers. It was Hagen, dressing better than the club
members, spending more than the club members and tipping
better than the club members, who finally put an end to
the nagging rejoinder "yes, but would you want a golf pro
as your next door neighbor?"

The world in which Walter C. Hagen stood out was
not a kind one for golf professionals and it took two back-to-
back Sundays in Florida for old Walter C. to set the record
straight. The man he set it straight against was a symbol
of all things to all people. He was out of that "other world"
and his name was Bobby Jones. He was a symbol of the
exclusiveness which was the country-club set. He was a
symbol of the purple-tinted prose which pumped the gospel
of the 1920s and the early 1930s as the "Golden Age of
Sports." He was also a genuine athletic marvel. But most
important of all to the generations of professional golfers
who would follow Walter Hagen, Bobby Jones was a very
badly beaten symbol on those two Sundays in 1926.

The golf pros' horizon was a very limited bag back
when Walter Hagen was pounding down the gates. It is
best typified by the memories of Dutch Harrison, the man
who won more golf tournaments than any other professional
in history. It was a world where "you spent your time and
what little money you had trying to get to where the other
money was. You traveled light and fast and generally in a
broken down old car in which you slept a great deal because there were a lot of hotels which wouldn't have you

even if you could afford it, which most of the time you
couldn't. You lived by your putter and your wits. You
hustled any way you could."

This is the world to which Walter Hagen brought dignity. He did it with no more flash then, say, Joshua blowing
down an electrified storm-fence around a restricted country
club with the aid of the Boston Pops Orchestra. When
Walter Hagen was around, everybody knew it.

He had begun as a caddie at the Country Club of
Rochester in 1912. That same year, he asked the club pro,
Andy Christie, for permission to enter the U.S. Open in
Buffalo. Christie said he could go but he couldn't play. He
told him to watch the real golfers and learn something.
Walter Hagen went and Walter Hagen watched and when
Walter Hagen returned to the club he said he'd had a
nice trip but he wasn't too impressed by the group he had
seen, which only happened to be comprised of the best
golfers in the world. A year later, he played in it at The
Country Club of Brookline and slipped unobstrusively into
the locker room the first day with the casual announcement
that since the British kept whipping them, he'd come down
to straighten things out.

Nobody forgot Walter Hagen after that. For the record,
he won four British Opens, two U.S. Opens and five P.G.A.
match-play titles. So much for the record. The rest of it,
was something else. He was the first of the flashy dressers
off the tee. He was a master of the art of gamesmanship. No
dividing line cut between his nights and his days. Sleep
was a vastly over-rated commodity. He could out-maneuver
the opposition, out-drink them, up-stage them and infuriate
them. But he got a lot of things done.

He went off to England, where the golf professional's
social lot was no better than it was over here. Walter

Hagen put things in perspective right away. The day began with Hagen pulling up in his rented chauffer-driven Rolls-Royce. Still wearing his dinner jacket, he stepped out to exchange pleasantries, excused himself, returned to the car, pulled the blinds and changed into his work clothes. And through it all, he was the consummate professional. A man captures people's imagination with flair and Walter Hagen had it. He was wild off the tee. So what? It only made life more exciting. With his magnificent short game and his putting touch, he was forever scrambling back from impossible situations. He and his opponent might halve a hole but nobody would ever remember how the other guy did it.

"There was nobody like him," recalls Johnny Farrell, himself a former U.S. Open champion, who lived through the Hagen era and who played against him many times. "He could drive you crazy. He had a habit of talking to his caddy and making sure that you overheard every word he said. If you had the honor, he'd pull a club out of his bag and step back and wiggle it and you'd get to watching him and wondering because until you got to know him you had no way of knowing that he wasn't going to use that club at all. What he wanted was for you to use it.

"I remember once I was up on the tee on a par-three and he had this wood in his hand and I thought 'well, he's Walter Hagen and if he has to use a wood here then I know damned well Johnny Farrell better use one.' So I did. I knocked the ball over the green. Then he put it back and took out an iron and knocked it stiff.

"Once he was going head-to-head with Leo Diegel and Leo had a fairly tough four-foot putt. Hagen dropped a long one and then he picked up Diegel's ball and conceded his putt. Poor Leo got up to the next tee and all he could think was 'now why in the world did he do that?' He thought so much about it, he blew his tee shot.

"Sometimes he'd be waiting and he'd say to his caddy 'I'm scared to death this fairway is so narrow. And that green, it's a cinch to wind up taking three there.' And you'd be listening and if anyone took three putts to get home it would be you because he would have talked you into it. And sometimes he would show up at a course, ask what the record was, bet $1,000 he could break it—and he would."

This, then, was Walter Hagen, striding through the country clubs and the taboos and the opposition, moving toward two days in the year 1926, which gave professional golf its first thrust toward universal respectability.

The other man was Bobby Jones. He was, in truth, the genuine symbol of what the newspaper-reading public believed sports was and should be all about. As an amateur golfer, he won the U.S. Open four times, the British Open three times and the U.S. Amateur title (a key event then but a crown now roughly equivalent to being elected Apache war chief for 1968) five times.

He was up from the affluent side of Atlanta society. At the age of seven he was better than most of the adults at Atlanta's East Lake course. He was 14 years old when he went off to play in his first U.S. Amateur. On the first day, he beat a man named Eben Byers, who had already won the tournament 10 years earlier. This was at the plush Merion Golf Club in Philadelphia and before the day was over, he had the largest gallery in the field. The crowd grew as he moved all the way to the third round before losing. Bobby Jones was never without a crowd from that day on. Women loved him. Grown men marveled at his skills. And America picked up its newspapers and went positively breathless.

He simply went on and on and on. In 1930, four years after his historic meeting with Hagen, he put together the greatest single individual season in the history of golf, winning the British Amateur, the British Open, the U. S. Amateur and the U.S. Open. He came home to a ticker-tape parade in New York. If ever two worlds met on the golf course, it happened in Florida in 1926.

The world looked like this on the day the first half of the 72–hole match began. A much caricatured political party under the leadership of a small man with a comic-opera mustache claimed 49,000 members in Germany. Adolph Hitler said it would grow and commissioned a stunted mouthpiece named Joseph Goebbels to make sure it did. At home, Calvin Coolidge was leading with brilliant inertia and Jimmy Walker posed for so many photographs that skeptics wondered if he were mayor of the City of New York or a paid lobbyist for the fashion industry. The Studebaker Big Six sedan was selling for $1,895 and two men named Sacco and Vanzetti were helplessly watching the final year of their lives slip away in a Massachusetts' jail cell.

Bobby Jones had agreed to meet Walter Hagen in a two-day, 72-hole match-play affair for the unofficial world championship. The first 36 holes would be played on Feb. 28 at the Whitefield Estates Country Club with the balance of the match set for the following Sunday at the Pasadena Golf and Country Club. Hagen would share in the gate receipts. Jones, as an amateur, would receive a set of gold cuff links. It is interesting to note here that nobody objected until the final score was posted. When it was, the United States Golf Association (the governing body of amateur golf) said that amateurs ought not to do such things in the future because it was not in keeping with the spirit

of amateur golf. Whatever it did to the spirit of amateur
golf is incidental compared to what it did to the body.

The crowd was pretty much pro-Jones. After all, they
had lived with him in the newspapers ever since he was
a high school kid. Moreover, they cherished that boyhood
appeal of his. The Great American sports public had not
yet reached the era of the anti-hero.

Five days before they teed off, Walter Hagen was
stricken with ptomaine poisoning and had to withdraw
from an international team match. As they waited on the
first tee, surrounded by a crowd of more than 1,000 spectators, the gallery speculated on what the illness might have
done to Hagen's chances. They did not have to wait long
to find out. What it did was absolutely nothing.

Hagen was still very much Hagen although, in truth,
there were times when Jones must have wondered because
Walter Hagen was not playing it the way most people
expected. It may have been psychological and it may have
stemmed from the fact that the pro knew that Jones wanted
to win so badly. What he did was to play virtually everything safe over the first 18 holes. He made Jones take the
gambles, which was not the way it had been figured. Hagen
won it with his putter and he won it with consummate
ease. Shooting steady 71–70–141, Walter Hagen made it
look easy. Bobby Jones was the scrambler on this first day,
scoring 77–74–151 and when the first 36 holes were finished,
Walter Hagen had stunned the world by piling up an eight-
hole lead.

They moved to Pasadena the following Sunday and now
the crowd swelled to 2,500, which at the time must have
been a record for a two-man match for a way-stop like that.
On the 61st hole, it looked as though Jones might prolong
the agony when he knocked in a 40-footer. But Hagen,

finishing with the Hagen flourish, dropped one from 30 feet and a self-taught pro from Rochester, N.Y., had beaten the world's greatest amateur golfer by the humiliating count of 12 and 11. America's newspapers were purple in their prose. America's golf fans were somewhat astonished. And Walter Hagen didn't waste much time reading about it. He simply picked up the $8,600 which was his piece of the action.

It was a rivalry which was to have an astonishing impact on the future of the professional golfers. Combined with color and flair of Hagen the man, which, by the way, rubbed off on the men he played against, it opened a new horizon. Years later, at a testimonial dinner at a swank country club, Arnold Palmer was to put it rather well.

"If Hagen weren't Hagen," Palmer said," things might not have changed and we'd be holding this dinner in the club kitchen."

Color became the golfing pro's stock in trade after Hagen, and from the late 40s through the mid 50s two men who had it in very different ways gripped the emotions of the American golf fan and helped splash professional golf into larger and larger headlines. Let Dutch Harrison tell about the first man. Dutch and a man named Bob Hamilton were scrapping for groceries back in 1934, which is a polite way of saying they were doing a little plain and artistic golf hustling. This is an art much frowned upon today (although much practiced on a great many golf courses) but of dire necessity then because Hagen may have brought the pros glamour but he didn't do anything to increase the prize money.

The test of a good hustler is to win golf matches for money but to leave the victim enough hope so that he will test the hustler again. The closer the score, the better the hustle. In 1932, Dutch and Bob Hamilton had a couple of vacationing school teachers on the hook at Pinehurst, N.C. The device was called syndicate golf. Whenever a man won a hole all by himself, he picked up 50 cents from each of the other players.

"So we came up to the first tee one morning and here is this guy sitting there in the heat with a long-sleeved shirt and a tie and knickers and I look at Bob and he looks at me and says 'see if he's got any money.' He said he did and I said well if he wanted to join us we could have a match because, shucks, he couldn't lose more than nine little old dollars at this thing.

"Well, he said yes," Dutch recalls, "and the next thing I knew I had a feeling we were in terrible trouble because he asks 'any side bets allowed?' Then he cranks up that swing and I know we've got a bear by the tail. He won 12 clear holes and he took everybody's money and he wanted to know about tomorrow and I told him that I didn't ever want to see him again because it was a big course and he could work some other side of it."

That was Dutch Harrison's introduction to Samuel Jackson Snead. Mr. Snead had a hold on the American public that was positively delightful. He was out of West Virginia where he had been an amazing high school athlete and he moved up and down fairways across America with his palmetto hat and his picture swing and the world's most colorful vocabulary. He was tough on the course and he was even tougher in business as witnessed by the day when two fast buck gentlemen approached him in Chicago to tell him that they had a money-making scheme they wanted him to under-write. They had tried to reach him down South and had failed but it was so good that they had followed him North.

"You mean," drawled Samuel Jackson Snead, "that you fellas come all the way up here just to make some money for me? Well, that's about as neighborly as you can get. You sure are good friends. Is there a little chance that you fellas might make some money too?"

In the words of the poet laureate of the Yiddish theater, Menasha Skulnik: "A country boy, Sam Snead ain't."

He was a golfer of consummate skill and he was a golfer plagued by his own private doom. Samuel Jackson Snead could hit a golf ball a ton. He could win tournament after tournament. He could charm gallery after gallery. But he simply could not win the U.S. Open Golf Championship. He found more ways to lose it than any other man in history. If every other player were to withdraw on the eve of the tournament, you can rest assured that he still couldn't win it because it would probably rain for 40 days and 40 nights.

And because of that, he was all the more human. Because of that, the galleries loved to follow him.

The other man had a different appeal. In a sense he had two different appeals. His name was Ben Hogan. He was born in 1912 in a place called Dublin, Tex., an hour's drive from Fort Worth. His father, a mechanic, died when Ben was nine. By 11 he was a caddy in Fort Worth and at a very early age, he was scrambling on the public courses, where education comes quickly or not at all.

By 1940 his name was up near the top of the meager money lists which represented the prize money in professional golf. In 1948 he won the U.S. Open. He attracted attention at that stage by his magnificent concentration and his fantastic ability to rally down the stretch. He was mechanical and devoid of color but he won and the drama was mostly centered around his ability to recover from early difficulties. Snead had the following because Snead had the color.

Then there was a foggy night on a highway 29 miles east of Van Horn, Tex., and Ben Hogan suddenly had an emotional gallery all his own.

They were driving back from a tournament in Arizona, Hogan and his wife, Valerie, when the bus came out of the night and halfway through Ben Hogan's windshield. The date was Feb. 2, 1949. The bus had pulled into Hogan's lane from the other direction in order to pass a truck. As it headed straight for Hogan's Cadillac, he swerved. Then he flung himself in front of his wife, who escaped with only a black eye. Ben Hogan's pelvis was fractured. His collarbone was shattered. A rib snapped like a wooden match. His left ankle was broken. Doctors at Hotel Dieu Hospital in Fort Worth, did not expect him to live.

As Hogan lay near death in the hospital, newspapers all over America detailed the accident, recalled his career and kept a daily vigil on their pages. Suddenly, the mechanical man was very, very human. He began to gain. Then there were blood clots. He licked that, too. Again the papers carried the story. Hogan would live. He might never walk again and nobody played golf from a wheel chair.

Which makes what happened at Los Angeles just a year later all the more remarkable. There was Ben Hogan on the practice tee announcing he would play in the Los Angeles Open. Photographers hounded him although he was playing with great pain. Snead was there, too. Snead had his colorful hat and his colorful swing and his colorful vocabulary. But on Jan. 6, 1950 at the Riviera Country Club, the mechanical man who had suddenly become flesh and blood, had the gallery.

The emotional wedge which was developing among golf fans found its impetus in Los Angeles that week. Ben Hogan was in the clubhouse with a four-stroke lead on the final day and then from out of the pack came Sam Snead to birdie the last four holes and send the thing into an 18-hole playoff the next day. As Hogan sat in front of his locker, he looked at reporters with the strain of it clearly visible on a face which they had previously known as devoid of emotion in the face of adversity.

"I'm damned tired," he said. "I wish I didn't have to play tomorrow. Rather than that, I wish he'd won it all today."

After several rainouts, Snead won the playoff. Hogan went down to Palm Springs to rest. Emotions were building. The 1950 U.S. Open would find Snead and Hogan in direct conflict.

The Open was played at the Merion Golf Club and Snead, despite the jinx which had shared his locker in every U.S. Open, was favored to win. In those days the Open began with 18 holes on Thursday, 18 holes on Friday and concluded with a grueling 36 on Saturday. With that Saturday session in mind, Hogan had the most discussed legs since Marlene Dietrich.

On Wednesday, Sam Snead unwrapped a brand new putter in the clubhouse and said "so here I am in Philadelphia again." Eleven years earlier in the same city he had managed to avoid winning the Open by taking an eight on the very last hole.

Hogan shot a 71 in his practice round. Snead was the heavy favorite to win it all. Only Jimmy Demaret, a colorful pro from Hogan's native Texas, gave Ben a chance. "The way he's playing," Demaret said to everyone's surprise, "he is a cinch to win this thing."

On the first day, an unemployed pro from Alabama named Lee Mackey shot a record 64. Hogan was lost in the shuffle eight strokes back. Snead has his usual Open problems and the next day put himself out of the running by missing the kind of putts which Sam refers to as "them-six-seven-footers." Hogan's second round of 69 turned the galleries into an emotional mass of jelly. It was no longer a question of any other golfer defeating him. The whole thing boiled down to Ben Hogan's legs.

A thousand times throughout the tournament, Ben Hogan told well-wishers "thank you very much I feel fine." But when they came down to the 14th hole of the final round, Hogan was near collapse. Doctors had worked a surgical miracle with him, delegating functions normally carried out by large veins to smaller ones. But Hogan would have to work his own miracle from that point. He did it with a courage which turned all the mechanical-man scoffers into Hogan fans. He finished at 287 in a three-way tie for first with George Fazio and Lloyd Mangrum. "It was enough," medical logic said. "You can do it," the gallery pleaded.

That night as Ben Hogan lay in extreme pain on his bed, the doctor and his wife Valerie massaged his legs in shifts. At 4 a.m., they quit. There was nothing left to do but hope.

On Sunday, Ben Hogan went back out to Merion and shot himself a 69. He beat Mangrum by four strokes and Fazio by six. For an added flourish, he banged home a 50-foot birdie on 17. Hogan fans—and suddenly there was a whole army of them—would never be passive again.

For the next four years the emotional followers of Snead and Hogan fought a running battle. In 1952, Hogan and Snead were deadlocked into the final round of the Masters.

Snead was off the tee first. Hogan played later in the day. Pressed by the knowledge that Hogan was in position to know exactly what score he must make, Sam Snead began to force. At the 12th tee, Snead dropped his shot in a creek. His second was almost as bad. But with his left foot above the embankment and his right foot deep in the weeds, Snead made a remarkable recovery. He finished at 72–286 and then to his amazement learned piecemeal during the long wait that Ben Hogan had three-putted five greens. Score that one for Snead.

The next year, Snead made his best run at Hogan in U.S. Open competition. After three rounds he was only one stroke back. But much to the consternation of his large gallery, Sam Snead couldn't buy a putt over the 18 and Hogan put him away with ease. Still, there was a live controversy in the wake of the final round. Snead rapped the USGA over his late starting time. He was still playing his first round on Saturday when Hogan had already begun his second. "They shouldn't give the leader the early schedule all the time," Sam said. "They ought to give everyone a fair shake."

So it came down to 1954 and the most dramatic head-to-head meeting the two ever had. Once again the tournament was the Masters but for much of its run the spotlight belonged to a surprising amateur golfer named Billy Joe Patton. On the first day, Hogan grumbled about the pin placements. He shot a 72. Snead shot a 74. And "Billy Joe Who" led the Masters with a score of 70. At the end of two rounds it was Billy Joe at 144, Hogan at 145 and Snead at 147. As they went into the final day, Hogan led at 214, followed by Snead at 217 and Billy Joe Patton at 219.

The fourth round was a dandy. It got even better when Billy Joe What's-His-Name scored a hole in one. It couldn't last, the Hogan-Snead fan clubs insisted. They were right. It didn't. At the end of the long day, Ben Hogan and Sam Snead were in a dead tie for the title. There would be a playoff the next day. The galleries would have their show-down after all.

The day was a beauty to behold and despite the fact that it was Monday, roughly 14,000 people turned out for the match. There were no neutrals in the gallery. The meeting at the first tee set a record for short-distance drama.

"Good luck, Sam," Ben Hogan said.

"Good luck, Ben," Sam Snead said.

They did not kiss.

They teed off and they moved down the fairway and from the very start each exhibited the trademarks which had earned him his private gallery. Hogan plugged ahead, steadily, quietly, his face set in the studied concentration which his people had come to appreciate. A furious chain-smoker he lit one cigarette after the other. Snead, five inches taller than Hogan at 5–11, bounced along with that magnificent athlete's stride of his, the usual straw hat covering his balding head. And as usual he kept up a running conversation with his admirers.

After nine holes they were still all even. A remarkable recovery after he had cleared the green at 10, brought Sam Snead a birdie and the lead for the first time. Hogan caught him at 12 but at 13, Snead out-drove him, played a splendid two iron for his second shot and once again held a one-stroke lead.

So they came to 16 and the marshalls tried to keep the huge crowd under control. They were successful. Nobody drowned in the water which guards the green. The Augusta National Course calls this the Rosebud hole. It is a 190-yard par three over water with a drop in elevation of 10 feet.

Standing on the tee the green is clearly framed by the mass of humanity which rings it in a tight semi-circle. Hogan could have caught him here. His tee shot left him with a 12-footer. He rolled it up short and now he needed a three-foot putt to keep Snead from pulling two strokes in front. Hogan studied the putt. He puffed on his cigarette. He moved back over the ball. Snead took a deep breath and wondered where he could find that insurance stroke. He didn't have to wonder for long. Ben Hogan blew what week-end golfers call a "gimmee." Sam Snead was two up and the putt ice-water Ben failed to make was the putt that decided the debate. Snead shot 70, Hogan shot 71 and in the locker room afterwards, Samuel Jackson Snead, mindful of the times when Ben Hogan had beaten him and the 99 out of 100 days when Ben Hogan would have made that putt, summed it up as only Samuel Jackson can:

"I just guess the sun don't shine on the same dawg's tail every day."

Hagen and Jones had been, in its way, a war of the worlds. Hogan and Snead had been a battle of pure professionals. But a new rivalry shaped up for the decade of the 60s. It is hard to say what it was the battle of. People who didn't know a putter from a driver took definite and noisy sides.

Think, for a moment, of Jack Armstrong with a college degree. Think of the boy next door in his varsity sweater. Think of Pauline, from the Perils of the same name, rolling off the railroad tracks as the Super Chief thunders by, kicking the great big saw off center just the necessary millimeter. Put him in the cockpit of his private airplane. Give him nerves of steel, reflexes of a brain surgeon and an All-American smile.

You are thinking about Arnold Palmer.

Why not? Half of America does at one time or another. His career reads like the classic introduction to a long-gone soap opera: "Can a young boy from a small mining town in Pennsylvania find health, wealth, happiness and affection on America's fairways?" He can find it like this:

"Arnold Palmer Putting Courses have become a way of life in Japan," reports the "Arnold Palmer Dispatch," the official organ of Arnold Palmer Enterprises. "Arnold Palmer Indoor Golf Schools are having a banner year. The Pleasantville Division of Arnold Palmer Enterprises has appointed a real estate director. The Jeepstakes (no purchase, no entry fee required) is currently being held at all Arnold Palmer facilities."

General Motors should have it so good.

On the other hand, General Motors simply does not work at it the way Arnold Palmer does. There has never been a golfer like him. His father, Milfred Deacon Palmer was the head pro at the Latrobe (Pa.) Country Club and when Arnie Palmer was still in the bubble gum stage, he gave him the two most important things he ever got. The first was a set of cut-down golf clubs. The second was some advice. "Hit it hard," Mr. Palmer told Arnold. Nobody ever had a more dutiful son.

Arnold Palmer hit it hard all the way down to Wake Forest University in North Carolina. He came out and turned pro in 1954. By 1960, he was the hottest golfer in the world. He took permanent possession of the world's largest private army that year, winning the Masters with back-to-back birdies and the U.S. Open, by coming from so far off the pace it looked as though he would have to mail his score in. He shot an incredible 30 for the front nine of the final 18 and wrapped it up with a blazing 65.

He did it before two national television audiences, and

anyone who gives it any thought will have to concede that television may have created the stage but it was Arnold Palmer who delivered the message, and it was Arnold Palmer who brought them out to the golf course every time the touring pros came through.

And so that strangest of all sports fraternities was born. It was immediately nicknamed Arnie's Army. There has never been a group like it. When Arnold Palmer is on the course, it will kill anyone or anything which gets in its way . . . whether that someone or something is another golfer, a wounded spectator or a portable comfort station. It has no economic common denominator. Its membership is not restricted by race, color, creed, sex or national origin. It has the legs of a centipede, the armor of a Panzer division, the determination of a kamikaze pilot and—at times the manners of Henry VIII. It sweeps across the fairways like Genghis Khan on a winning streak. But most of all it suffers and it triumphs with Arnold Palmer and anyone who short-circuits the victory is treated like the loser in a deodorant ad.

It is a complex, highly nervous organism. When Arnold Palmer gave up smoking, it suffered with him. When Arnold Palmer is on a losing streak, it suffers with him. When Arnold Palmer exhibits any emotion whatsoever, it exhibits the same feeling.

Interestingly, it is made up of equal numbers of female and male enlistees. During the 1967 U.S. Open at Baltusrol Golf Club in Springfield, N.J., a reporter surveyed several of the women corporals. "Why," he asked, "do you belong to Arnie's Army?"

"You wouldn't understand," one woman replied, "but it's the way he hitches up his pants when he walks onto the green." The same woman and her female companion had just twisted their bodies painfully as Palmer ran a particularly tough putt toward the cup and in chorus they had implored the ball to "fall, baby, fall."

"I just like to watch him walk down the fairway," the other one said.

For the masculine members, the appeal seems to be rooted in two definite factors. The first is Palmer's fantastic track record for bold performance, turning abject adversity into personal triumph and doing it by driving over mountains, recovering from man-made deserts and, in short, accomplishing everything every Walter Mitty ever dreamed of accomplishing. The second factor is economic. Arnold Palmer wins a lot of money. In the 1960s when a Joe Namath pulls down $400,000 for one signature and a variety of baseball players bring home six-figure paychecks, money has become the ultimate measuring stick.

American morality plays, however, do not settle for faceless obstacles. If there is to be a flesh and blood hero then there must be a flesh and blood enemy. The members of Arnie's Army found him on a beautiful and historic golf course just 35 miles from the commander-in-chief's ancestral home. The battlefield was called the Oakmont Country Club. The battle began on June 14, 1962. The enemy was named Jack Nicklaus.

Jack Nicklaus was pudgy. He wasn't obese. He couldn't have been despite the number of front line troops in Arnie's Army who called him "Fat Guts", "Fat Jack" and "Ohio Fats." In the first place he was an athlete of some ability, having played baseball and averaged 18 points a game for his high school basketball team in Columbus. He was, however, not the muscular boy-next-door whom the army was devoted to and the comparison made it easier on the image-lovers.

When he was 10 years old, his father had given him his first set of clubs and taken him out to the Scioto Country Club where Jack Nicklaus had shot a 51 for nine holes the first time he tried it. At 16, he was the Ohio State Open champion. He won two U.S. Amateur titles. And then, in January of 1961, he turned pro and entered the Los Angeles Open, where his first paycheck came to $33.33. He won money in every tournament he entered and in early June, he finished second in the Thunderbird at Clifton, N.J., to win $25,000. He came to Oakmont just 24 hours before a driving thunder storm. It wiped out most practice rounds but because Nicklaus had refused to take Monday off, he managed to get in 18 holes.

If this were going to be a battlefield, however, Arnie's Army had a decided advantage. The object of their affection lived just 35 miles away. Over the years, he said, he had played Oakmont "at least 200 times." The terrain was familiar. The gallery was "just family."

On the first day, a San Diego pro named Gene Littler took the lead with a 69, one stroke ahead of a man named Bobby Nichols. They could wait. Arnold Palmer and Jack Nicklaus were having their own thing. They were paired together for the first two rounds. The army missed reveille that first morning. By the time it assembled, Jack Nicklaus had ripped off three straight birdies. A wave of humanity engulfed them. The wave grew larger and larger as the tournament progressed.

Palmer had always been a quick decisive player. Nicklaus, a total stranger to the large gallery, approached his shots like a wounded snail. The army, its ranks swelled by off-duty Pittsburgh steel-workers who had begun their weekend early, grew decidedly impatient.

The character of accepted spectator amenities at golf

tournaments is somewhat alien to traditional American behaviour patterns at sports events. Golf demands a kind of
silence in various situations which fluctuate between decent
respect and the absolute absurd. The gallery at Oakmont on
June 14, 1962 was prepared to give neither.

"Hey, fatty," they yelled at Nicklaus. "Hey, Crisco, fats
in the can." As the day warmed up, the beer consumption
kept pace with it. And as the two moved down the fairways
toward the end of the round a new chant began. "Step on
his ball, Arnie. Kick it into the rough." The Nuremberg
Jury was more objective. As the huge gallery struggled—
and staggered—toward the 18th, crowd-control marshalls
began to feel like they were policing Omaha Beach. Palmer
shot a 71; Nicklaus a 72. Arnold, who possesses all the quality a super-star should, was genuinely embarrassed by the
crowd. Nicklaus said nothing.

On the second day, management had to mobilize 27
helmeted marshalls to police the crowd. Walking a precarious trail between the mob and the golfers, reporters trying
to follow the round got the distinct impression they were
covering a lynching. As each of Palmer's putts fell, the huge
gallery raced violently toward the next tee. In most cases,
they only succeeded in running into each other. But the
noise was constant. In the middle of it stood Jack Nicklaus,
trying to hole his putt. As the Friday round ended, Arnold
Palmer and Bob Rosburg were tied for the lead at 139.
Jack Nicklaus was three strokes back with two 18-hole
sessions scheduled for Saturday.

Nicklaus chipped a stroke off Palmer's lead during the
morning round. After lunch, he went out and finished with
seven straight pars. He caught Palmer and now he sat in the
clubhouse, watching it on television as Arnold Palmer and
the Chinese Eighth Route Army came struggling up to the

18th green. Palmer needed a 12-foot birdie putt to win it out-right.

The crowd massed 20 deep around the green, zeroing in on destiny with their cardboard periscopes. It looked like Homecoming Day for the Ancient and Loyal Order of Cyclops. Palmer's putt broke to the left. It skittered past the hole and the collective groan sounded like the tearing of human flesh. They finished in a tie at 283. Armageddon would play a one-night stand on Sunday.

June 17, 1962 was hot and muggy. So was the crowd. Roughly 11,000 of them showed up and a disproportionate number of them insisted on trying to walk with the competitors instead of staking out strategic vantage points. Tempers in the gallery were past the boiling point. At one stage, a beer-soaked customer, angered by the huge press contingent following the players inside the ropes, reached out just as Don Weiss of the Associated Press was threading his way across the narrow strip of turf guarding a very deep bunker. "Lousy free-loader, I paid to get in here," he announced. And then pushed the startled Mr. Weiss head over heels down the incline and into the sand below. Happy Valley was positively jumping.

It was a noisy, angry crowd but it seemed to bother Palmer more than it did Nicklaus. While Palmer fidgeted, Nicklaus' rate of play seemed to get even slower. After eight holes, Arnie was four strokes back. But then it was time for the kind of finish which Arnold Palmer seemed to have invented. He birdied nine and 11 and 12. He was just one stroke back. They came up to the par-three 161–yard 13th. The Army surged forward for the kill.

There was indeed, a killing at the 13th hole. Palmer barely made the front of the green with his tee shot. He was 40 feet from home and he took three putts to get down. Jack

Nicklaus led again by two. The final scores read Nicklaus, 71; Palmer, 74. In 90 holes of golf over some of the trickiest greens in the country, Jack Nicklaus had three-putted just once.

He had committed the unforgivable sin. He had beaten Arnold Palmer. He had beaten him in his own ball park. There was never any of the tension between Palmer and Nicklaus which Arnie's Army would like to imagine there was. But it was there between the new U.S. Open Champion and the troops. It was not going to evaporate.

There are a lot of ways to try to explain it but performance is perhaps the best. Nicklaus plays his absolute toughest when he is either paired with Palmer or meeting him head on. That same year, for example, he beat both Palmer and Gary Player in the World Series of Golf. The pattern has held throughout most of their competition. This is a tough thing for the Army to handle. The Army is emotional and it is not about to give Jack Nicklaus a chance. During the 1968 Open at Rochester Arnold Palmer was in the throes of the worst slump of his career. As he missed a putt, a middle-aged lady in Bermuda shorts right near the green shook her head and sighed:

"Poor baby, he looks so lost."

Her sentiments were echoed by other women. It did not bode well for the establishing of diplomatic relations between the Army and Mr. Nicklaus. Hell hath no fury like a distressed mother.

As for Palmer, he undoubtedly felt the strain of similar situations. There was the time that Arnold led the Thunderbird Golf Classic in Clifton, N.J., in 1967. He had already finished and he sat in the clubhouse, watching the Giants-Cowboys football game on television and receiving bulletins on the survivors from a club member with a walkie-talkie.

"It doesn't look like Casper can catch you," the man told him.

"Uh huh," Palmer said, "Where's Jack?"

"Well, he looks like he has too much to make up."

Moments later the man said "Casper blew, you're safe."

"Yeah," said Palmer, "Where's Jack?"

"Oh, I'll find out. Oh, he's only one stroke back."

"Arnie," said Darrell Brown, who pilots Palmer's private plane, "do you want another coke?"

"Hell, no," Palmer said, "I want to go home."

At that point Palmer took two golf balls out of his bag and gave them to Brown. "Hold these, Darrell, just in case there's a playoff."

"He's on the green at 18," the guy with the walkie-talkie said apologetically. "He's putting for a bird."

Arnold Palmer got up and walked down to his locker. "He's straight up," Palmer said. "It's the same putt I had."

"He missed," the guy shouted, "he blew it."

"Ask again," Palmer said.

"No, he missed it."

Palmer smiled that magnificent smile of his. It spoke volumes. There has never been a greater golfer in this country but the Jack Nicklaus thing is as much of a problem in a different way for Palmer as it is for Arnie's Army.

The Army, on the other hand, continued to fight its own battle in its own way after the trauma at Oakmont. The following year, Jack Nicklaus was in the middle of his backswing at the Masters when a southern-fried corporal hollered out:

"Ahnie just buhdied thuh'teen. How d'ya lak that, Fat Guts?"

It is about as much a gentleman's game as snooker.

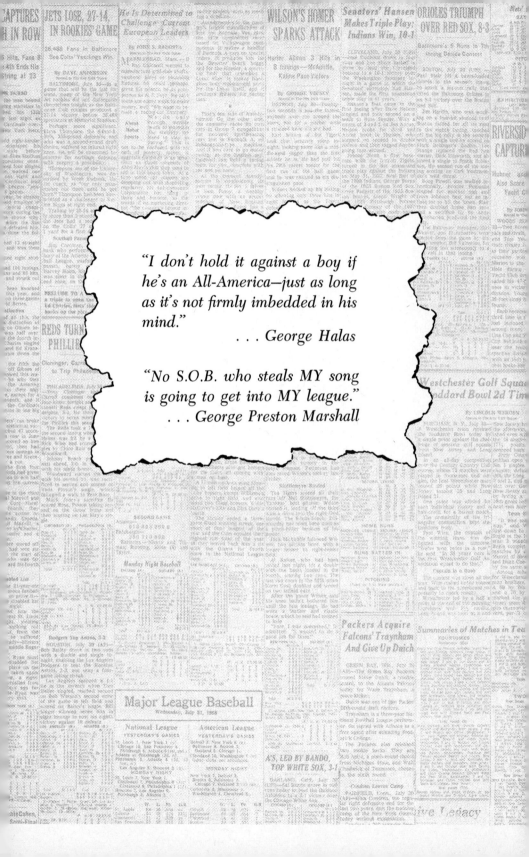

"I don't hold it against a boy if he's an All-America—just as long as it's not firmly imbedded in his mind."

    . . . George Halas

"No S.O.B. who steals MY song is going to get into MY league."

    . . . George Preston Marshall

ONLY ON SUNDAY

The concept was born of boredom. Life in the mill towns was six days of blast furnaces and machinery; six days of carbon-copy drudgery. On Saturday afternoon, they made their choice (or their wives made it for them). Saturday was a half-day and they either brought their pay-envelopes straight home or else they got a head start. In either case, Saturday night was escape in a beer-and-a-shot world and it melted all too quickly into Sunday.

Sunday was church. It was a big family dinner. It was a nap in the afternoon. It was Dullsville. There are 52 Sundays in a year. Somehow, some way, they reasoned, there has to be something better to take into Monday than the raw ends of Sunday morning's hangover. The mill towns found it first.

They found it in places like Latrobe and Jeanette; Canton and Dayton; Rock Island and Duluth. The Harvards and the Yales belonged to the bankers and the brokers. They were somebody else's hang-up. So Green Bay, Wisc., found what it was looking for on a fenceless plot of ground called Hagemeister Park. Pottsville, Pa., found it on a rocky stretch of turf on the out-skirts of town where other coal miners

189

brought their ball clubs and their side-bets down from
Shenandoah and Coaldale and made Sunday afternoon come
alive.

It was a study in controlled—and sometimes not-so-con-
trolled—violence. It was triggered by boredom, nurtured by
chauvinism and pushed down a long, painful highway. It
was the neolithic dawn of professional football.

Sunday is still no bell-ringer in Canton or Rock Island or
Duluth. But it's better. On Sunday, Canton sprawls around
its living room and watches the Cleveland Browns pop
leather on the television screen . . . Rock Island pushes itself
away from the dinner table at 1:15 and settles back to
watch the Chicago Bears . . . Duluth takes its after-dinner
coffee in front of the boob-tube and projects itself into the
real-life *noe* play which is the flesh and blood of Minnesota's
Vikings. From mid-July when the teams assemble at their
pre-season training camp, through a half-dozen meaningless
exhibition games, on down through the regular season schedule and over into January when the last touchdown for
money is scored in the Super Bowl, professional football is
what Sunday afternoon in this country is all about.

They can cite Curly Lambeau, leading his Green Bay
Packers into the big cities and throwing the cry of "rube"
back into the slickers' teeth. They can cite old Tim Mara and
Art Rooney, holding off the financial wolf like separate but
equal Cyrano bookends. They can tell about the Hutsons,
the Baughs, the Luckmans and the Heins. In truth, all of
them were a part of it. But all through the thread of this
violent game's survival and ultimate success, in virtually
every facet of it, you keep coming back to the same two
names.

George Halas and George Preston Marshall rode this
precarious whirlwind through economic famine, two world

wars and off into the candy-striped, U.S. Mint-scented horizon of televised affluency. They rode it as bitter, table-thumping rivals. They rode it as shoulder-to-shoulder allies in a war for bread and butter. And there are people who owned other franchises who will tell you that sometimes they quibbled and shouted and fumed at each other in public but all the while they were secret conspirators for their own purpose of the moment.

There were two key ingredients which gave professional football the muscle to survive long enough to reach television's Great Nest Egg in the Sky. The first was the continued manifestation of pure violence in a country where the worship of young bodies, young muscles and young faces is a positive fetish and where the legal safety valve of other people doing the hitting provides a vicarious complement to the spirit of Dodge City, Superman and trial by combat.

George Halas, who began tilting with violence as a kid by fighting his way through the ethnic street gangs in order to get to the old Chicago Cubs' ball park a mile from his home, took care of that phase very nicely.

But there was something else, too. It took a peculiar kind of vision to foresee, and it was an approach destined to turn professional football into a modern gladiatorial game. It took flare and daring and a lot of trumpets. It stamped the weekly 100-yard war as America's own peculiar bread and circuses.

George Preston Marshall, born to reasonable affluence, enchanted in his youth by the lure of the Broadway stage and mindful of the slender line between emotion and corn, handled that end of the business.

Make no mistake about it. The sum total of what pro football would become can be measured directly through the strengths and weaknesses of these two men. Each was stubborn, a quality which, in the end, would betray Marshall but which, in his earlier years, would do much to keep professional football growing in the face of other executives who, left to their own unimaginative devices, would have taken the safe, comfortable and conservative role to continued anonymity.

Ironically, at a time when society was caught in the powerful vortex of social change, it would be stubborn old George Preston Marshall who would refuse to join the latter half of the 20th Century and whose total loss of touch with reality would trigger the ludicrous sight of diametrically opposed pickets circling his ball park.

He would be the last NFL clubowner to hire a Negro athlete and the NAACP and the Department of the Interior, which owned the huge ball park to which George had finally moved, would apply extreme pressure. And because of his ultimate stupidity, unwanted forces which made him cringe would rally to his side with the sadly laughable slogan: "Keep the Redskins White." This was one battle he would lose and it was the one defeat he suffered which made his world a much better place.

Marshall and Halas battled off the field. They clashed violently over expansion among other things. But this was a House fight and it had little impact on the emotions of the country. There was, however, a day in Washington, D.C., when George Marshall's football team and George Halas' football team acted out the strangest charade in the history of professional football. It slipped up on the world with little fanfare. It had so little appeal two hours before the game that shrewd, tough ticket-scalpers went broke. But it triggered a storm of emotion in the days and even the years which followed. It hounded one of the participants, Wayne Milner, half-way around the world. It made Marshall and his Redskins the butt of thousands of jokes on hundreds of radio programs. Its nuances lived on in the wake of late-night arguments in bars across the length and breadth of America and in even later night phone calls to newspaper sports desks to determine "who scored the first touchdown in the 73–0 game and will you please tell this idiot with me?"

The date was Dec. 8, 1940. But you cannot begin to understand its impact without first understanding what George Halas and George Preston Marshall were all about. In Halas' case, you begin with the second floor of a three family house at 18th and Wood in Chicago where George Halas, the son of an immigrant Czech tailor who turned to real estate, grew to young manhood. It was on Saturday afternoons here that George Halas and his buddies began their trek through the territories of the highly stratified ethnic neighborhoods which were Chicago of the early 1900s.

"We had to get through three different street gangs," he recalls. "Some of us had money and some of them did not. It was here that I acquired my great speed."

It is doubtful that young George Halas really did much running. Contact was his strong suite and a good fight was always a good fight. Mark Duncan, who is the National Football League's supervisor of officials, can testify that more than half-a-century after 18th and Wood, George Halas was stomping the sidelines at Wrigley Field, laying into Duncan's official from the opening kickoff and on into the Tuesday morning mail.

At the University of Illinois, Bob Zuppke took Halas' raw genius for contact and made him into an end of substantial violence. "As I remember George's last game," says an Illinois teammate named Bert Ingerwersen, "it was a bad one. He knocked out only two opponents."

The turning point for George Halas, and perhaps in a way for generations of pro football teams yet-unborn, came at Great Lakes Naval Training Center during World War I, where he played with a group of former college athletes who proved an old Zuppke theory that there is something positively wasteful about football players hanging it up after they had used four years of college to approach their peak.

George Halas and the mill towns made this discovery at roughly the same time. To implement it he approached a man named A. E. Staley of Decatur, Ill. Mr. Staley owned the Staley Corn Products Co. and he agreed to sponsor Halas' new pro ball club. On such things do the fates of national pastimes hinge. You have to wonder what would have been the end product if Mr. Staley had looked back across his big desk and told George Halas: "A football team? You have to be out of your mind. Go out and find me six basketball players."

A year later George Halas had the club in Chicago. His partner was a man named Ed Sternaman, one of his halfbacks. If one left the game, so did the other. Counting the gate receipts did things like that to a man.

What the Bears did as a franchise is simply old and ofttold history. They were good and they were tough and their rivalry with Green Bay and its Packers, is a classic competition which required no bands and no halftime shows to sell. But the battles which Halas fought during those years shaped both himself and the destiny of a league in which he was to play a major role in running behind the locked doors of its executive sessions.

He had to battle most college athletic directors who behaved as though playing a little boys' game for money was akin to spitting on the American flag. He wrote his own propaganda and he bundled it up in the back seat of his old car and passed it out in front of college stadiums in Evanston, Champaign and Chicago. It was George Halas who bought the pencils and the stamps, who took the bids on the tickets, who went down to the newspaper offices and tried to plant his own press releases.

The Bears' organization evolved this way and later when professional football became an elaborate chain of command, George was still riding herd on the office materials, handling each tedious detail himself. This is the framework within which the Bears' franchise operated. For most of the team's existence, George Halas also coached it. He had little interest in the nuances which so fascinated George Marshall. He was of football and by football and for football. He would not spend the money for the frills which Marshall cherished and which helped to draw entire families to the park. He would spend it to produce touchdowns. When the time came, he would not be miserly. But he always made damned sure that he was convinced it was, indeed, the time.

As a case in point, nobody in pro football fought the players harder when they tried to form a kind of semi-pro union which they called the Players Association. Like Henry Ford sending the Pinkertons with their clubs out to "convince" the strikers, George battled furiously. And then, like Henry Ford when he realized he would run out of Pinkertons before he would run out of strikers, George simply said "O.K., what do you want?"

In later years he would make a major contribution from the executive side of his office by leading the National League toward expansion in a direct confrontation with Marshall. But for the most part, the significance of Halas is to be found out on the football field. "I don't hold it against a boy if he's an All-America," Halas once said, "just as long as it's not firmly imbedded in his mind." His teams were shaped in his image and likeness. They thrived on violence. One afternoon in Fairfield, Conn., where he was serving as line coach at the Giants' pre-season camp, Ed Kolman, who had played tackle for Halas for five years, explained something of the complexities of life with Poppa Bear.

"The one thing which used to infuriate him was if you got thrown out of the game by an official. He always told us that nobody was going to win a game for him by sitting on the bench. He said if the league could take 50 bucks from you for it, then so could he. He nailed me once when I got caught taking a punch at a guy in a game with the Giants."

"He fined you?" a visitor asked Kolman.

"Yes, for trying to hit the guy and getting caught."

"Like hell he did," interrupted Ken Kavanaugh, who also played in that game. "He fined you for missing."

Halas provided the football with which people from all sections of the country could identify. It was Halas who signed Red Grange out of Illinois, put the show on the road from coast to coast and brought the scoffers out to see what pro football was all about.

With George Preston Marshall it was somewhat different. Marshall was not a charter member of the National Football League. His father owned a chain of neighborhood laundries in Washington, D.C. He had gone up to New York and tried his hand briefly at acting. After the death of his father in 1918, he returned home to run the family business.

This was George Preston Marshall. All day long his trucks rumbled through the big city with the legend: "Long Live Linen" emblazoned across their sides. He was a restless showman without a stage. Try as he would there was simply no glamorous way to say "easy on the starch." In 1932, he and two other partners purchased the Boston franchise of the National Football League for a total outlay of $30,000.

The team was the Braves and it played in Braves Field and in one season Marshall lost more than he had paid for the ball club. He decided it was time for a change.

Operations were shifted to Fenway Park and the club was re-named the Redskins. Now Marshall had something to work with. Appropriately he immediately hired a full-blooded Indian named Lone Star Dietz as his coach. He also hired several ball players whom he claimed were Indians, too. Then on a cloudy day in Boston he tried to make an Indian out of everybody on the ball field.

He covered their faces with war paint in a promotional stunt worthy of the Palace. But rain swept the field and drove the few huddled fans for shelter. The harder it rained the more the theatrical grease paint ran down the faces of the players. It oozed into their eyes. "Let's get this stuff off," one of the players suggested. "You tell Marshall," another suggested. "I won't."

The gimmick days were soon joined by some genuine talent. In 1936, Marshall's Redskins won the Eastern title. This triumph was greeted with frenzied yawns from Back Bay to Boston Commons. Boston had Harvard and Boston College and Boston University and Holy Cross. Boston couldn't have cared less. Incensed, Marshall did something that no other promoter in the history of sports would have dared. If Boston didn't like the Redskins, Marshall wasn't going to like Boston. He moved the site of the title game . . . not to Green Bay, whose team would provide the opposition, but to New York City. He drew almost 30,000 out of sheer novelty. But George Preston, as he was known in some circles, was just beginning. He took the team all the way down to Washington.

Its arrival coincided in a dead heat with the arrival of a tall, slender Texan named Sam Adrian Baugh. Marshall

went high to get him because Baugh, a magnificent thrower
of footballs, was also a baseball player of genuine talents and
had several major league offers. But Marshall knew what he
wanted. He knew what a passer could mean to his box
office. He knew it because he and George Halas, of all
people, had already proven it to the league. Together, in
1933, they had fought to institute a major rule change which
allowed the passer to throw the ball from anywhere behind
the line of scrimmage. Other owners had scoffed at the idea,
particularly when Marshall presented it along with a plan
to put the goal posts up on the goal line instead of 10 yards
back as an aid to the kicking game and to split the league
into two divisions, setting up a championship match which
has come to be one of the premier attractions in sports.

Halas listened. He bought the idea (he knew it would
benefit his personnel) and he helped sell it to the other
owners. Its wisdom was soon demonstrated and now Marshall had a passer of his own in Baugh. That same season of
1937, Sammy Baugh beat the Bears and Halas for the league
title. He threw the ball for what was the incredible total of
33 times, completing 18 for 335 yards. The 'Skins won it
28–21, and so violent were the Bears in their eagerness to
neutralize Mr. Baugh that it ended with Sam Baugh chasing
the Bears' Dick Plasman to the front of the Washington
bench where everyone joined in the fight.

The artistry of Baugh and the Redskins was established.
The artistry of Marshall was just around the corner. On Aug.
9, 1938, George Preston Marshall, the Long Live Linen Kid,
out-did himself. He announced the formation of the Redskins Marching Band. Eight days later, an unsuspecting
world was assaulted for the first time with the strains of
"Hail to the Redskins"—a battle hymn written by Corrine
Griffith Marshall and a Washington Society bandleader

named Barnee Breeskin, with an assist from untold Evangelical tent meetings. The words were pure slush with a release which featured pigeon English. The music—"Yes, Jesus Loves Me"—was pirated off the revival-meeting circuit and had been heard all over the South in the name of religion. His enemies said that when Marshall approved it, it was like Satan and Gabriel signing a mutual non-aggression pact.

The song itself was a hit. This was 1938 and everyone was trying to run away from a world where the name Munich leaped out of the headlines. Corn was a much desired commodity. Nearly two decades later, it would figure in a strange charade which could only have involved George Preston Marshall. When Marshall and Mrs. Griffith terminated their marriage, the rights to the song kicked around without anyone paying much attention. As part of a debt, a man named Ted Webb took over ownership. Mr. Webb did it as something of a joke because he worked for a man named Clint Murchison, who was then trying to obtain an NFL franchise for Dallas. And he knew that Murchison, a practical joker in his own right would appreciate the dandy gag.

Marshall was livid. Technically, his Redskin Marching Band could have been prohibited from playing George's alma mater. It was the last straw in a running battle which also happened to include George Halas. Halas, ever the realist, saw the danger of the embryonic American Football League as clear and present. He wanted to expand and, indeed, it was Halas who played a major role in kidnapping the Minneapolis franchise from the other side. Halas understood the import of all the money millionaires like Lamar Hunt and Bud Adams could throw into the battle for the other side. He insisted in a bitter session that the league must expand.

Marshall was adamant. He wanted to protect his tele-vison network, which encompassed the entire South. He saw no reason to slice the dollar bonanza up among more people and of course there was something else.

"I don't understand you," Halas told him. "How can you fight against something which has to benefit all of us? How can you possibly object to a man like Clint Murchison in a city we want and need?"

"That does it," Marshall thundered. "No son of a bitch is going to steal MY song and get into MY league."

When Dallas finally did come in, Murchison had to sign the strangest two-part document in the history of sports. He agreed, as expected, to protect Marshall from any law suits ensuing as a result of expansion and to indemnify him. He also agreed that on the day Dallas signed its first player, "Hail to the Redskins" would return to George Marshall's band room forever.

This was Marshall. The song and the team were what he was all about. He knew how to promote. "New York is the world's worst sports town," he thundered four days before the Redskins were scheduled to play there. Ticket sales mushroomed. This was an old Marshall trick. He had pulled it in the heart of hard-core North Carolina Baptist country once in an effort to sell tickets for an exhibition game he had scheduled there. A share of the proceeds had been ear-marked to benefit a police fund. Tickets were not moving.

"I like to drink. I like to shoot dice," Marshall told his horrified audience, "and that isn't all I like to do. Now get those cops out on the street selling tickets for my game so I can go off and enjoy my visit to your town without being bothered."

In 1939, George Preston Marshall led his Redskins and

his band and his fans into New York aboard 13 special trains. The prize was the Eastern Division title. The Giants won the game but the city was a long time recovering. Bill Corum of the New York Journal-American put it this way:

"George Preston Marshall and his 15,000 Redskin fans slipped quietly into town yesterday behind a 75-piece band and paraded up Broadway to the Polo Grounds."

Armed with cowbells and wooden tomahawks and liberal doses of firewater, the Redskin faithful snake-danced their way to the Polo Grounds. They had already destroyed the interiors of most of the 13 trains back in the yards downtown. They ran head on into the enemy, which was assaulting the ticket booths for the remaining 4,000 bleacher seats management had withheld until game day. When they got inside, it was discovered that management had put 62,530 people into a ball park which sat considerably less.

The game had a dandy beginning. Mel Hein, the Giants' all-pro linebacker tackled Andy Farkas around the neck and nearly recovered his head. Exit, Mr. Farkas.

It was rock-gut football and by the time they came down to the final seconds, the field looked like The Tub of Blood on a Saturday night. The Giants had scored on three field goals by Ward Cuff. The Redskins, despite their band, their fans and the great Sam Baugh, had managed seven points. They trailed with 45 seconds left when coach Ray Flaherty sent Bo Russell into the game to attempt what could have been the winning field goal. The ball was on the five but Russell's substitution cost Washington five yards for delay of game.

Frank Filchock dropped to one knee on the Giants' 12. He took the snap and spotted the ball. Russell kicked. Under the goal posts, referee Bill Halloran signalled that the kick was wide of the cross bar. The Redskins surrounded him in violent protest. Forty seconds later it ended—or began, depending on your viewpoint. Flaherty and Washington halfback Ed Justice rushed back to Halloran to argue again as the teams left the field. Just as they passed the end zone near the entrance to the clubhouse steps, the first wave of fans had cleared the wall and had him surrounded. A Redskin fan with a paper-feathered headdress swung on Halloran but umpire Tom Thump pushed in between them and diverted the blow. By that time fist fights raged all over the ball park, in and out of the stands. It took police a half hour to hold the line until reinforcements arrived to cart the bodies away. In the confusion, George Preston Marshall lost his $10 hat.

That was "Hail to the Redskins," too.

On such happenings, Marshall's promotional genius thrived. On Oct. 10, 1954, the Redskins had already lost 41–7 to San Francisco, 37–7 to Pittsburgh and would lose that day 51–21 to New York. But at halftime that afternoon, George Preston glowed the glow of the righteous from his private box in Griffith Stadium. Dr. Howard Mitchell, his baton raised on the 50–yard line, had led the National Symphony Orchestra in "Hail to the Redskins." The band, the trappings, remained very much the same thing with George Marshall and, in truth, they brought a lot of bored housewives into the ball park.

As a case in point, there came a blizzard to Washington one Sunday in the early 1960s when the Giants and the Redskins were scheduled to play at Griffith Stadium. The protective tarp had been laid down the night before and the snow was so deep, nobody could even hope to find the canvas. Wellington and Jack Mara, the co-owners of the Giants, stood calf-deep in the white stuff and pondered the solution when from across the field they saw old George

Preston go mushing toward the groundskeepers. He was a magnificent figure, his silvery hair bared to the wind, his expensive camel's hair overcoat turned up at the collar. The Maras watched him gesticulate wildly but commandingly at the grounds crew.

"You know," Jack said. "Dad was right. He is amazing. Look at all this snow. I don't see how they're going to remove that tarp. But he's already got it figured out. I'm going to walk over there and eavesdrop."

What Jack Mara heard as he moved into ear-shot was George Preston Marshall knowing exactly what he wanted. He heard: ". . . and put the trumpets on the 20 yard line so they have plenty of room. I don't want them crowding the base drum. . . ."

This was Marshall, whose promotional ideas were the antithesis of those of George Halas. And this was the orator who, like Halas, fought for the college draft. One day at a league meeting in the Willard Hotel in Washington, after hearing eloquent Jock Sutherland, himself a former college coach, attack the draft by saying: "Colleges teach the boy the value of amateurism . . . the value of the rules and it is simply not right that we come along before the mud on the boy's jersey is dry and smear him with the taint of professionalism," George Marshall rose to speak.

"The text of my sermon this morning is Let He Who Is Without Sin Among Us Cast the First Stone." Marshall proceeded to attack every college coach and every college athletic director who ever lived and by the time he was done only cooler heads kept the entire group from drawing up a manifesto against college sports.

He could bargain and he could argue. But there finally did come a day when he could neither argue nor bargain away the greatest humiliation of his career. It became a

national joke and George Halas was the man who made it
happen.

All Washington-Chicago football games have been surrounded by emotion. They play in different divisions and
most of their meetings have been with the title at stake.
One of the least known Boswells of this series was once a
man named Fred Gillies. He was a kind of volunteer coach
and fanatical Chicago fan. The team occupied all of his
waking hours each fall and most of his dreams. Three years
after George Preston Marshall's great humiliation, George
Halas would be on active duty with the Navy but Fred
Gillies would burst into the Chicago locker room on the eve
of yet another title rematch between the teams and faithfully
remind the troops of George Halas' credo. "You've got to
hit them . . . hit them . . . hit them . . . and if they get up,
hit them again."

In that game, which the Bears won, 41–21, on Dec. 26,
1943, Jim Logan, a Chicago guard was rushed to Masonic
Hospital. Harry Clark, who caught two touchdown passes,
was a bloody mess. Joe Pasqua, a Washington starter at
tackle had to be helped off the field, and Sam Baugh, the
passing arm of George Preston Marshall's Redskins, was so
badly mauled that he could not return to play the second
half. As a post-script, Ralph Brizzolara, the Chicago general
manager in Halas' absence, had George Preston Marshall
ejected from the field.

But that game was in the future. Now it was Dec. 8,
1940, a date George Preston Marshall suffered with the rest
of his life. It was 1940 and the world looked like this.
London was in flames. The Battle of Britain was in its full
horror and Hitler nightly boasted that the British were
on the verge of surrender. Selective Service was a fact of
life in this country and American generals were trying to

train an army which had to use old Model T fords to simu-
late tanks. America sought escape at the movies where
Wallace Berry was starring in "Wyoming" and Gary Cooper
held forth in "The Westerner." It sought escape in a lot of
ways. On Sunday, Dec. 8, it tuned in its radios to the National Football League's championship game in Washington
with mild interest. It was a way to kill Sunday.

Still, there was a pretty good feud going. On Nov. 17,
the Redskins had beaten favored Chicago 7–3 in a regular
season meeting at Griffith Stadium. Afterwards, Marshall,
about as reserved as, well, as reserved as George Preston
Marshall, had thundered in the Washington dressing room
that he wasn't surprised. "The Bears have a way of folding
up when the going gets tough."

Even for Marshall it was carrying showmanship dangerously far. The Bears were good. They were also big. By
today's standards they were an average-sized football team.
By 1940's measuring stick, they were monsters. They were
also a difficult team to defense because they played T-
formation football in a Single Wing world. This was a problem for everyone who played them. Opponents were simply
not used to seeing the quarterback with his hands up against
the center's rump instead of the more open Single Wing
alignment and they were not used to coping with the possibilities opened to the offense by its sending a back in motion
toward either side of the field before the ball was snapped.

Once, in a moment of frustration, the league's clubowners
had discussed the possibility of making it legal to run with
an incomplete pitch-out. The pitch-out was bread and butter
to George Halas' early version of the T Formation. A rule
change could only be aimed at the Bears.

They had met in Atlantic City and George Halas, whose
approach to oratory bore no resemblance to George Mar-

shall's stentorian formality, had, for possibly the only time ever at a league meeting, risen to speak with great passion. A hint of tears glistened in his eyes as he implored the club owners to remember the vast contribution of the Bears (although what that had to do with pitchouts was not quite clear.) At any rate, George Halas beat back the rule change.

In 1940, Halas had himself a quarterback who represented the total manifestation of all a quarterback could be under the T-Formation as it was then constituted. His name was Sid Luckman and he was off the unlikely campus of an Ivy League college named Columbia. It was his second year in professional football and his first championship game.

It had been a strange week in terms of preparation for both teams. The temperature hovered near zero for most of the week in Washington but the skies were clear and with a little Spartan control, the Redskins were able to get in their usual practice sessions. History doesn't show whether or not George Preston permitted his brass section to risk frost-bitten lips during the week.

Out in Chicago it was different. A foot of snow covered the Bears' practice field. They spent most of the week indoors, looking at film. Halas and his assistant, Ralph Jones, along with Clark Shaughnessy, a student of the T Formation who was about to coach Stanford to victory in the Rose Bowl, decided to concentrate on the counter series, hoping to tip the defense in the direction of the man in motion and come back the other way with the ball carrier.

They managed very little work on the field that week but Halas never let them forget George Preston Marshall's remark. They came to Washington by train. Sid Luckman recalls it vividly:

"Most of the time when a team rides a train, the boys play cards or read or hold bull sessions. But this ride was different. I have never seen anything like it before or since. There weren't five words spoken the entire trip. Then we got off the train and the Washington newspapers were echoing another one of Marshall's charges. They were calling us crybabies and front-runners."

Which may in part explain the incredible sight which the Redskins witnessed that afternoon when at the conclusion of their workout they showered, dressed and filtered into the grandstand to watch the Bears loosen up.

"I got back to the field just as the Bears were coming out," recalls Andy Farkas, who was Washington's best ball carrier. Farkas remembers everything about that week. When you are beaten 73–0 there is very little you could forget even if you tried.

"They actually came out screaming all kinds of things . . . like a pack of wild men. I'd never seen anything like it . . . none of us had. They took off and ran the length of the field. They circled the goal posts and started back and they were still screaming."

At that precise moment, Halas, noting the assembled Redskins, smiled faintly and said to his assistant, Hunk Anderson, in a stage whisper loud enough to dent Mt. Rushmore "My, but the boys are enthusiastic today. Get 'em back inside. I don't want to lose that kind of enthusiasm."

So the Bears did not work the day before the ball game, which is just as well because if they had been any better the following day, Marshall would have had to send his tuba section into the ball game.

The team Halas sent out onto the field on Sunday, Dec. 8, 1940, was the largest in the league by far. It was embarrassingly deep in talent. Among the backs were people like Luckman, Joe Maniaci of Fordham, George McAfee of Duke, Gary Famiglietti of Fordham, Bill Osmanski of Holy

Cross, Scooter McLean of St. Anselms and Ray Nolting of Cincinnati.

And this was the day on which they were to prove themselves. This was the day on which they would earn the nickname "Monsters of the Midway." But most of all, this was the day on which George Preston Marshall's classic remark about the Bears folding would draw a high place in history alongside the scout who told George Custer: "Beats me, general. Maybe they went up to Canada for Expo 67."

The game drew 36,034 customers or roughly 1/132 of the people today who claim they were there. Scalpers tried to peddle their tickets at half price dangerously close to Griffith Stadium. This is a reasonable barometer of the surprising lack of interest. Scalpers need a great deal of lack of interest before they will go that close to the front gate.

On the second play of the game, Luckman faked a handoff to Ray Nolting, who carried out his fake into the right side of the Bears' line. The ball went instead to Osmanski, who tried to move over his left tackle, found the hole sealed and slid off outside the end. The Washington linebacker on that side had been drawn off just enough to be an easy target. But Ed Justice and Jimmy Johnston had not been fooled. Now they converged from the Washington secondary to pressure Osmanski just past the Redskin 40 yard line. The crowd relaxed. A nice gain. An interesting start. But just as they were starting to breathe on Osmanski, George Wilson, the Bears' right end, came hurtling out of the pursuit straight at Johnston. He threw his body crossways at the Redskin defender, caught him flush. Johnston banged into Justice. Both of them tumbled out of bounds. Osmanski, perhaps as surprised as anyone, tightroped down the sidelines to score. The play covered 68 yards. The score was 7–0. The game was only 55 seconds old.

The Redskins took the kickoff and battled back. In his private agony, George Marshall leaned forward with a faint hope for an instant when Baugh found a receiver in the end zone but the pass was dropped. It was as close as Washington came that day and long after the game, exhausted and half naked Baugh stood in front of his locker and said "That was the most humiliating thing I have ever gone through in my life." Then a reporter pointed out that football games, like wars, often turn on little things. The Redskins had, indeed, rallied after Osmanski's early score. What if Baugh's pass had not been dropped in the endzone? What would have happened then? "Why," Sam drawled, "then the final score would have been, 73–7."

Which about tells it all. Before the first period ended, Luckman had slipped to score on a quarterback sneak and Maniaci had gone 42 yards for another to make it, 21–0.

A Luckman pass to Ken Kavanaugh produced the fourth touchdown and it was 28–0 at intermission. Not even "Hail to the Redskins" could bail this one out during the halftime show. Operating in pure panic when the teams returned to the field, the Redskins tried five, six and ultimately seven-man lines. They passed in desperation. The Bears ran three of the Washington tosses back for touchdowns in the third period. Insult piled upon insult.

Fans scrambled as nine footballs were kicked into the grandstand. Mercifully—or was it that old time Halas economy?—the Bears passed in their last two extra-point attempts to insure management that at least there would be a football for the ensuing kickoff. In all, there were 11 touchdowns.

But as the game reached its final 60 seconds, George Preston Marshall had not yet experienced his worst moment. With less than a minute to play, the stadium public address announcer, following pre-game orders, made the following announcement:

"The management thanks you for your support and would like to remind you that season tickets for next year are now on sale." The sound of the boos was enough to wilt the band's headdresses.

When it finally ended, Marshall met the press and with surprising calm, told them he didn't think Halas had piled it on. "That's the way it should be in this league . . . but I'll tell you this," he said with the old Marshall passion, "there'll be a little house-cleaning around here next year."

The impact of the game was enormous. First the radio comics took it up. Then the tavern set began to argue the details of Osmanski's run. And finally college and high school coaches all around the country began to scrap the Single Wing and try their hand at the T-Formation. As for the players, none of them—particularly the Redskins—have ever been able to go very long without somebody asking them something about that day.

Wayne Milner, a fine end on that Redskin team and the one who dropped Baugh's endzone pass was a pilot in the Pacific theater four years later when another flyer asked him:

"Milner . . . Milner, say, didn't you play in that 73–0 game?"

"Thanks a lot, big mouth," Milner told him. "Before you joined the outfit, I had the score talked down to 14–10."

It stayed with the football fans and it stayed with the players and it stayed with Halas and Marshall.

On Oct. 26, 1964, George Marshall was already suffering from the lingering illness which was to reduce him to a hollow shell. Within a matter of months he would never leave his hospital bed again. He was then 68 years old and he had obtained permission to attend the Redskins-Bears game at lavish D.C. Stadium. As Marshall's limousine drew up to the press gate, the Bears were piling out of their bus. Halas, then 69, and still coaching, rushed over to the car. He struggled against betraying the jolting effect his old rival's physical appearance had on him.

It's so good to see you, Chief," Halas said. "So really good."

Marshall looked at him dully. Tears ran down Marshall's face. It was his only sign of recognition.

"Why, it's just like old times," Halas said.

But it wasn't. And it never will be again.

"Heat not a furnace for your foe so hot that it do singe yourself."

William Shakespeare,
Henry VIII, Act 1, Scene 2

THE HATE THAT LOVE PRODUCED

It was born of that great under-dog syndrome which is as much a part of American folk-mores as Davy Crockett when the lack of a back door at the Alamo forced immortality upon him or little Harry Truman throwing it all back into Tom Dewey's moustache. Here were these over-matched kids from the cornfields of Indiana, so poor that many of them took their cleats off their football shoes and wore them on the train-ride East. They had a coach who had spent an entire college career gathering splinters on the University of Chicago bench. Behind him was a brief career as combination football coach-trainer-equipment-manager at tiny Wabash College. When the Eastern Press learned about that it wondered whether Wabash was a college or a freight train. His name was Jesse Harper and the Notre Dame team he brought to West Point off the flat farmlands of Indiana featured a prematurely bald pass-catching end with a face that looked like a Scandinavian road map. The end's name was Knute Rockne and he was a most unlikely hero.

There was all of this and, of course, at the opposite pole there was the United States Military Academy with a foot-

ball team which outweighed Notre Dame's varsity by more
than 15 pounds a man and a football reputation which out-
weighed Harper's poorly uniformed ball club by several
thousand light years.

But on Nov. 1, 1913, the little Davids of the Cornfields
hit Goliath right between the eyes with more air-borne
footballs than he imagined ever existed. It began just like
that before 3,000 people in the rickety wooden grandstand at
Cullom Hall Field in the Hudson River Valley. It ended 34
years later before another campus crowd within sight of the
Golden Dome of the University of Notre Dame in South
Bend, Ind.

But in between, somewhere beyond the genuine artistry
of the Rocknes and the Gipps, the Oliphants and the Cagles,
the Blanchards and the Lujacks, it turned to ashes. It tumbled free of the clearly-defined dimensions of an annual
college football game into a strange kind of vendetta which
dwarfed the magnificence of Notre Dame football and the
quiet dignity of the Army's annual battle against the
inevitable. It triggered more barroom brawls than a married
blonde with a short memory. It captured a great un-lettered
army, whose only alma mater was the Eighth Avenue Subway and whose motivation ultimately evolved into a complex
hang-up which ran the gamut from misplaced chauvinism
to outright hatred. Banded together under the catch-all mis-
nomer "Subway Alumni," they made the game everything
college football should never be. In the end, they killed
it.

It is hard to say when this game began to die but you
could take a shrewd if highly unpopular guess. You could go
back to an autumn afternoon in 1944 when this lunatic fringe
cheapened the raw courage of a hopelessly out-manned
Notre Dame football team comprised of teenaged kids

and war-time military rejects . . . cheapened it obscenely
when the Army football team, which bore no resemblance
to the windmill tilters, who had lost 10 and tied two of the
12 previous meetings with Notre Dame, trotted up the dugout steps and took the first tentative strides onto the playing
field at Yankee Stadium.

You could follow the team captain, quarterback Tom
Lombardo, as he jogged past the lower stand endzone seats
where the Subway Alumni—that splendid group of vocal
chords which was about as much a part of the genuine
values which are Notre Dame as a pack of leeches at bleeding time—and listen to the first words which greeted Tom
Lombardo:

"You draft-dodging son of a bitch."

Six years later, on Sept. 24, 1950, 1st. Lt. Tom Lombardo,
platoon leader, I Co., 38th Infantry Regiment, lay dead
10,000 miles from home on a Korean battlefield. You could
say that the series began to die on that day in 1944.

The Subway Alumni . . . don't for a second confuse it
with the thousands of graduates who poured out of the
great educational institution which Notre Dame became
during the years which followed that dramatic confrontation
on The Plains in 1913. The Sunday Alumni had never been
further West than Hoboken, N. J. It contributed nothing
to an institution in whose name it offered banalities, obsceni-
ties and a pseudo-religious crusade which was a mockery.
It was a loud-mouthed army of frontrunners, spot-lighting
everything abysmal which college football can—and never
should be permitted to—become. If as responsible authorities
at West Point and Notre Dame insist, the Subway Alumni
was just one side of a many-faceted problem, it was, most
assuredly, the major one. It could almost make you forget
what this series had once genuinely been.

The first Army-Notre Dame game had slipped up on college football with little recognition. And yet this genesis, the well-spring which triggered a collegiate football rivalry which gripped this country from coast to coast for more than 30 years, was itself compounded of several myths. Notre Dame, to be sure, was unknown in the East but it could play football and Army knew it. Just the year before, the Irish had demonstrated that they had a reasonable idea of the objectives. They had beaten somebody named St. Viateur, 116–7, Adrian, 74–7, and Marquette, 69–0, en route to a perfect season. The names may sound like settlement house glee clubs but 116 points is 116 points even if you get them against The Little Sisters of the Poor.

Moreover, in winning its first three games prior to the Army match, Notre Dame had rolled up 169 points to only seven for Ohio Northern, South Dakota and Alma. Notre Dame could play this game and the Army coaching staff knew it.

Then there was the business of the forward pass. It had been thrown before and it had been thrown in the East. What the Army did not appreciate was how well, how far and how often it could be thrown. A young man named Gus Dorais explained it to them and the over-aged hands of Mr. Rockne brought the lesson home.

But the little college from Indiana was indeed an underdog and when it inched away to a 14–13 halftime-lead, the Corps of Cadets and the scattered visitors from New York City settled back to watch the home side put things back in perspective. In truth, the home side was lucky to get out of the park with its underwear. Notre Dame scored three touchdowns in the final period and Gus Dorais threw, what then was, the incredible total of 17 passes, completing 15 of them. As Army staggered off the field, Bill Roper, one of the game officials commented with unabashed admiration: "I've always believed such things were possible under the rules but I have never seen a forward pass used to such perfection."

So it had begun. Its impact on Notre Dame football was immediate. From St. Viateur and Alma, the little college at South Bend, Ind., graduated to a whole new horizon. The glee club-set was off the schedule. In its place the very next year were Yale, Army, the Carlisle Indians and Syracuse. Nobody ever again would have to ask the question: "Notre Who?"

Notre Dame came back to West Point in 1914 and lost. It won in 1915 and lost in 1916. It was a nice little series but it was hardly enough to grip an entire nation. Then came Gipp.

George Gipp was a great football player. He was also a pool hall hustler, a gambler, a tragic figure, a factor in a football game eight years after his death and a starring vehicle for a man named Ronald Reagan, who went from movie halfback to governor of California. No player in the history of college football can lay claim to all those qualifications.

George Gipp was raised in Laurium, Mich., a mining and industrial town near Lake Superior. He was, of course, an extremely gifted high school athlete but there is no record of his ever having received his high school diploma. He did, however, spend a great deal of subsequent time in the pool halls and saloons of Laurium. In 1916, at age 21, he accepted a baseball scholarship to Notre Dame. Rockne, who by then had become an assistant coach under Harper, saw him kick a football 60 yards in street shoes and goaded him into coming out for football. It was an historic turn of events. Without it Notre Dame would have lost its first genuine All-

America and Lord knows how many votes Ronald Reagan
would have lost. With stakes like that it is apparent we are
dealing with a very unusual man.

As a freshman, George Gipp drop-kicked a football 62
yards for the winning field goal against Western Michigan.
There is no record of the number of fast cues he drop-kicked
into side pockets at Hullie and Mike's poolroom in downtown South Bend. Football was a delightful game, college
was a delightful diversion but pool was a delightful liveli-
hood. Ronald Reagan didn't quite play it that way on the
silver screen.

In 1917 Gipp led Notre Dame to victory over Army. The
following season he was a standout on the first Rockne-
coached Notre Dame team. And in 1920 he was expelled,
blew a shot at professional baseball, received an appointment
to the United States Military Academy (an ironic turn of
events in view of the fuss Army would make in a similar case
which went the other way roughly two decades later) toyed
with offers to play football for Michigan and the University
of Detroit and ultimately passed a make-up exam and found
his way back to Notre Dame.

He gambled heavily on his own team. He moved to a
downtown hotel and continued to shoot pool. He did a lot
of things. Sleep was something for other people to worry
about. And through it all he was one of the most gifted
football players of his time.

The late-night pace took its toll. George Gipp was obviously sick through most of the 1920 season. Naturally, the
1920 season was his greatest.

On Oct. 20, 1920, George Gipp coughed his way past the
Army. He gained 124 yards rushing, he passed for 96, he
ran back punts and kickoffs for another 112. He was plainly
the difference as Notre Dame whipped Army, 27–17. When

he left the field that afternoon, the entire Corps of Cadets stood and gave him a grudging but genuine ovation. Ironically this peculiar rendering unto Caesar would be the rule between athletes and student bodies all through this emotional series. It would not be the genuine participants who would destroy the magic of these annual confrontations.

Gipp's health continued to move downhill after the Army game. He helped beat Purdue and Indiana in flamboyant fashion while managing to work in a three-day bender in Chicago. Against Northwestern, he was obviously ill and played little. When the team played its final game that year against the Michigan Aggies, George Gipp lay dying of pneumonia in St. Joseph's Hospital. The end came on December 14, 1920.

There are two versions of those final minutes. The one keeps George Gipp firmly in the Cyrano character he had played so well throughout his Notre Dame years. The other insists that he asked Rockne to have a Notre Dame football team win a game in his memory one day.

In any event, eight years later, George Gipp figured in the game which perhaps more than any other, gained millions of uncommitted football fans for Notre Dame and focused their attention on games yet unplayed against the United States Military Academy.

Before that, the Four Horseman—Miller, Layden, Crowley and Stuhldreher—would come riding out of the West on Grantland Rice's royal purple prose. Notre Dame under Rockne would be everybody's favorite. The Army-Notre Dame game would be a national institution. And then it would be 1928. Critics were calling football an exercise in brutality. Teddy Roosevelt and Knute Rockne joined forces to silence them.

Knute Rockne's 1928 Notre Dame football team won

just five of nine games, the worst record in Rockne's career. Army, led by All-America Chris Cagle was a prohibitive favorite. After this, the Notre Dame-Army game would never be the same.

Notre Dame won it, 12–6. Despite the drama of that long afternoon on the field at Yankee Stadium, the real story took place in the Notre Dame locker room. It didn't become a matter of public record for 48 hours. Meanwhile, 85,000 people inside the park and Sunday morning newspaper readers around the country had this to think about:

For two quarters Notre Dame and Army played violent but scoreless football. Army finally took the lead in the third period but Jack Chevigny, who was superb all day, got that touchdown back for the Irish and tied the score at 6–6. Enter, One Play O'Brien.

John O'Brien was a tall slim kid from Los Angeles. Now you know as much about him as anyone in the press box that day and more than anyone on the Army bench. He was a track star with a track star's lean body and elongated strides. He could also catch a football. Rockne had seen to that, running him up and down the practice field at South Bend hour after hour while John Niemiec, the Notre Dame passer threw football after football at him. As O'Brien trotted slowly onto the field to replace Chivegny, Frank Carrideo, the Notre Dame quarterback, looked up, thought about all those lonely hours O'Brien and Niemiec had spent together and immediately called the only play in which One Play O'Brien could have possibly participated. The ball was on the Army 40. Niemiec would throw it and O'Brien would catch it.

There was an instant of doubt. Niemiec's pass was high. As Rockne had figured, the tall O'Brien was able to out-reach stumpy Billy Nave, the Army defender. But because of the arc of the trajectory, O'Brien had to lunge. He got his hands on the ball, juggled it, nestled it to him and fell into the end zone even as Army was trying to figure out who the devil he was.

Notre Dame had taken a 12–6 lead. It stood up despite a brilliant effort by Cagle, who drove Army within three yards of the tying score as the game ended.

Then it was Monday morning and New York opened its newspapers. What it read was pure Jack Armstrong out of the Riders of the Purple Sage. Francis Wallace, the sports writer who broke the story, told it like this in the New York Daily News:

"Football people knew Rockne would fire up his boys in his speech before the game. This is what he told them:

"On his deathbed, George Gipp told me that some day, when the time came, he wanted me to ask a Notre Dame team to beat Army for him."

That's the way it was . . . honest. Chevigny even threw the ball in the air after he scored the tying touchdown, looked toward heaven and shouted: "That's one for The Gipper." It was the way Knute Rockne told it in the Notre Dame dressing room at Yankee Stadium and it was the way Ronald Reagan told it to Pat O'Brien who told it to the whole cast and still tells it every time they play "Knute Rockne-All American" on the Late Late Show. The Army couldn't have neutralized that emotion with a mace and chain.

Wallace broke the story and with time it moved further and further beyond the genuine facts which he reported. Grown men, who never asked themselves "would you want your daughter to marry a pool hustler?" suddenly made George Gipp the very essence of the American Dream. The qualities they began to ascribe to him far transcended his magnificence as a football player. Nurtured by sports writers, the story of Rockne's emotional pre-game ploy took on supernatural aspects for the great mass of the Subway Alumni. But unless George Gipp had a very long reach, it was still One Play O'Brien who caught the ball.

Rarely, if ever again, would a Notre Dame team come into an Army game as the underdog. In the years which followed, Notre Dame's growth as an outstanding educational institution was matched by its ability to recruit the biggest, fastest, strongest football players in America. Army, for its part, went exactly the other way. But somehow the Cadets managed to play excellent defensive football in these meetings and kept the score and the drama respectable. Despite the fact that Notre Dame won 10 and tied two of the last 12 meetings prior to 1944, it was undoubtedly the most bitterly played series in the history of college football.

But along the way something happened to this college kids' game. It began to go sour— although nobody could have foreseen it—when they took it off the campus at West Point and moved it down to Yankee Stadium. They did it, they said, because you could get 85,000 people into Yankee Stadium and they wanted more people to see the game. This may be so but there is no record of either school planning to give the added revenue to the Community Chest. They could put their 85,000 inside the park but that still left 120,000 prospective ticket-buyers who couldn't get any closer than Jerome Avenue. What followed, therefore, is what always follows the law of supply and demand. What followed is called scalping.

The re-sale of Army-Notre Dame football tickets and the prices they brought would have made a Mississippi River pirate blush. At Bear Mountain Inn, where Notre

Dame teams traditionally pass the final hours before combat, nice and not-so-nice people began accosting the athletes . . . "100 bucks if you can just get me inside the park and no questions asked." More than a few got their tickets and more than a few got them from Notre Dame football players.

On the other side of this emotional tightrope things were just as serious. In order to purchase a ticket from the Army Athletic Association you had to be a West Point graduate if the game you happened to pick was Notre Dame. The demand for tickets was so great that the ticket office couldn't have functioned otherwise. The Army A.A. sat its members in the grandstand by classes. Suddenly, strange faces began appearing among the sea of captains and majors. It was painfully clear that even United States Army officers are not above a little moonlighting at 100 bucks a copy. The game was slipping away from the schools.

Certain people at Notre Dame were frankly worried by the confusion at Bear Mountain. The few that were not, should have been. Frank Tripucka, a quarterback of consummate skill first at Notre Dame and later with the pros, recalls:

"The lobby was so packed with well-wishers and people who wanted tickets that it was worth your life to sneak out of your room for a drink of water. They even mobbed the practice field. Looking back now, I can see that it wasn't a good situation."

Frank Leahy had come on to coach Notre Dame by then and Earl Blaik had moved in at Army. Both were exceptional leaders of men, brilliant football strategists and extremely strong-willed. There was no love lost between them.

This became apparent to the inner circle at both colleges

when a highly secret but nevertheless intense brush-fire war broke out over an outstanding schoolboy athlete from Connellsville, Pa., named Johnny Lujack.

Lujack could play baseball. Lujack could play basketball. Lujack could do magnificent things at track meets. But most of all he was a football player; some said the best high school prospect in the country.

John Lujack received a principal appointment to the Military Academy at West Point. What happened between the day he got it and the day he matriculated at Notre Dame is a maze of confusion. Blaik, pointing to the obvious difficulties in recruiting athletes for West Point, was furious and relayed his feelings to both the Athletic Board and Maj. Gen. Francis B. Wilby, superintendent of the Academy. As a result of the heated correspondence which followed, Father John W. Cavanaugh, chairman of Notre Dame's athletic board, and Leahy himself traveled to West Point for a secret meeting. Relations between the two schools—and some say the two coaches—had rubbed raw.

No official minutes were kept of this meeting and no announcements were made. Each school presented its point of view and a mild non-aggression pact of sorts in the area of recruiting was agreed upon. Everyone shook hands and agreed to carry on in the best traditions of Rockne, Gipp, Cagle and Eisenhower. It is interesting to note, however, that the real danger, the total distortion of the meaning of the series and very real emotions that distortion evoked from coast to coast, was not a point at issue. When the meeting adjourned, however, there were people on each campus who were suddenly struck with a very new idea. The Notre Dame-Army series might just not necessarily endure 'till death do us part.

There was an interesting postcript to this first semi-official hint that all was not good, true and beautiful. In the fall of 1943, using a second-string quarterback after starter Angelo Bertelli had been called into the Armed Forces, Notre Dame whipped the Army, 26–0. The kid substitute was 18 years old. His name was Johnny Lujack.

To be sure there was another factor beginning to influence the Army's thinking. Although the series between the two schools had become totally lop-sided in Notre Dame's favor, there was something almost demented about the way the Army football team approached the game each fall. Always out-recruited and always out-manned, Army's peacetime position against Notre Dame was virtually hopeless. Nevertheless, its football players labored under the delusion that they ought to win the game. If you didn't know better you could have sworn that "Don Quixote" had replaced "The Manual of Close Order Drill" as required reading the week of the game. The players worked themselves into a state of positive hysteria.

It had long been felt at the Military Academy that such temporary insanity ought to be nurtured and stored for the final game of the season when it could be used to trigger intense damage upon the Navy football team. As a result of this mood, there were people at The Point who insisted that the Notre Dame game was beginning to cost Army three victories a year . . . the game before, when everyone looked ahead to their kamikaze mission against the Irish . . . the Notre Dame game itself, which was always lost . . . and the game after that when the infirmary had to canvass for volunteers.

Notre Dame, for its part, had no such problem. Army was the big game for it and the Irish would have kept on playing Army regardless of which direction the series took just as they have always scheduled any major team regardless of the potential outcome. Notre Dame believed that the Army-Notre Dame series, which had done so much good for the school since that day in 1913 ought to be kept alive.

And then it was 1944. And the Subway Alumni settled the debate in its own dainty way. When it was finished, it was a miracle that the two institutions didn't play the break-off game with Mongolian cavalry and flame-throwers.

The fall of 1944 swept across the war-weary face of America. Both Europe and Asia were in flames. In Europe, Aachen and Belgrade fell to the Allies. In Asia, a massive wave of American infantrymen were advancing on Leyte. And back home college football was being played by fuzzy-cheeked 18-year olds and military rejects. Only Army and Navy had representative teams and what they represented was just about all the football talent left in the country.

The 1944 Army team, which would win the national championship, was indeed one of the most impressive teams ever assembled. Blaik ran it in inter-changeable units. Its wealth of talent included people like Doc Blanchard, the massive fullback, and Glenn Davis, the slick halfback, who earned for themselves the title of "Mr. Inside and Mr. Outside." Blanchard, so powerful that a game-film of him laying out two different opponents on a kickoff return is considered the classic demonstration of downfield blocking . . . Davis, so good that he could even take a whirl at professional football long after a torn knee and a military career had made it seem impossible.

The list of talent under Blaik's command that fall was enormous. It was apparent that nobody—not even Navy— was going to bother this Army football team. As Army humiliated Villanova, 83–0, just a week before the Notre Dame game, the deluge of hate mail which certain semiliterate segments of the Subway Alumni began to pour into the cadets' mailboxes reached a vitriolic peak—at least West Point thought it did but West Point was wrong, it was only beginning. It is possible to offer a rational explanation for this kind of emotion surrounding a football game but only with the assistance of several thousand analysts' couches.

In truth, nobody has ever been able to explain the lower regions of the ranks of the Subway Alumni. Brains was never its strong point. There were even among it those who insisted on putting the Army-Notre Dame game into a religious bag. There had been many Catholics on the Army teams over the years but it wouldn't have made any difference to this vocal minority of the Subway Alumni if St. Francis of Assisi played left halfback for West Point. Much to the chagrin and distaste of the vast majority of Notre Dame supporters, they insisted on turning this football game into the Second Crusades. They were never a majority but their ranks were considerable and they did much to hasten the end of this series.

This was brought sharply into focus shortly after the series was terminated during a speech by Joe Cahill, then director of sports information at West Point. Cahill was himself a Catholic and in answer to a challenge from a primarily Catholic audience of non-Notre Dame alumni as to why the series died, he determined to get something said which had been rankling him ever since he had come to the Military Academy. It was something which he felt was an inexcusable affront to the sensibilities of the Notre Dame people as much as it was to the Corps of Cadets.

"The Army football team," he said, "could no longer afford to be hated."

He found this particularly puzzling since all along he

had assumed that the Army it represented was the United States Army. Moreover, he had been appalled at the people who had injected religion into the game. "It was stupid and it was totally false. I remember," he told them, "seeing a huge picture of the Notre Dame team taking Communion the week of the Army game. I think that's the way it should be but in view of the stupid emotions around this issue I don't think the picture belonged in the paper. Listen, we had Army football players doing the same thing and if I had wanted to take their picture they would have chased me out of the chapel. One of them was Doc Blanchard. What about him? Did playing for Army make him anti-Catholic? Hell, I'm a Catholic. What about me?"

Religion, in all candor, did enter into the thinking of a great many non-college affiliated people who worked themselves into a frenzy over this football game. But the real trouble in 1944 and the years which followed went far beyond that. The West Point cadets were training for military careers. Very few Army football players, as the future casualty lists would show, did not elect to serve. But for some highly emotional, irrational reason, the Subway Alumni was incensed that Congress didn't order the entire Army football team to either agree to lose to Notre Dame or to be parachuted into Hamburg the same night. They were draft-dodgers and worse, the Subway Alumni wrote them. As more and more letters reached the campus, a feeling of anger, later to be replaced by depression, set in.

So it came down to 1944. Leahy was in service and Ed McKeever was the interim Notre Dame coach. He knew that other colleges had been decimated by the war and against those same schools his team did deceptively well. It ripped through Pitt, Tulane, Dartmouth, Wisconsin and Illinois before it ran into Navy and got whipped, 32–13. Why no hatred of Navy? Well, Notre Dame football from a national standpoint began with Army. It began with the underdogs licking the establishment. The Army remained the emotional focal point. George Gipp never asked anybody to beat Navy for him.

There was irony to what followed the Army-Notre Dame Game that year. Army would win, 59–0, and the Subway Alumni would howl that brave, little Notre Dame had been deliberately humiliated. This is particularly interesting in view of the fact that when Notre Dame beat a Dartmouth team that was fortunate to field 11 men by the score of 64–0 earlier in the season, nobody said anything.

Sports writers knew that Notre Dame was over-matched. They weren't the only ones. A New York bookmaker, furious over hopelessly trying to balance the few Notre Dame bets against the flood of Army money which rolled in, sighed and said: "People who bet the Notre Dames are men. People who bet Army are mouses." He was wasting his breath. The Subway Alumni, which had thrived on a sure-thing for so long, would not support its venom with its money.

It began the minute Army came up the dugout steps and onto the field at Yankee Stadium. It rolled out from the endzone seats of the lower stands where genuine Notre Dame alumni rarely sit. Tom Lombardo, the captain and quarterback, was the first man out. "You draft-dodging son of a bitch," he heard. It gained in intensity as the Army team, which had lost 10 and tied two of its last 12 games with Notre Dame and which suddenly bore no resemblance to the losers which preceded it, ran onto the field. The invective had thundered down on the massed Corps of Cadets during their pre-game parade and now the football team caught even more hell.

Out on the field among the non-footballers standing at attention were Cadet Arthur Truxes, Jr., captain of the cross country team, and Cadet Jared Morrall, captain of the track squad. They too, would die in Korea. Of the Army students—both football players and non-football players in Yankee Stadium that afternoon, more than 60 would die in combat. The list of wounded would be so long it would be virtually impossible to compute. And a cadet named Wally Hynds, the team manager who brought up the rear, lugging the footballs, would last be seen over North Vietnam in 1968 as his jet fighter went down in flames.

Perhaps it was the severe cold. Surely a great deal of alcohol had been consumed in the grandstand that afternoon before the team made its entrance. But whatever the cause, the West Point people would realize their own peculiar philosophy (ie: the long gray line, today's plebe is tomorrow's general) meant nothing to anyone but themselves. The United States Military Academy, controlled by public funds and public legislators and dedicated to turning out career soldiers, had very definitely become the most hated college in the country that day. Among those most angered was Maj. Gen. Maxwell Taylor, superintendent of West Point.

The game itself was a farce. Notre Dame had already sent 8,675 graduates and former students off to war. Its contribution was total. Now its student body had been decimated. Just two weeks earlier, Chick Maggiolli, whose 65-yard touchdown run had beaten Illinois, had enlisted in the Marines. It was a monumental mis-match.

Army scored the first three times it handled the ball. By half-time it was 33–0. After intermission it was just as bad. In the fourth period, Army added the final touch by permitting Hal Tavzel, a substitute tackle to catch a touchdown pass. The score was 59–0 and in the storm which followed Blanchard said: "If there was anyone to blame for the size of the margin, it was Notre Dame, which fired our desire to win with its long humiliation of Army teams." This is somewhat overstated but it does indicate that the Army players were not without their own George Gipp on this particular day.

Far more to the point was Earl Blaik's comment. "What Army did find sharply distasteful was that segment of the Subway Alumni, neither small nor quiet, which had, in the 1930s and early 1940s come to regard the Notre Dame-Army game in Yankee Stadium as a sporting event only so long as Notre Dame continued to win it."

Consequently, for sheer venom, 1945 far surpassed what had happened the previous fall. Notre Dame had again played well under Hugh Devore, the new interim coach. It knocked off Illinois, Georgia Tech, Dartmouth, Pittsburgh and Iowa before it ran into Navy. The Iowa score was 56–0 and again nobody said anything about that.

Against Navy, Notre Dame played magnificent football. Led by Boley Dancewicz, its quarterback, it battled to a 6–6 tie and came within inches of winning. Buoyed by this false optimism, the Subway Alumni mailed its hate letters up to West Point and descended on Yankee Stadium in search of a miracle. While the Corps of Cadets marched on to the field in its traditional pre-game parade, the invective thundered down. "It surpassed 1944," Joe Cahill recalls. "It came from people who really didn't represent Notre Dame except in their minds. I really believe that the restraint under which the game was played was something of a tribute to both schools. If things like that had been shouted at games involving any other teams there would have been a riot."

Down in the Notre Dame locker room, Hugh Devore knew that his team was totally out-manned. He tried to simply put the game in perspective for his kids in order to get the most out of them. "I know," he told them, "that we can sit around here and feel sorry for ourselves. But we are men. And believe me if we are not men now, we will be when we come back in through that door."

This time the score was 48–0. Once again the Subway Alumni poured it on. But the war was over. It had ended a month before the football season began. Next year the boys would be home. Next year, these two institutions would take part in one of the most emotional football games ever played.

It was also apparent that nothing involving the united football fortunes of these two schools could ever again be the same. The Army would notify Notre Dame that following the 1947 game at South Bend, the series would be terminated. Years later, in discussing that decision, Blaik would voice the belief that because of the Subway Alumni "we never made one friend out of that game." He would also say that the game had begun to engender "a form of psychological hatred detrimental to the best interest of the Army . . . (and it) could hardly tolerate a condition that bred such ill will for the service and the Military Academy." This would launch yet another fierce battle which would echo across the country and through the halls of the Pentagon and of the Congress. But before that there was 1946 and Johnny Lujack and all the others had come marching back to Notre Dame. The Army still had Davis and Blanchard and a talented quarterback named Young Arnold Tucker. New York bookmakers estimated that close to $25 million were bet on the outcome of that single football game.

"There was something about the week leading up to it," Frank Tripucka recalls, "that is almost impossible to explain. Remember, these were very tough guys who'd been away to war . . . guys like, say, Bob Livingstone, who'd fought all the way up from the Boot to Berlin, and Lujack, who'd been on a submarine chaser. They had pretty much had their fill of discipline and I remember how earlier in the year they sat in the back of the room at squad meetings and just grinned when Leahy tried to give them that old college try stuff. But the Sunday before we played Army all of that changed.

"Jack Lavalle came in and gave us the scouting report that night and you could hear a pin drop. The next day we were on the practice field and Ziggy Czarobski was leading cheers in the huddle. Normally, Leahy never would have stood for that but he let us go and we got higher and higher. It was only Tuesday and we were acting like a pack of mad dogs."

Bear Mt. was its usual mob scene that November week in 1946. Notre Dame had run through Illinois, Pitt, Purdue, Iowa and Navy, scoring 177 points and yielding only 18. Army, too, was unbeaten in seven contests but its victims included patsies like Villanova, Columbia and Cornell. Despite the fact that Lujack was limping, Notre Dame was a slight favorite.

"I can remember the bus ride down to the ball park and I can remember the pre-game locker room," Tripucka says. "I have never in my life seen a football team so emotionally high. Nobody had to tell us anything. I imagine it was the same way in that other locker room."

There were 74,000 people in Yankee Stadium that day and they saw some amazing things. They saw Lujack play the entire game on a bad leg and they saw him catch Doc Blanchard in the open field from behind when a touchdown seemed inevitable. They saw Army fail to cash in on six scoring opportunities. They saw Notre Dame stopped on the Army three yard line. They saw Tucker of the Army and Lujack and Terry Brennan of Notre Dame dominate the defense with interceptions.

They saw just about everything which can happen in a football game but what they did not see was anybody score a point. Nobody cashed a bet despite the millions of emotional dollars which had been wagered with actuaries at candy stores, cigar stands and in the grandstand. The final score was, 0–0.

So now it was just about over. Army was scheduled to visit South Bend. the following year and congressmen were raising hell with the Pentagon, which in turn was raising hell with the Academy. The Pentagon had to get its money from Congress. It needed a reason to explain the end of the series.

Maxwell Taylor, the superintendent at West Point, took them all on. Fortified by his athletic board's decision and determined to reverse the flood of anti-West Point feeling, he refused to budge. There are others who say that he liked the attention the debate focussed upon him. Whatever his reasons he did gain Congressional support by pointing out that now the Army could play one more game each fall against schools from any number of Congressional constituencies. The message fell on sympathetic ears.

The series ended in 1947 on the Notre Dame campus. Army football had slipped a little and to the great disappointment of a magnificent Notre Dame team, Columbia upset the Cadets just two weeks earlier, thereby denying them the privilege of ending Army's long defeatless string which had reached 33. There was precious little left for Auld Lang Syne.

For all intents and purposes, the divorce-game ended almost before it had begun. Terry Brennan took the opening kickoff for Notre Dame. He juggled it on the seven, dropped it, picked it up on the five and started up the middle of the field. He cut toward the Notre Dame bench and Notre Dame's precision blocking opened the alley he needed. He went 95 yards to score and it happened so quickly that his father, who had been delayed en route to the stadium did not get to see it. Army never caught up.

Late in the first half the score was 14–0 and Leahy was mildly concerned that Army might take advantage of Notre Dame's natural tendency to coast. He needed a psychological peg to goad them at halftime. He had already told them that he didn't want them to be remembered as the team which lost the last one to Army. Now it was Frank Tripucka, the B unit quarterback who would give him his spur.

With less than two minutes remaining in the first half, Notre Dame had a fourth and one situation. Leahy watched the Irish break their huddle and prepared to see Tripucka shift into kick formation. Instead, the Irish came out in a straight T.

Tripucka could hear Leahy all the way from the sidelines. He swears he will never forget it.

"Oh, Francis. . . . Oh . . . no. . . . Francis . . . don't. . . ."

"I popped our fullback, Floyd Simmons, off tackle and he went for about 30 yards. Then he fumbled. Army recovered. The noise was unbelievable but I swear I could still hear Leahy.

"When I started to come off the field he ran out and grabbed me. He was saying things like 'Oh, Francis. How could you, Francis? Francis, why do you hate me? You do, you know. You hate me. You hate your teammates. You hate Notre Dame. You even hate the lady on the Golden Dome.'"

"Thank God Army didn't score but he followed me all the way into the locker room talking like that and all through halftime he told them 'Look at this boy. This boy hates me. He hates you. He hates Notre Dame. He let us down. Why do you hate us, Francis?'"

It worked. Notre Dame was loose and relaxed when it came out for the second half. It won easily, 27–7. And Leahy let Frank Tripucka play the whole last quarter.

"I remember one other thing about that day," Tripucka recalls. "My wife, Randy, and I hadn't been married yet and she was out there for the ball game. Afterwards the cadets visited on campus and dropped by the different parties and everything was so friendly. I remember her saying how much that impressed her."

The series as it was constituted died that afternoon. It went out on a college campus in much the same way it had begun. Red Smith, Notre Dame alumnus who went on to become America's premier sports columnist, described it as "an atmosphere of studiously courteous assault." Absolutely none of the acrimony of the recent games was apparent. Nobody can speak for the yo-yos in front of their radios down in the bottom of the subway. They weren't there and it was a delightful afternoon for both institutions because of that fact.

The Army and Notre Dame football teams took a 10-year vacation from each other. The Subway Alumni continued to root for Notre Dame but in a far healthier vein. Somehow the break in athletic relations (it was more a mutually agreed-upon separation proceeding) had a sobering effect upon them. When the teams met again for the first time in 1957, Notre Dame won a thrilling football game, 23–21, before 95,000 people in Philadelphia's Municipal Stadium. But it was different. The bitterness was gone, the pseudo-religious atmosphere which the Subway Alumni had injected into the game appeared to be buried forever.

It was simply a football game. For the first time in years, it was a very nice affair.

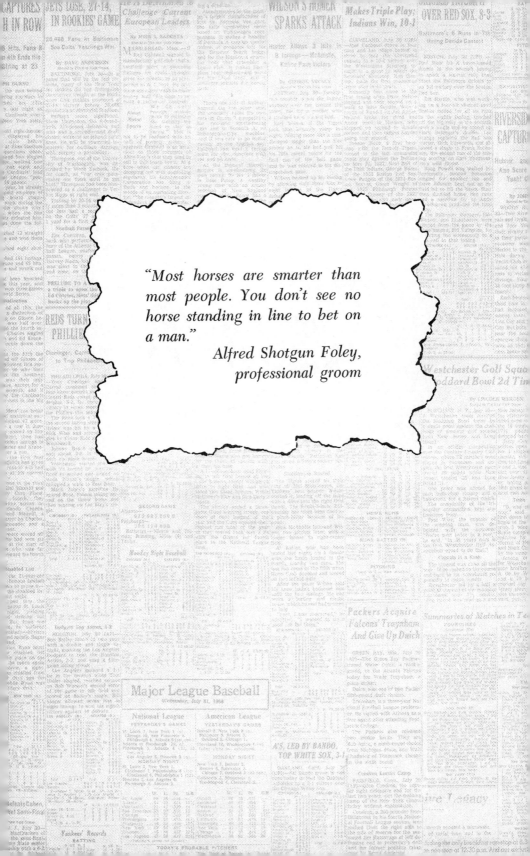

"Most horses are smarter than most people. You don't see no horse standing in line to bet on a man."

Alfred Shotgun Foley,
professional groom

VANITY, OH, VANITY

It is a business of sharp angles and quick hustles . . . of whispered bar-room coups and the idle clubhouse luxury of the rich. Jockey clubs will point to 100,000 exhibitionists, stepping on each other's toes, picking each other's pockets, necking in the infield and destroying perfectly good booze by soaking sickly-sweet flora in it and they will tell you that this is tradition as personified by the Kentucky Derby. But let them shut down the mutual windows just once *before* the Derby is run and you won't have enough people left in the joint to get together for a trio for the singing of "My Old Kentucky Home."

The Belmont Stakes, for example, that wonderful marathon which completes thoroughbred racing's Triple Crown cycle, is a slice of snobbish history written by, for and mainly about that chubby set which tells you it is sacrificing itself for "the good of improving the breed" but which will kick you in the patella—or worse—if you crop any one of them out of the winner's circle photograph.

Once, there was a bricklayer named Chicago O'Brien who earned 14 bucks a day. Mr. O'Brien laid aside his trowel one day, took his weekly paycheck out to a race

track and by judiciously parlaying show bets, ran his wad
up to 10 grand. After that he became a professional horse
player and ultimately decided to breed his own. Once he
beat the millionaires in the Belmont Futurity and the millionaires never had a formal ceremony for him. They simply
left the Gold Cup in the jocks' room and sent a message that
he could pick it up.

So much for myths.

Make no mistake about it. The idle rich plays the game
for vanity and the working stiff plays it for money. Horse
players are not by nature a sentimental breed. The story has
often been told about the two guys watching the post parade
with two buck mutual tickets in their hands.

"Look at that animal. I had to bet on him." The first one
said. "Look at the style and grace . . . the classic lines . . .
the powerful fetlocks. You just have to love a horse like
that."

"What's his name?" the other guy asked.

"Number Six."

America will pour dollar after dollar on the horses in
both on and off track betting but, with a few very notable
exceptions, it is simply not going to fall in love with them.
Still, there have been moments when two horses going head-
to-head all by themselves in a private moment of truth have
captured this country's imagination and held it. In one case,
the purse was negligible. In the other it was substantial.
But without that marvelous vanity of vanities, which makes
an owner determined that he must have the fastest animal
in the world this side of the African gazelle, neither race
would have taken place. Because of it, this country experienced a brace of match races which gripped everyone from
the habitual horse player right down to Aunt Emma from
Des Moines.

It began in 1938 with two men named C. S. Howard and Samuel D. Riddle at a place called Pimlico Race Track, hard by the outskirts of Baltimore, Md.

Mr. Howard was not born to his Jockey Club membership, which is perhaps why he loved his horses so deeply and wound up with one of horse racing's classic Dear John letters. The object of C. S. Howard's affection in 1938 was a marvelous animal named Sea Biscuit.

There were valid reasons for this deep and abiding affection. C. S. Howard had started from the ground and clawed his way up. He had, through long hours and a tigerish business sense, fashioned a small empire of automobile distributorships out on the West coast. Money was no problem after that and money could buy him the thing he wanted most. C. S. was positively crackers about horses.

In 1930, he founded the Howard Stables when he came up with $8,500 to acquire a good, solid workhorse which had been mainly used to help condition more affluent stablemates at the famous Wheatley Stables. The horse, a bay stallion by Hard Tack—Swing On, was named Sea Biscuit.

Howard ran him everywhere he could. He campaigned him so many times in so many places that railroads nicknamed the horse Marco Polo. The more he ran, the more C. S. Howard banked. By the time his racing career would end, C. S. would have made $427,770 off him. Sea Biscuit was the rock upon which the Howard Stable was founded. He was C. S. Howard's passport into an inner circle which read like a Reader's Digest condensation of the Social Register. The Howard Ranch in Mendocino County, Calif. was a showplace. C. S. Howard had reached what he considered the best of possible plateaus.

But in 1938, that plateau was suffering from over-population. A horse named War Admiral was stepping all over Sea Biscuit's headlines. Just a year earlier, with Charlie

Kurtsinger in the saddle, War Admiral had made 19 other horses look like they were running in quicksand during the 1937 Kentucky Derby. He had displayed terrible manners during the walk up to the starting gate but once they banged those stall doors open, War Admiral had accelerated with amazing speed. After a quarter of a mile, Kurtsinger had to take him under restraint but at the head of Churchill Downs' scarred, old stretch he had turned him loose again. He won in what winning teams in one-sided baseball games refer to as a laugher.

This was a stout son of Man o'War, both bred and raced by Riddle. He was only four years old when he went head-to-head with Sea Biscuit in 1938 but already, in a day of infinitely smaller purses, he had earned $263,800. Both owners had strong feelings about their horses. Without that kind of emotion, nobody could have brought these two animals together alone on the same track.

The man who made the match was named Alfred Gwynne Vanderbilt. Mr. Vanderbilt—of the right Vanderbilts—was no Mike Jacobs but then Mr. Jacobs, who had produced Louis-Schmeling and Louis-Conn, did not get invited to the same parties as Mr. Vanderbilt. The match was made for Nov. 1, 1938 at Pimlico Race Track over a distance of a mile and 3/16 with $15,000 at the stakes. The date was chosen because it was a Wednesday and management did not want to interfere with its regular stakes program. Moreover, there was no radio contract and television was still an evil gleam in the eyes of technicians in places like the Dumont Laboratory. But the people knew and the reason it gripped them relates to that earlier piece of intelligence concerning horse players and sentiment.

There is, it should be stated here, one thing which does touch a horse player's heart. The thing is called money and since War Admiral and Sea Biscuit were nearly always favorites and nearly always won, it must be assumed that a great many people made a lot of money off both of them. It was simply a matter of choosing sides now. People in office buildings, barber shops and bars all over America did. This may come as a shock to various Jockey Clubs, but that's the way it really was and still is.

The terms of the race were simple. Since only two horses would be on the track, major fouls were not anticipated. They would begin at the head of the mile and 3/16 chute from a walk-up start. History doesn't substantiate this but it is probable that this last term was insisted upon by Riddle since War Admiral had a distinct dislike for starting gates. George Cassidy, the track starter, would send them on their way. Charlie Kurtsinger would again ride War Admiral but Red Pollard, Sea Biscuit's regular jockey, had smashed his leg in an accident and a veteran jock named George "The Iceman" Wolff was named to replace him.

On race day, a crowd of 40,000 went out to Pimlico in mid-week. In a beauty contest, Sea Biscuit did not belong on the same track with War Admiral. This was not a beauty contest but racing crowds have made their wagers for stranger reasons. Whatever the motivation, they had bet War Admiral down to a 1–4 choice (obviously win-betting only) by post time. Sea Biscuit, the ugly duckling with the swan's bank account, the horse which had been sold to C. S. Howard because the Wheatley Stables had lightly regarded him in the first place, would have to prove himself all over again.

There had been added skepticism at this Eastern track because Sea Biscuit had campaigned so heavily in the West. California horses were held in high contempt east of the Mississippi, a fact of racing life which still exists today. But from the moment George Cassidy turned them loose, Sea Biscuit gave this crowd a whole race to regret its haste to back the home team.

War Admiral had drawn the rail but this was not expected to be much of a factor in a two-horse race. In truth, a two-horse race is a thing of sheer beauty. One horse is going to finish first and one horse is going to finish last and nobody is going to finish anywhere else. It takes an enormous burden off the hunch bettor.

The start was a shocker. War Admiral was supposed to be the great accelerator but Sea Biscuit caught him flat-footed and opened up two lengths on him. This was a tribute to C. S. Howard's four-legger mint but an even greater one to his jockey. Woolf had out-hustled Kurtsinger on the very first turn. He took back a hair on The Biscuit and his mount's churning hind quarters were right in front of War Admiral. Kurtsinger had to take back to avoid trouble.

The large crowd held its breath and waited for War Admiral to move again. War Admiral did not come this far to lose a race right at the start. He made another run at Sea Biscuit down the backstretch. He flew at him with the great fluid power which had humiliated everything in sight a year earlier in the Derby. And the crowd roared its love of both War Admiral and the money it had bet on him as Kurtsinger's mount got his nose out in front.

It didn't stay there. Georgie Woolf went to his whip for the first time and the horses were dead even again. It became apparent then that this was not going to be a battle between two paper tigers. This was a horse race and, indeed, it would stay a horse race right down to the stretch. They swung around the bend and hit the top of that final flat-out run, stuck so close together that railbirds swore they were watching a two-headed, eight-legged horse run.

But that great early effort to get back into contention had cost War Admiral. Woolf went to his whip again now and there was Sea Biscuit pulling away. At the finish line, he had a growing three lengths of daylight on War Admiral.

The object of C. S. Howards affection had clearly settled this argument for all time. He had set a Pimlico track record in covering the mile and 3/16 in one minute, 56 and 3/5 seconds. In less than two minutes, he had broken the chalk players' hearts and returned $6.40 for every two bucks the underdog bettors had slipped through the mutuel windows. It was Howard's greatest triumph. He had loved well and wisely and had won. But the next time he fell in love with a horse things would be different.

Riddle and Howard had been willing to settle their argument through a method which had its roots in the colonial horse racing history of this country. Few others had been confident—or, perhaps vain enough—to try it. The precedent they had hung on the modern tote board would not be forgotten. Seventeen years later another non-club type horse owner would claim supremacy for his animal against a challenger who was born and bred for the inner circle of racing elite. He would agree to risk settling it just as Riddle and Howard had and when he did, the red-rimmed, ubiquitous eye of television would take the debate into every bar in the country. Once again, support for both horses would break down along East-West battlelines.

The year was 1955. A muscular young golfer named Arnold Palmer made his debut on the pro golf tour and came from left field to win the $150,000 Canadian Open. Doctors confidently announced that Sen. Lyndon B. Johnson (D., Tex.) was rapidly recovering from his mild heart attack and in New York's Radio City Music Hall, a very sad lady, the product of press agents, key-hole-peeping newspaper columnists, sycophants and her own purely physical assets, was starring in a movie called "The Seven Year Itch." Her name was Marilyn Monroe.

It was in May of that year that a colt named Nashua had shipped down to Louisville for what figured to be the mere formality of winning the Kentucky Derby. He was owned by the very, very correct Belair Stud. Founded by millionaire sportsman, William Woodward, Sr., and now the province of his son, William, Jr., Belair was rich in the right kind of tradition . . . Gallant Fox, Omaha, Johnstown . . . Derby winners all. And now there was Nashua. Trained by Sunny Jim Fitzsimmons, who had saddled all three Belair Derby winners, ridden by battle-wise Eddie Arcaro and driven by his own fantastic ability to come thundering from off the pace, Nashua was the over-whelming favorite to bring another blanket of Kentucky roses back to Belair.

But there was another colt on the grounds that year who deserved some notice. His name was Swaps and most rail-birds conceded that without Nashua in the race, this son of Khaled—Iron Reward might very well have been the favorite. But he was, they pointed out, a California horse and California horses, as every schoolboy with the price of a racing form knew, made their reputations by running against nothing on tracks that were rumored to be downhill. True, Willie Shoemaker would ride him but then Arcaro was still up on Nashua.

Swaps was owned by a West Coast rancher named Rex C. Ellsworth and trained by his life-long friend, Meshack Tenney. Mr. Ellsworth was surely not in the club. Moreover, both he and Tenney were saddling their first Derby horse.

What happened on that day in Louisville broke the chalk players' hearts, thereby tying a record held by several million other "invincible" horses. First, a drizzle. Then humid, sticky 85-degree weather. And finally, Swaps dealing both the two dollar bettors and the Establishment a royal bath and rub-adub-dub to you, Belair Stud.

Swaps stole the race. Shoemaker sent him after it right at the start of the mile and a quarter cavalry charge. By the time they hit the upper turn, he had broken the heart of a hopeful rabbit named Trim Destiny and broken it in so many pieces that the early challenger would finish dead last in this 10-horse field. Still, the huge crowd waited for Nashua. Arcaro had him well-placed. Just before they got by the mile mark, Nashua moved easily past the gasping Trim Destiny and into second place, a half-length back of Swaps. And now with three eighths of a mile to go, Arcaro sent him at Swaps and the crowd caught it deep down in its throat and poured it out on the sticky Louisville air as a hymn to money. Nashua moved boldly on the outside of the track as they thundered down the stretch. Shoemaker went to his whip and Swaps took up the challenge. He was not going to be caught. That was clear in the low moan which inadvertently escaped the mouths of a large portion of the 100,000 sardine-tight spectators.

The debate might have ended right there. But Ellsworth did not choose to chase the Triple Crown with his new champion. The rest of the three-year-olds shipped east to Pimlico and the Preakness. Swaps went west to face lesser opposition. The stage was beginning to be set.

Swaps knocked over everything in sight out west but Nashua had come on with a kind of super violence. He won the Preakness and then he destroyed the field in the marathon Belmont Stakes, winning by nine lengths and paying a lousy 15 cents on the dollar.

By Aug. 21, Swaps had run his winning streak to eight by capturing the $146,425 American Derby at Chicago.

People around the country were winning money consistently on both horses. When a horse player can cash more than one bet on a horse, he comes as close to love as a horse player can get. Somebody had to supply the answer.

The man who did was named Ben Lindheimer. As head of Chicago's Washington Park Race Track, he proposed a match race . . . Swaps against Nashua over a mile and a quarter. . . . $100,000—winner takes all. The date would be Wednesday, August 31. It would be the seventh race on a nine-race card and through its television cameras, the Columbia Broadcasting System would carry the shoot-out into every bar and living room that wanted it. Most of them did.

The choice of Washington Park was interesting. The track's homestretch—the longest in the country at the time—measured 1,531 feet. The horses would carry 126 pounds as they did in the Derby. Nobody would steal this race. It would go to the better horse and the shrewder jockey under the prevailing conditions. This was going to be a dead honest debate.

Nashua drew the rail. An empty stall separated the two horses. Arcaro would ride the Belair colt and Shoemaker would again handle Swaps. On this sunny but unseasonably cool August afternoon, the crowd made Swaps a solid 3–10 choice.

But there was, indeed, another factor in this race. A few days earlier the track had been muddy and in later years, Shoemaker would claim that Swaps had hurt himself over that same track. More important, however, it did not dry well, according to Shoe. Eddie Arcaro used that piece of information to expert advantage.

Arcaro went for the money right at the start. He opened up a length on Shoemaker, who cut the margin in half at the first turn. But down the backstretch, Nashua broke it open.

He moved to a length and a half advantage and Shoemaker
had no choice but to go to the whip early. He could have
also used a gun and an axe for all the good it did. Nashua,
embarrassed in the Derby, and put down by the bettors in
Washington Park that day, won it by six and one-half
lengths.

Arcaro picked up $10,000 for his day's work. Shoemaker,
second in a two-horse race, got the standard riding fee for
losers—35 bucks. It was his tuition fee to the Eddie Arcaro
School of Gamesmanship. Shoe explains it this way:

"Mr. Arcaro really gave me a riding lesson. He rode a
dynamic race. There was a dry path around the race track.
Every time I tried to get Swaps on it, he pushed me off. I
didn't know too much about riding match races then. Had I
done a little research," he candidly admits, "I'd found out
that 99 per cent of the time, the horse that takes the early
lead wins."

Willie Shoemaker, of course, needs no apologies. He is a
professional's professional. But then so was Eddie Arcaro
and on that August afternoon he re-enforced an old axiom:

"People who want to ride in match races and do not do
their homework are a cinch to finish second."

As a matter of fact, people who do not do their homework *before* agreeing to put their horse in a match race are
in even greater difficulty. Which brings us back to old C. S.
Howard.

Mr. Howard was involved in another match race nine
years after his moment of triumph with Sea Biscuit. It didn't
grip the country—as a matter of fact it was supposed to
have been run behind locked doors—but the reason he got
himself into it in the first place goes back to the warm glow
Sea Biscuit had brought him in his only previous match race
experience. Again, love was the trigger.

C. S. had a deep personal conviction about each of his

horses. It was natural that he should feel pure, un-fettered love when he obtained a classic English sprinter named Fair Truckle, a beautiful animal which ran short distances at clock-shattering speeds. And while Fair Truckle was out terrorizing the opposition up and down the West Coast, the seeds of C. S. Howard's greatest embarrassment were being sown by as cool a gang of rustlers who had ever hustled a bet. Their legs were bowed, their cheeks were tan and they had spurs that jingled-jangled-jingled. They also had a sinfully ugly bag of greased horseflesh named Barbra B.

As far as history can determine they were a band of anonymous Arizona cowboys and Barbra B was their meal ticket. They ran her at county fairs and dirt tracks and at the so-called bull ring tracks where thoroughbreds and quarter horses were thrown into the same races to fill out the card.

Barbra B was a quarterhorse. A quarterhorse, the cow people will tell you, is big in the haunches, supple in the withers, stout in the neck and wide across the chest. If this makes her sound like your mother-in-law, then go argue with the cow people. They will also tell you that a quarter-horse can beat anything this side of Cape Kennedy at a quarter of a mile. This is somewhat overstating the case but it is true that they are bred for this distance, that they accelerate with a quickness which rivals a moderately irri-tated cobra and that non-quarterhorses which race them under their ground rules are generally horses which are owned by people who do not like money. It is also true that quarterhorses have run 400 yards in something under 20 seconds.

And, most of all, it is true that one day during one of those sloppy bull ring races, Barbra B beat a thoroughbred to a frazzle. Somehow one of the cowboys learned that this same thoroughbred had given Fair Truckle all he could handle. Armed with this knowledge, the Arizona Mafia pulled up its sage brush and sat down to consider the possibilities. Many years later, a prison psychiatrist would talk to Willie Sutton, then America's single greatest bank robber, and would wonder:

"Willie, why do you rob banks?"

"Because," Willie would reply with embarrassing simplicity, "that's where the money is."

Like Willie, the cowboys knew that to rob a bank you must first find one. Their bank, they knew, would be sitting in Box 47 at Hollywood Park, soaking up the sun and bathing in the reflected glory of his horses. Well, if Mr. Howard wanted a bath, the cowboys would be more than happy to oblige.

They descended upon Box 47 during the final week of the Hollywood Park meeting in their faded jeans and their wide-brimmed hats, smelling faintly of what horsemen in their position generally smell of. They milled around outside the box and began to talk innocently but loudly about the fact that Sea Biscuit had to be one of the world's most overrated horses. C. S. Howard did a slow burn. Then they called Fair Truckle a plough horse and C. S. turned medium rare. By the time an apologetic usher had offered to evict the intruders, C. S. was positively charcoal gray. Then they mentioned Barbara B and dangled the bait.

"For how much?" snapped C. S. Howard in uncontrolled anger. "Put up or shut up."

"Waal," a cowpoke drawled thoughtfully, "I reckon we could get together 50."

"Fifty what?" C. S. snorted.

"Why $50,000," the man in the stetson said quite clearly and suddenly it was no longer a game.

It had simply gone too far for that but if C. S. Howard

was intensely loyal to his horseflesh, he was also loyal to his wallet. He—and nobody else—would set the ground rules. Barbra B and Fair Truckle would race 400 yards as the cowboys requested. But there would be a stationary starting gate. There would be stewards and a film patrol and he would be able to use his regular rider, Johnny Longdon. The cowboys quickly agreed. Quarterhorses had been running their distance in this country ever since the first Spanish settlers had reached Florida. Quarterhorses could be a rocket at 400 yards. And just so it shouldn't be a total loss, the cowboys had a few hole cards of their own.

The site would be Hollywood Park after the current meeting closed. Mr. Howard, who had more than a little to say about how Hollywood Park was run in those days, went to management and told them what he wanted. He wanted the track for his exclusive use the morning after the meeting closed and under no circumstances was the public to be invited. Everybody in the room tried to run. A man named Jimmy Stewart had the misfortune to be the last man out the door. He was chosen to supervise the race.

"The first thing that happened," Mr. Stewart, who is now vice-president of the track recalls, "is that a bunch of us went out the next day to see Barbra B work. She had been vanned onto the grounds during the night. Right away we knew Mr. Howard was in a hell of a lot of trouble. The second thing was that the press found out about the bet, wrote stories about it and on the morning of the race a crowd of about 10,000 people smashed down a fence and stormed the track. There was nothing to do but let them sit in the grandstand. Suddenly, it looked like we were going to have half of California in on the thing.

"I had a money truck parked in the infield with the stakes in it, you know one of those big armored cars, but it got to be a lot more complicated than that."

The reason it got so complicated was that the entire grandstand seemed to be crawling with free-lance book-makers and most of them were wearing big, stetson hats. The cowboys walked through the stands accepting man-to-man bets. Even Mr. Stewart has no idea to this day how much extra money changed hands that morning. But he does remember one thing quite clearly. He recalls seeing those big, tough cowboys and very hard city slickers whose action they were booking. Then he remembers seeing Barbra B's brain trust and C. S. Howard. And, most of all, he remembers looking toward that money truck in the infield.

"Lord," he said that morning, looking toward the sky, "Lord, I am a young man and Lord more than anything else in this world I want to live to be an old one. Please, Lord, if you have the time and if you hear me, I don't care who wins this damned race. But Lord, don't give us a photo finish today."

The cowboys themselves had taken a few well-calculated steps to guard against that same possibility. The first was the placing of the starting gate scrupulously on the starting line instead of a jump behind it in order to give Barbra B every possible chance to make use of her superior ability to accelerate.

The second became apparent to Stewart and the other track employees when the jockeys made their appearance. Longdon, tough, able, shrewd, and race track wise, climbed aboard Fair Truckle wearing the traditional racing silks of the Howard Stable. There was a great reassurance in watching all of this for Mr. Howard. The best jockey, the best horse, he'd teach amateurs to mess around with him.

Then they brought out Barbra B. "She was," Jim Stewart recalls, "one of the stringiest-looking animals I have ever seen on a race track." And aboard her was a jockey who now rode mainly on Mexican tracks at the invitation of several

American tracks. This was something of a shocker but C. S.
Howard conceded that he had imposed no conditions con-
cerning the jockey's prior legal behaviour. Moreover, with
what was happening up in the grandstand, it was impossible
to call this thing off without first checking to see whether the
track's fire insurance was paid up.

But what was more alarming than this horse which
looked more like Rocinante than Pegasus, more alarming
than the jockey whose reputation seemed to worry Mr.
Howard, was what the jockey wore.

Barbra B's jockey had taken advantage of one of the
things which C. S. Howard in his assumption that all men
were fair, honest and improvers of the breed had failed to
consider. "He wore," Jimmy Stewart says, "the biggest,
longest, sharpest set of spurs I have ever seen in my life."
They looked like separate but equal knitting needles. Hopefully, C. S. Howard called for the ground rules again. He
had written those rules. He had no comeback.

So they came out onto the track at Hollywood Park and
even as the cowboys and the city slickers were still hustling
each other up in the grandstand, the starter got them into
the gate. The crowd fell silent. Suddenly, the starter turned
them loose. For some incredible reason, the most incredible
of possibilities happened. Fair Truckle got the jump and for
an instant, C. S. Howard's heart sang. Then, just as quickly,
the resident rider of the Arizona Mafia's mascot jabbed those
two spears into Barbra B's flanks. Nobody is sure when her
feet touched the ground again but there is reason to believe
it wasn't until well past the finish line and forget it, C. S.
Howard. It's hootenanny time down in Arizona.

"Barbra B ran Fair Truckle into the ground," Jimmy
Stewart says. 'She won it by three lengths. The photo camera
was never a factor. We paid off at the money truck and the

crowd paid off in the stands and then everybody just went
home."

"It was a very nice race. Nobody was killed."

"Human virtue demands her champions and her martyrs and the trial of persecution always procedes."

. . . Ralph Waldo Emerson

"I guess it might have been better if the 61st home run had never come. A lot of people felt I wasn't supposed to be the one to do it."

. . . Roger Maris, six years after the asterisk

THE MAN WHO WASN'T RUTH

August smothered the city. A faint breeze struggled off the East River and spent itself hopelessly against the big, square piece of concrete gingerbread which is the United Nations Building. It was only 3 p.m. but the rush-hour traffic was already beginning to build. As the big car nosed its way up the F.D.R. Drive, Roger Maris turned to look at the river. The driver, a labor leader-fight manager-sports fan named Big Julie Isaacson, was trying to keep Maris' mind off the ball park.

"What is it with you?" he said. He is a large man with a voice designed for cracking turtle shells and his laughter filled the car. "I mean really what is it? Every day now you got us eating baloney and eggs for breakfast. Every day. Look, kid, I'm Jewish. I know. Baloney and eggs is something you are supposed to eat at midnight."

Maris laughed but the laugh died abruptly. "I wish it were over, Julie," he said suddenly. "I mean it. I wish it were done."

"What done? You're just beginning now."

"I mean it," Maris said. "I wish it were November."

It was August 4, 1961. He was just 26 years old. He

was the biggest single sports story in the country. Before the season would end, 71 reporters would follow him all the way to Baltimore, Md., because no self-respecting editor was going to get caught without at least one special story about him every day. He was on the verge of earning more money then he had even dared think about eight years earlier when he had played his first professional baseball game at Fargo, N.D. He was only 26 years old and his bat was a huge ash-blond eraser bearing down on Babe Ruth's single-season record of 60 home runs, a record which was now in its 34th year. It should have been a great, big cotton-candy world.

But it doesn't work that way within the folk-myth framework of American sports. Records, the Great-American-Dream hucksters say, are meant to be broken. What they do not say is that the time and place of the breaking is something they would rather decide for themselves. So, for that matter, is the identity of the breaker. Roger Eugene Maris was caught in the greatest single emotional squeeze-play in the history of American sports. He was bracketed between a ghost on the one hand and an All-American Boy idol on the other. Before the long hot summer of 1961 would melt away, he would be booed in every American League ball park in the country, a tiny patch of his crew cut would turn white with nervous tension and the ritual baloney and eggs breakfast would lie in his stomach like a lump of low-grade asphalt.

First, there was the man whose record he was chasing. America is fussy about its heroes. It expects a certain standard of behavior from them. That behavior can be good or bad but above all it had better be what people want it to be. George Herman Ruth (1895–1948), the man who hit 714 home runs over an incredible major league career with the Yankees, who in 1927 hit 60 in a single season, who even before that had set a World Series record of 29⅔ scoreless innings when he was a pitcher with the Red Sox, George Herman Ruth was America's idea of what its premier athlete should be. The round face, the pigeon-toed trot, both stamped him as unique. You didn't need a scorecard to pick him out of a crowd. But most of all there was the over-powering simplicity of the man. In the 1920s America liked its heroes simple. And America thrived on Ruth. With his trigger-quick wrists and his dramatic power, he rescued baseball from the ugly truth of the 1919 Black Sox scandal which had threatened to destroy the game. America hated to be wrong about anything. Babe Ruth made them forget the Black Sox scandal because, most of all, America wanted to forget it.

On top of that, there was Babe Ruth on Grantland Rice's radio show saying: "As Duke Ellington said, the battle of Waterloo was won on the playing fields of Elkton." There was Babe Ruth, photographed with crippled kids in the hospital and Babe Ruth saying he loved hot dogs and Babe Ruth, surrounded by people, people and more people. America's heroes do not have to be articulate but they do have to be available. No wonder Grade B war movies pictured the Japanese infantry pouring across the beaches at Guadalcanal in a saki-inspired frenzy, shrieking: "You die, Yankee, and to hell with Babe Ruth."

There was all of that and it is the stuff of which American legends are made. And once the legend is made, woe unto him who would unmake it.

The second thing was Mickey Mantle. He was out of Oklahoma and into Joe DiMaggio's shoes. This is no small thing. The Yankees were a franchise of groomers. There was Whitey Ford to follow Vic Raschi. There was DiMaggio

to follow Ruth and Mantle to follow DiMaggio as the next
Golden Boy in the line of succession. Heirs apparent were
the logical order in the Yankee scheme of things and who in
all of baseball was more logical and more orderly than the
Yankees of New York?

Surely you couldn't quarrel with Mickey Mantle's cre-
dentials. He arrived young. Yankee heroes almost always
arrive young. For a long time there was a theory that the
Yankees bred them themselves so that they could always
have three . . . one leaving, one there and one on the way.
Mantle was glamour. He could switch-hit, a plus. He hit
balls so far that the club bought tape measures to chart
them, an even larger plus. He was good-looking, a proven
clutch-performer and he played in the face of enormous
physical handicaps, which added up to the largest plus of
all—a total justification of an in-bred pioneer legacy sometimes called "the don't give up the ship syndrome."

If anyone was supposed to break Babe Ruth's single-
season of 60 home runs, it wasn't Willie Mays or Ted Williams or Stan Musial (well, they might have bought Musial
or Mays because of their ubiquitous smiles. They might
have bought them under another American cliche known
as "the scouting rounds a guy out syndrome.) If anyone
should do it—and mind you the great American sports
public was not sure anyone should—well, then surely the
somebody would have to be Mickey Mantle.

And then there was Maris. The year before, Roger Maris
had hit 39 home runs, far and away the most of any of
his previous four major league seasons. He was shy and
introverted. He did not like crowds. He had come to the
Yankees from two other major league teams. Worst of all,
he was there at a time when Mickey Mantle had a shot at
the record. If this were a two-cornered race between the

living, hundreds of thousands of people made no mystery of which warm body they were backing. All Roger Maris had to do was listen every time he walked up to the plate. As for battling Ruth's ghost, the task was so formidible that even Mantle had trouble with that one.

Others had tried it and had reported with some agitation that the battle was not a happy one. Johnny Mize once hit 51 home runs and had a shot at the record, or so it seemed, in late August. "I think I could have beaten it," Mize once told Kenny Smith, who was then the baseball writer for the New York Mirror, "but I used to swing for average and it was more important to me to hit .300. But even with the outside chance I had, I could feel enormous pressure from the crowd. I could feel they didn't want me to do it."

Mize was lucky. Hank Greenberg was not. Hank Greenberg hit 58 home runs in 1938. He hit the last one with five games left on the schedule. Then Howard Mills and Buck Newsom of the Browns and Bob Feller, Denny Galehouse and Johnny Humphries of Cleveland stopped him. The words Hank Greenberg says he very often heard from the crowd when he was going for the record were "kike and Jew bastard." Outside of New York's garment center, the American Dream apparently was not rooting very hard for Hank Greenberg.

Others had come close, too, but no other year had ever been like 1961. There was Maris hand-wrestling with the shadow of Ruth and with Mantle, who was one of his closest friends. And there was the irritating, thoroughly cheapening intrusion of Ford Frick's asterisk.

Ever since baseball had settled upon a eight-team, two-league format, its schedule had been rigidly set at 154 games. It was 154 games in 1921 when Ruth set a record

with 59 and was still 154 games six years later when he set
another by hitting 60. But then baseball began to add new
teams. By 1961, the American League already had ex-
panded to 10. Schedule adjustments brought the new length
of the season in at 162 games. Nobody gave it much thought
until Maris had pulled himself up to Ruth's elbows by mid-
September. It was then that Ford Frick, who was commissioner of baseball, ruled that while all American sports
might be created equal, baseball was more equal than the
others. Should Maris eclipse Ruth's 60 home runs, baseball
would then have two home run champions . . . one for a
154-game season and one for a 162-game season. Naturally,
Ruth's name would appear first in the record book. Naturally.

So this is the way the thing stood on Aug. 4, as Roger
Maris and Julie Issacson drove up to Yankee Stadium for a
night game against the Minnesota Twins. Roger Maris,
who hit third in the Yankee batting order, had already
slammed 40 home runs. Mickey Mantle, who hit fourth,
had 39.

Before they parked the car, Roger Maris told him: "I
don't understand it. There's only one Babe Ruth and there's
only one Mickey Mantle. I'm really not trying to be either
one of them. All I want to be is Roger Maris." He ran his
home run total to 41 that night with a first-inning home
run off Camilo Pascual. Mantle was shut out.

Again, that night, on the way back to the apartment he
shared in Queens with outfielder Bob Cerv, Roger Maris
repeated what he had earlier said about Babe Ruth. "I'm
trying to break his record. I'm not trying to run him down
or take his place. I just don't understand why they keep
saying that."

There were good and valid reasons why Roger Maris

wouldn't understand. Several years later, after things had torn apart between him and most of the sportswriters, none of his most severe critics would be able to say that Roger Maris had lied to them about anything. This may come as a shock to worshippers of batting averages and fielding records but most people in this world are capable of not telling the truth in situations of extreme stress and athletes are no different than most people. But during that cruelest of baseball seasons and during the total chaos which marked Maris' relationships with the press and with baseball fans in the following year, Roger Maris never failed to give a straight answer to a straight question. Lesson number one on how not to become an American idol.

When you are dealing with legends and when people can read what you say the next morning, then you damned well better preface everything with "naturally, Babe Ruth was a great man and naturally it would be an honor for me to break the record and, of course, the money is secondary."

When they asked Maris about the money, he told the truth. When they asked Maris what he thought of an umpire's call, he told the truth. When they asked Maris what he thought about unfair intrusions upon his privacy, he told the truth.

This is fine if you happen to be hitting .257 because nobody is going to ask you in the first place. If they do, they are going to make paper airplanes out of their notes in the press box during the seventh-inning stretch.

But Maris' case was different. Nothing he said, nothing he did and, at times, nothing he ate went un-reported. Maris was trying to set a home run record. Babe Ruth held the record Maris wished to break. Babe Ruth was gregarious, extroverted and not without his share of platitudes. Ergo:

Roger Maris was supposed to be the same way. It was, of course, impossible.

In the first place, Ruth himself never had to contend with the unbelievable demands modern American journalism made on Roger Maris in the second half of the 20th Century. It wasn't the fault of the reporters. It wasn't the fault of their editors. It was an out-growth of televised baseball into every remote American hamlet. It was an out-growth of millions of ex-American G.I.s whom the war had taken out into the world and who had taken something of the world with them when they went back home. It was an out-growth of the insatiable craving for more and more detailed information about American celebrities. It was what mass communications had suddenly become all about.

Contrast it with the day Babe Ruth hit number 60. The date was Sept. 30, 1927. The Yankees had already won the pennant and were killing time until they could dispose of Pittsburgh in the World Series. Ruth had tied his own single-season record the day before at Yankee Stadium against the Senators by hitting home runs in the first inning off Rod Lisenbee and in the fifth off Paul Hopkins. Now he would go after the record. Thousands and thousands of fans would storm the Eighth Avenue Subway and fight their way into Yankee Stadium for the final game against the Senators. Like hell they would.

New York was positively indifferent. The rest of the country couldn't have cared less. So Ruth hit 59. So maybe he would hit 60. So what. In two years he would probably hit 72. Because baseball was a daylight game in those days and because the world had not yet begun to demand information about why a man did things rather than how, a writer could move quickly at the end of the game, file his story and be home in his own dining room in plenty of time for supper. No sports writer was about to make a big deal out of home run number 60.

As far as the record shows nobody else was either, with the exception of Ruth, who was moderately excited about beating himself, and a man named Tom Zachary. Mr. Zachary wound up pitching in the major leagues for 18 years with the Philadelphia Athletics, the Washington Senators, the St. Louis Browns, the Boston Braves, the Brooklyn Dodgers and, ironically, the New York Yankees. He won 186 games and lost 191. Nobody would remember him for any of these statistics. Tom Zachary was a smart cookie. He figured it would be a long time before anyone, including Babe Ruth, ever hit 60 home runs again. He did not want to be remembered as the man on the front of that 60th home run pitch.

"I said to myself," Tom Zachary would recall years later, "that if he wants to hit that home run he had better come up there swinging. I'm not going to give it to him."

It was a dark, cold day and the small crowd rattled around inside the huge ball park which Ruth's bat had indirectly built. George Pipgras was the Yankee pitcher. On Oct. 6, his next start, Mr. Pipgras would beat the Pittsburgh Pirates, 6–2, in the second game of the world series. This was his tune-up, a baseball euphemism, meaning you'd-better-take-a-turn- now-before-your-arm- dries-up-but-don't-throw-too-hard. Mr. Pipgras was not exactly approaching it like a life and death struggle. Except for Tom Zachary, the whole joint was about as enthusiastic as the Happy Hour Nursery School at vaccination time.

In the first inning, Ruth walked. In the fourth, he singled and in the sixth, he singled again. Now it was the eighth inning, the score was tied 2–2, the Yankees had a man on base and the crowd began to applaud for a rally,

possibly on the theory that movement is the best known
weapon in the war on frost-bite. Some of them did, however, apparently remember that Babe Ruth could break his
own record. They thought it would be very nice if he did
and conceded that the new mark would probably last all
of one season.

Out on the pitcher's mound, Mr. Zachary was experi-
encing the tortures of hell. Where to throw the ball? After
a long pause he gave it a whirl. It was, he later explained,
supposed to be a curve ball. What it looked like was a
plain old-fashioned bean ball. It is difficult to believe that
Ruth could have hit it with anything but his head because
that's exactly where it appeared to be going.

But Babe Ruth, with his marvelous reflexes, stepped
back, brought those whip-quick wrists around and pulled
the ball to right field. It went a long way and so did Mr.
Zachary right into the record books where, hopefully, some
as-yet-unborn Roger Maris would hit a pitch thrown by
some as-yet-unborn Tracy Stallard and get Mr. Zachary
off the hook. Unfortunately, some baseball commissioner
dredged up some unheard of asterisk and Mr. Zachary remains in the book 'til kingdom come.

Afterwards, commenting on the spot where he had
thrown the ball, Tom Zachary said "I don't see how he
hit that pitch. I don't see how anyone could have hit it."

But Ruth, being Ruth, could and did and when he did,
he set the stage for a summer of acid indigestions which
Roger Maris never dreamed possible. It was a cruel fate
to hang on a baloney and eggs man.

Despite the magnificence of the accomplishment nobody
has ever come forth to indicate that Babe Ruth ever really
had strong feelings about the record. Ken Smith, who
covered him for years, said he cannot recall a single ref-
erence which Ruth ever made to it.

But the deed was done. It was done in relative privacy and it was done to the total absence of pressure on anyone except Tom Zachary. This is, perhaps, the prime factor which should have been taken into account 34 years later. There were other factors, too. Ruth, indeed, did have only 154 games in which to hit his 60. But Babe Ruth did not have to play night baseball, where an entirely different optical approach is necessary for the hitter and he did not have to play day baseball after a night game where an entirely different gastronomical approach is necessary for the hitter's stomach. Moreover, he did not have to play baseball in three different time zones in the same week and fly all night to get there. All things considered, Maris and Mantle should have been given 154 extra games to break the record.

As August of 1961 melted into September, Maris had 51 home runs and Mantle had hit 48. Maris also had an added problem. Around the country they had been pointing to Roger's previous major league totals and deprecating his ability. They had thought it was positively disgraceful for a man with his batting average to menace a record held by Babe Ruth. Now that September was here and Mantle was still in the race, they began to talk about something else. Maris hit third and Mantle hit fourth. Mickey was so much more dangerous, the emotionally-involved contended smugly, that the reason Maris got the chance to hit so many home runs was that they didn't dare walk him because they would then have to pitch to Mantle. This was an interesting theory for the decimal-point readers but it still didn't rationalize away the fact that Maris had, indeed, hit 51 balls into the seats and managers who thought that wasn't dangerous were managers who considered unemployment good for the soul.

Still, they clung to the idea and a new sound began to

fill the ball parks. Roger Maris began to be booed for the sin of excellence. He was booed as he stuck his head out of the dugout, as he walked to the plate and as he returned to the bench after failing to hit a home run. Just to keep the hedge-your-bets-front-runners in good standing, he was cheered when he hit a home run. Mantle, who followed him, received support which bordered on a standing ovation. The baloney and eggs had turned sour . . . when he could eat them, that is.

For the most part, the added attention from the public, which never held tact too dearly, spilled over into out-right rudeness in public places. Breakfast or late lunch at the Stage Delicatessen, one of Maris' favorite haunts, had now become impossible. Mickey Mantle had been a major leaguer for 10 seasons and a star for virtually all of them. He knew how to handle situations like this. Roger Maris had been a good major league ball player at Cleveland and a good one at Kansas City but when it comes to rudeness, New York can give each of those cities 10 points and still beat them without a field goal kicker. Roger couldn't handle them.

It was September now and the Detroit Tigers were coming in to settle a little matter which everyone seemed to have overlooked. It was called the American League pennant and when the three-game series opened on Sept. 1, the Tigers were just a half-game back. When they left town two nights later they were lucky to still be in the league. The Tigers started Don Mossi in the first game and the Yankees beat him, 1–0, Neither Maris nor Mantle homered.

"What happened?" Roger was asked.

"When you're lousy, you're lousy."

"Mossi had good stuff," Mantle told the press.

Everyone made whatever they chose to make out of the contrasting quotes.

The they-don't-make-'em-like-the-Babe-anymore glee club took heart. Maris was in a slump. In his last 30 trips to the plate he had managed just two hits. Mantle was down by just 51–48 in the home run sweepstakes. Both were running ahead of Ruth. It was a dandy Indian summer afternoon and 52,530 took advantage of it. In the second inning, Mantle, a genuine team player, bunted home the leading run. He remained in the game despite the fact that he injured his back. He hit no home runs.

But Roger Maris came up swinging. In the sixth, he homered off Frank Lary. In the eighth, he hit another off Hank Aguirre. In the dressing room all he wanted to talk about was Mantle's bunt. It was impossible for a late-comer to get anywhere near Maris' locker. It was a wall-to-wall battle zone, surrounded by reporters.

"Mickey could have wheeled for the home run," Maris said. "But he got the run home with a bunt."

"What about you?" somebody shouted out of the mob. "How come you hit today and not yesterday?"

"If I could tell you," Maris said with extreme patience, "then this game would be easy, wouldn't it?"

The next day Mantle hit two. Maris hit none. Mickey trailed, 53–50. In the excitement everyone forgot the Tigers. The Tigers were so dead that even the Tigers wanted to forget the Tigers. By Sept. 10 each had hit three more. After Maris hit his 56th off Cleveland's Mud Cat Grant, he told the growing mob of historians around his locker:

"I don't know if I can do it. My chances are the same as they always were. I just don't know."

Across the way in the Indians' dressing room, Mud Cat Grant indicated that this war of attrition was about to enter a new phase. "He's hot. He's hitting anything you throw up there. We know it. But if he does it after this then he'll deserve it. I can tell you that starting now the pitchers are going to be extra careful with him." On the same day a fan suffering from extreme hyper-tension mailed off the results of a personal survey which has to rank as the greatest all-night waste of time this side of income-tax eve. According to his abacus—or whatever he used—Roger Maris should be required to hit 170 home runs that season in order to get credit for the record. When Ruth hit 60, he reasoned, the major league total was 922. Ruth's output represented .065 of the overall total. But in 1961 the total figured to pass 2600 and .065 of that would be 170. Exhausted, he closed his letter, presumably to go off and drink a toast to the memory of Babe Ruth.

Mantle began to drop from the race at that point—perhaps he'd read the letter, too, and 170 home runs would be pushing it a little. At any rate, the tension belonged solely to Maris and tension is hardly the word to use. Take Maris' hair for instance.

Somebody must have been. Every time he ran a comb through it that September it came out in bunches. The front of his pale-blond crew cut had developed a patch of white in it. "Nerves," a physician told him. "Thanks," Roger said.

As the pressure and the attached press corps began to mount Maris tried hard to please but there were moments when it was impossible. Somebody asked him about the rightfield fans in Yankee Stadium and again Maris gave an honest answer. "They are terrible," Maris said, explaining why. When the story hit the papers, New York baseball fans took violent exception to it. But, in truth, the rightfield fans were terrible. They shouted unprintable epithets at

him all through early September possibly because he wasn't
Ruth and possibly because he wasn't Mantle and just possibly because they weren't anything. When he objected, they
objected to his objections with more unprintable epithets
under whatever system of logic disturbed minds use.

Then he got nailed for criticizing calls on balls and
strikes. Everybody criticizes balls and strikes. But not everybody will do it honestly to a reporter and not everybody
gets quoted. Roger Maris could and did. Again he was in
trouble with that great jury in the cheap seats.

"The Babe wouldn't do it," they said.

No, the Babe wouldn't do it. All he would do was to
go to the owner of the ball club and try to get him to fire
the manager of the ball club because he had had the te-
merity to fine the home run hitter of the ball club (one
Babe Ruth) for keeping his curfew time with a sun dial.

The press corps which headed west with the Yankees
on the last road trip was a study in logistics all its own. It
was enormous and more were joining the club at each city.
It was easy for some strange reason for a lot of writers to
forget this when the period called "the trouble" broke out
between Maris and the press in subsequent seasons. It was
easy to forget that he had tried to be cooperative, that
once he had broken free of a huge circle of writers and
asked one of them privately "Can't you get them to ask me
some new questions?" or that a whole brigade of magazine
people and non-baseball writers had joined the club and
that Maris had patiently answered their questions for hours
although they were elementary and had been already asked
a thousand times. One, however, had not been asked. It
had to do with Roger Maris' sex life. For the first—and
possibly only time—the other writers who heard it agreed
that one of their number had finally set an indoor record

for gall. Maris' answer "I'm a married man and what you do with your life is your problem" was roundly applauded.

But the strain was there. After the balls and strikes story and after failing to hit home runs in Chicago and in a doubleheader in Detroit, he declined to meet the press. It was the only time all year that it happened. The reporters had problems of their own. They had deadlines to meet and they had editors back home demanding they go in and ask "what pitch did you hit?" It was genuinely unfortunate. But the miracle was that it had not happened sooner.

It was at this juncture that Mantle, who in his earlier days on the ball club had not always been the elder states-man he now was, suggested that Roger accept it and learn to live with it. Mantle was, of course, right and Maris knew it. He would be cautious but he would try again.

On September 17, Roger Maris hit number 58 off a Detroit pitcher named Terry Fox. The team headed back east to Baltimore. Roger Maris had already used up 152 games. He would have just 18 innings left to hit three and tie the record. He would have to do it in the town where George Herman Ruth was born.

It was in Baltimore that Babe Ruth spent most of his adolescence at St. Mary's Industrial School. It was in Balti-more that Jack Dunn of the International League Orioles signed him to his first professional contract as a left-handed pitcher. It was in Baltimore that Babe Ruth played for the Orioles and beat three major league clubs (the World champion Athletics, the National League champion Giants and the Phillies) in spring exhibition games. It was in Balti-more that Ruth launched his minor league career by shutting out Buffalo in the league opener of 1914. And it was in Balti-more, where the franchise discovered it was going broke when only 17 people paid to see a league game, that the deal was made which originally sent the Babe to the majors.

Maris was in Baltimore and Baltimore knew exactly who it would root for.

Baltimore was not a good town for Roger Maris. On July 17 he had lost a homer there when the game was rained out in the fifth inning. Ironically, that homer would have enabled him to tie Ruth within the framework of Ford Frick's half-asterisk season. The park, moreover, a converted football stadium with depressing dimensions, was a distinct disadvantage to the hitters in their regular war with the pitchers. Roger Maris was going to have to be very good to save it.

On Sept. 19, the Yankees and the Orioles split a doubleheader. Roger Maris hit no home runs. The Ford Frick version of the race now came down to a single baseball game in a park where he had been unmercifully hooted the previous night. The jeers were coming from the stands and through the mail and courtesy of Western Union. As soon as they spotted the number 9 on his back, the crowd opened up. But Maris didn't have the time or the opportunity to hear them. He was in the middle of one of the largest press corps ever assembled for a baseball game, which by itself was not critical for either team. True, the Yankees could clinch the pennant by winning. If not, they still would have eight more games and needed only one victory.

There have been a lot of things written about Roger Maris and the things which happened to him in 1961. But nothing anyone ever writes can begin to describe what he must have felt that evening in Baltimore and what he thought as he did the things he did there. He didn't break the record. He didn't tie. But he gave it a magnificent shot.

Milt Pappas was the Baltimore pitcher. Pappas had been one of those bright young smoke-throwers discovered by Paul Richards back in the days when Richards was the Orioles' general manager and he was signing every muscular young pitcher in America. Pappas made it big. In 1961 he was still a very smart pitcher.

In the first inning, Maris hit one on the nose to right but he didn't get under it and the ball lacked height. Earl Robinson, the Baltimore rightfielder, took it after a brief run. In the third, with Pappas still pitching, the count went to 2–1. Pappas took his sign and wheeled in with the pitch. Maris swung. Everyone in the park knew it was gone. It carried 390 feet and over the fence where it rattled into the bleacher seats. Roger Maris had 59 home runs. And suddenly, like all crowds which think that in some peculiar way they can be a part of history, a lot of people rooted for Roger Maris for the first time since this long, weary season had begun back in April.

Now it was Dick Hall, a big, tall relief pitcher who had replaced Pappas. Hall was all arms and legs and his forte was motion. When he was going right, the ball was very hard to pick up coming out of all those limbs. Hall slipped two strikes past Maris. He swung again and the crowd began a scream which died somewhere between its collective voice box and its adam's apple. The ball hooked foul. Hall fired strike three past him. In the seventh, there was another swing and another crack and again the ball soared toward right field. Again it hooked foul. He flied out to right center.

So in the ninth, it had come down to this one turn at bat and the pitcher was Hoyt Wilhelm. . . . Hoyt Wilhelm, who possessed a knuckleball so treacherous it had to be caught with an over-sized catcher's mitt . . . Hoyt Wilhelm, who during his halcyon days with the Giants threw knucklers so puzzling that batter, catcher and umpire often flinched as one man . . . Hoyt Wilhelm, who knew that he was not going to get his name in that book with Tom Zachary as long as he had a knuckle left to fight with.

It took two pitches. Maris fouled the first one back. Then he tried to back away from one of Wilhelm's dancers. He twisted back with his body but he was too slow with his bat. The ball hit it and trickled toward Wilhelm, who tagged him out near first base.

The legions of ghost-worshippers had won. The Mickey Mantle Fan Club had won. The Ford Frick asterisk had won. The Yankees had played their 154th game and won the pennant. Roger Maris walked into the clubhouse one short of Ruth.

"I'm tired," Maris said in front of his locker. "I'm tired. I'm lucky I hit as many as I did. Let's face it, I would have liked to hit 60 or 61 within the 154 games. I tried like the devil tonight but all I got was one and I'm tired."

On Sept. 26, in the 158th game, Roger Maris hit a curveball thrown by Jack Fisher of the Baltimore Orioles in the third inning at Yankee Stadium. "I threw it," Fischer said, "and the minute I did I said to myself that does it. That's 60." Maris' body corkscrewed with the effort and it seemed to freeze there as he followed the flight of the ball. It cracked against an empty seat in the second row of the upper deck close to the foul line. As he circled the bases the crowd roared in genuine approval. In a box seat near the Yankee dugout, Clair Ruth, Babe Ruth's widow, left her seat with tears streaming down her face.

"I was bewildered by it all," Maris said afterwards. "The fans were so wonderful and I appreciated their ovation. But I didn't know what to do. I didn't know whether to step out of the dugout or not. I'm glad I did. I've just never been through anything like this before."

There were four games to go now. And Maris took the first one off. On Sept. 29, the Red Sox came in for the final series of the season. Pat Maris flew in from Independence,

Mo., to be with her husband. Roger Maris hit no home runs
on Friday or Saturday. Now it was Sunday—the last game
of the season. Now it was Roger Maris, the man who said he
didn't want to be Babe Ruth, and Evan Tracy Stallard, the
man who knew he didn't want to be Tom Zachary. The
Yankees won it, 1–0. The only run came on a fourth inning
home run by Roger Maris. Asterisk or no, Roger Maris had
hit his 61.

It was over and the questioning in front of Roger Maris'
locker lasted two-and-a-half hours. "I have to give him
credit," Maris said. "He wasn't trying to walk me. He was
pitching to get me out. The mental pressure was worse than
the physical. The interviews and all that stuff. I'm happy
about a lot of things. But I'm happiest because it's all over."

But it wasn't.

He is not comfortable in large gatherings. The glamour
of the right table from the right head waiter doesn't move
him. In the off-season he prefers to be with his family. But
the winter which followed was not an ordinary winter and
Roger Maris was not an ordinary ball player between seasons
and he reluctantly conceded this. He went on the banquet
circuit and the winter was a mess. He was misquoted in little
towns. He was bum-wrapped in big ones. He was accused
of running out in the middle of a major sports dinner when
he didn't. By the time spring rolled around, he was resentful
of the bum-raps. He put all the writers into one bag marked
trouble. It angered some who had genuinely been his
friends. The others took advantage of it.

When the Yankees went to camp in 1962, Maris twice
refused interviews. Tempers were lost on both sides. Things
were never going to be the same. Some of the digs the
writers took at him came under the heading of what pro
football players call cheap shots. A few were justified.

Although he hit .281 in 1964, Roger Maris was never the same. He played well when he was physically sound. He played poorly when he was not. And then during the 1965 season, the Yankees, the people who always pride themselves on class, did something they should never have done. One can only chalk it up to stupidity or indifference.

On a close play at home plate, Roger Maris came sliding in and jammed his hand under the umpire's shoe. He didn't play much after that. As the days melted into weeks the front office issued a running bulletin which never changed: "Roger Maris' case is a day-to-day proposition."

"All I had to go on was what they told me," he would explain later. "I couldn't swing a bat without pain and after a while I couldn't throw the ball without pain but what could I do? You can't hold your hand out to people who don't believe you and show what pain looks like."

It happened in June of that year—a year in which Roger Maris played only 46 games—and the operation, which ultimately became a matter of tying shoes and knotting neckties instead of things like gripping bats, wasn't performed until Sept. 28. Up until then a great many people—puzzled by the Yankees' inference that he would soon be better—believed that Roger Maris simply did not want to play. He was booed so often that it is worth a little thought.

Roger Maris, who wasn't supposed to want to play (and who at times tried very hard to give that impression) ran into a lot of fences and slid into a lot of people when he was a Yankee. When the Yankees needed home runs in 1961 they got them from Roger, who must have been doing something which won ball games because he also won the RBI title that year. And when they needed a big throw from the outfield to win the 1962 World Series they got that from Maris, too.

You cannot question Mickey Mantle's courage, which is a kind of toughness hard to come by. But every time Mantle so much as put a band-aid on people rushed off to typewriters to recall the world of Mantle's genuine agony. Nobody was killed in the rush, making a case for Roger Maris in 1965.

On Dec. 8, 1966, Roger Maris was traded from the Yankees to the St. Louis Cardinals in exchange for a journeyman third baseman named Charley Smith.

That spring in the strangely disquieting uniform of an alien league, Maris stood by the batting cage at St. Petersburg, Fla., and thought about that whole dizzy year of 1961 and the strange events which followed it.

"It might have been better if the 61st home run had never come," Maris said in total candor, "because a lot of people thought I was the one who wasn't supposed to do it."

"Listen," one of his close friends said when he heard that, "it wasn't Babe Ruth's fault and it wasn't Mickey Mantle's fault and it certainly wasn't Roger Maris' fault. But if Mickey Mantle had hit 61 home runs that year and Roger had hit 60, then Roger Maris would have gone on to be a very popular Yankee—asterisk or no asterisk."